Max Weber's Politics of Civil Society

Civil society has made a surprising comeback in our time. Its detractors, however, have charged that, as both an analytical concept and a blueprint for political practice, civil society has already run its course, or its promise was based on a myopic euphoria to begin with. While acknowledging the problems in the contemporary theorizing of civil society, this book still argues for its usefulness by relocating the source of civil society from the question of a legal-institutional framework to that of public citizenship and civic education. And it does so by revisiting Max Weber.

In fact, this book is the first in-depth interpretation of Weber as a political theorist of civil society. On the one hand, Weber's ideas are considered from the perspective of modern political thought rather than from that of the modern social sciences; on the other, the book offers a liberal assessment of this complex political thinker without apologizing for his shortcomings. From this perspective, the book effectively foregrounds Weber's concern with public citizenship in a modern mass democracy and civil society as its cultivating ground. Weber's civil society, thus reconstructed, is neither a communitarian haven for mutual trust and solidarity nor a liberal-juridical sphere of deliberation and communication, but an arena for competition and struggle in which a certain ethical personality – what he called the "person of vocation (*Berufsmensch*)" – can be constantly fashioned and sustained. It is when we recognize this hitherto neglected vision of Weber's pluralistically organized civil society that his misgivings about the modern "iron cage" as well as his ethico-political project conceived of as its antidote can be properly accounted for. Despite some serious questions that Weber's politics of civil society raises, Sung Ho Kim argues, it still harbors an alternative vision of civil society, which is useful for the contemporary conceptualization and politics of civil society.

All in all, Kim has successfully resuscitated Max Weber as a political thinker for our time, in which civic virtues and civil society have once again become urgent issues.

Sung Ho Kim teaches modern political and social thought at Yonsei University in Seoul, Korea. Previously, he was a professor of political science at Williams College in Massachusetts and at the University of California in Riverside. His articles have appeared in, among other journals, *Political Theory, History of Political Thought*, and *Max Weber Studies*. This book is based on his doctoral dissertation, which won the 1998 Leo Strauss Award of the American Political Science Association.

Max Weber's Politics of Civil Society

SUNG HO KIM

Yonsei University

CAMBRIDGE
UNIVERSITY PRESS

CAMBRIDGE UNIVERSITY PRESS
Cambridge, New York, Melbourne, Madrid, Cape Town, Singapore, São Paulo

Cambridge University Press
The Edinburgh Building, Cambridge CB2 8RU, UK

Published in the United States of America by Cambridge University Press, New York

www.cambridge.org
Information on this title: www.cambridge.org/9780521820578

First published 2004
This digitally printed version 2007

A catalogue record for this publication is available from the British Library

Library of Congress Cataloguing in Publication data

Kim, Sung Ho, 1966–
Max Weber's politics of civil society / Sung Ho Kim.
p.   cm.
Revision of the author's thesis (Ph. D.)–University of Chicago, 1997.
Includes bibliographical references and index.
ISBN 0-521-82057-X (hardback)
1. Weber, Max, 1864–1920 – Contributions in political science.   2. Civil society.
I. Title.
JC263.W42K56   2004
300′.1–dc22   2003055592

ISBN 978-0-521-82057-8 hardback
ISBN 978-0-521-03656-6 paperback

Contents

Acknowledgments   *page* vii

1. Of "Sect Man": The Modern Self and Civil Society
   in Max Weber   1
   Agency, Citizenship, and Civil Society   1
   Reading Weber: Between Politics and Science   8
   In Search of the Protestant Ethic Thesis   18
   Outline of the Argument   25

2. The Protestant Ethic and the Spirit of Individualism   27
   Introduction: "The Last of Our Heroisms"   27
   "A Rationalization toward an Irrational Conduct of Life"   30
   Calling: Sanctification and Regimentation of Everyday Life   33
   Predestination: Objectification of the World and
       Disempowerment of the Self   37
   Empowering the Individual Agency: Self-Mastery
       and Discipline   43
   Conclusion: Value, Rationality, and Freedom   50

3. The Protestant Sects and the Spirit of Civil Society   57
   Introduction: Sociability of the Puritan Berufsmensch   57
   Gemeinschaft, Gesellschaft, *and* Amerikanismus   60
   Modes of Sociability: America versus Europe   68
   Sect contra Church: Particularism and Voluntarism   75
   Secularization of Charisma: From Sect to Status Group
       and Bureaucracy   84
   Conclusion: The Public and the Private   91

4. Politics, Science, Ethics   95
   Introduction: Götterdämmerung   95
   Disenchantment and Reenchantment   99
   Conviction, Responsibility, and Decision   110
   Practice of the Self I: Realpolitik   117
   Practice of the Self II: Ideal Type   123
   Conclusion: Modernity, Conscience, and Duty   130

5. Liberalism, Nationalism, and Civil Society   133
   Introduction: Liberalism and Nationalism   133
   National Identities, Nation-States, and the Political   137
   Nationalism, Citizenship, and Personality   145
   Politics of the Classes: Refeudalization and
      Embourgeoisement   151
   Politics of Checks and Balances: Corporatism
      and Parliamentarism   160
   Conclusion: "The School of Men"   169

6. Max Weber's Politics of Civil Society   173
   Statecraft and Soulcraft in Max Weber   173
   Purpose, Contestation, and the Political   180
   Bowling Alone   187

References   191
Index   211

Acknowledgments

This book has been long in making. It began its life as a doctoral dissertation at the University of Chicago and then matured through many stages of rewriting subsequently at Williams College and Yonsei University. Naturally, its growth is deeply indebted to many institutions and individuals.

Chicago was my intellectual home and still is at heart. Were it not for its unsurpassed intellectual vibrancy and exemplary community of dedicated scholars, the ideas presented in this book would not have seen the light of day. Susanne Hoeber Rudolph represents those academic values and cultures in person, and it is to her that I have incurred the most substantial debt during my Chicago days and ever since. This book was in fact first imagined in her Weber seminar, a venerable institution in Chicago's graduate curriculum, which I joined in my first term. It did not take long for her to turn around a young yet relatively firm mind of a left-Hegelian bent by introducing me to the open-ended theoretical horizon of Weber. Ever since then, she has stayed with her pupil throughout the journey as a guide, mentor, and exemplar. I owe her much – simply too much. Two of my advisors, who also contributed much to build Chicago as the institution that we all recognize now, passed away before the completion of my dissertation, let alone of this book. Hopefully, the late Edward Shils and François Furet would have been pleased to recognize their ideas, voices, and spirits (and disagreements, too) in the final version of the project they warmly encouraged long ago. It was my good fortune that I met scholars with no less intelligence, learning, and commitment, who also saw in my project what I failed to see in the first place. Bernard Manin, Gary Herrigel, and Charles Larmore had graciously agreed to oversee the maturation of my dissertation, and their guidance proved to be critical for the new direction and form it took subsequently. I thank them all dearly.

Williams provided me with an ideal environment for the substantive revision of my project. It differed from Chicago in certain respects; many ideas for rewriting were conceived, for example, as I strolled around the bucolic Berkshire hills. And yet, it still shared much with Chicago; for one thing, my colleagues forced me relentlessly to revisit my arguments in a fresh light. Many evenings of lucid conversations with Michael MacDonald, Gary Jacobsohn, and Monique Deveaux are and will be sorely missed. Graeme Garrard has produced incisive comments on the entire manuscript. I could not have asked for a better reader than this learned Rousseauite, who is thoughtful and balanced in judgment (his theorist side), honest and straightforward in communication (his Canadian side), and sharp-tongued and dry-witted in presentation (his British side). I have nothing but gratifying memories of Williams and its people.

Yonsei, my alma mater, has welcomed me back with open arms. In fact, it was not until I returned home that I realized how much of who I am and what I think first germinated here on this beautiful campus. My belated recognition has gradually dawned upon me in the course of many pleasant conversations (and some fierce debates) that I have had with my new colleagues and students, prompting me in the end to rewrite the introductory and concluding chapters. I especially thank Chin Wee Chung, Chaibong Hahm, Dong-Jin Jang, Youngjae Jin, Dalchoong Kim, Ki-Jung Kim, Yongho Kim, Shinheang Lee, Yeon-ho Lee, Chung-In Moon, Myungsoon Shin, and Seungham Yang.

I am also grateful to those who have, on different occasions, read parts or all of the manuscript. Harvey Goldman has time and again produced the most helpful comments, and it was my good fortune to be able to consult one of the most accomplished Weberians of our time in the course of revision. John A. Hall read the entire manuscript in its infant shape; his comments were critical in determining the direction and scope of the subsequent revision. Their support is truly appreciated. For their careful reading and penetrating comments, I also would like to thank David Blaney, Peter Breiner, Erik Carlson, Mary Dietz,

John Houston, Mark Lichbach, David Mandel, John McCormick, Gianfranco Poggi, Marion Smiley, and Tracy Strong. My editors at Cambridge University Press, especially Lew Bateman, deserve my sincere gratitude. They have proved to be the most insightful and supportive editors any author can possibly hope for.

Last but not least, I thank my parents, Kyung-ja Lee and Chang Yul Kim. It is through their exemplary lives of sacrifice and discipline that I have come to appreciate what Weber saw in the "person of vocation." It was my greatest fortune to be raised by lifelong seekers of knowledge and paragons of citizenship who have demonstrated by example that integrity is one virtue that can be compromised under no circumstances. To my parents this book is dedicated with the deepest gratitude.

Of "Sect Man"

The Modern Self and Civil Society in Max Weber

AGENCY, CITIZENSHIP, AND CIVIL SOCIETY

Civil society was a vision largely forgotten during the "short twentieth century." It sounded quaint and even irrelevant for the age of power politics, organized economy, and mass democracy, in which individual agency tended to be stifled by these gigantic institutions and processes that operated beyond one's practical comprehension and engagement. This was a time when the centralized bureaucratic state, whether the totalitarian or welfare variant, dominated public life, while the economy of scale, whether capitalist or not, was welcomed with little questioning. Democratization surely constituted an irreversible trend of the century, and yet its universal appeal was intrinsically tied to passive citizenship, in its worst case, of a mass consumerist kind. Neither society, increasingly cramped between the state and market, nor civility and civic virtues, increasingly displaced by the sovereignty of individual citizens' unreflective preferences, could claim much attention but in a romantic lament for their erosion. According to Eric Hobsbawm, the vision of civil society had no corresponding reality in the twentieth century and was merely reflective of a bygone era – that is, an "idealized nineteenth-century."[1] The twentieth century was not to be remembered as the age of civil society.

---

[1] E. Hobsbawm, *The Age of Extremes: A History of the World, 1914–1991* (New York: Vintage Books, 1996) 139.

Against this historical background, it comes rather as a surprise that its last decade witnessed the sudden triumph of civil society all over the world.[2] The unanticipated collapse of the communist bloc, third world democratization, and the crisis of the Keynsian regimes were all lumped together and seen as evidence that civil society, long thought dormant, had finally reasserted itself over the overbearing states. Much hubris followed these historical developments – most notably, the ironical celebration of the Hegelian "end of history" that had finally dawned with the demise of the Hegelian state.

For a while, it was widely believed that civil society was the answer to the governance and legitimacy crises of the Hegelian state, since it would make the state less intrusive while more responsive to individual citizens' daily concerns. This expectation was fueled by a formal-juridical understanding of civil society as embodying a set of determinate institutions that stand independent of or even in opposition to the state. Civil society was seen to consolidate a zone of institutionalized self-regulation, buttressed by the formal rule of law, which adjudicates the conflicts immanent in civil society and formed through spontaneous interaction among rights-bearing individuals religiously pursuing their own ends. Its inspiration came from, along with a Lockean liberalism, the social imagination of "commercial society" popularized by the Scottish Enlightenment thinkers, and its model, a laissez-faire market where ideas and opinions would circulate throughout the society as freely as money. In this view, the state is also an institutional agent that faithfully services and implements the mandates given by civil society, one that confers legitimacy on the state and sometimes withdraws it. The alleged Hegelian end of history was to inaugurate a profoundly anti-Hegelian age in a double sense: first, the relationship between the state and civil society was to be completely reversed from the way in which Hegel postulated it, and second, formal juridical institutionalism of civil society was to trump the ethical formative principles of the state as Hegel saw them.

This reversal, of course, does not mean that the reinvigorated civil society would be indifferent to the question of good citizenship. Quite the contrary. For, within a clearly walled citadel in which to pursue

[2] P. Hirst, "The State, Civil Society, and the Collapse of Soviet Communism," *Economy and Society* 20:2 (1991) 217–42.

freely their autonomously chosen ends, individuals would regain the ownership of their lives and an authentic sense of agency. In turn, reempowerment of individual agency would usher in a more participant citizenship that was to make the state (and market) more accountable; the increasing efficacy of the public participation that was to ensue would further motivate active engagement; and so would begin the benign cycle that would ultimately culminate in a more robust and efficacious liberal democratic regime. In other words, civil society was believed to be the harbinger of the public citizenship without which neither a healthy democratic self-governance nor the liberal moral ideals of individual autonomy, freedom, and agency could be realized to their fullest extent. Civil society sustains "conditions of liberty," which (re)produce a uniquely modern kind of moral agency that Ernest Gellner called a "modal self."[3] The difference from Hegel's project, then, lies less in a principled indifference to the moral matters in the public sphere than in the institutional framework advocated for the empowerment of individual agency. This ultimate ethical stage was reachable, according to the civil society advocates, through an institutionalization of local voluntary associational life free of paternalistic interference of even the benevolent state. The recent project of civil society, one might say, rejected a Platonic politics of the soul only to embrace a laissez-faire politics of the soul. Alexis de Tocqueville was to replace Hegel as the political theorist for our posthistorical age.

As the initial euphoria has subsided, however, a growing number of people are focusing on a different understanding of civil society that is conceived more explicitly in terms of human *capabilities*, both moral and political, than of legal and economic *institutions*.[4] The new focus is predicated on a recognition that many of the optimistic consequences that were to ensue from a robust civil society did not materialize as

---

[3] E. Gellner, *Conditions of Liberty: Civil Society and Its Revivals* (London: Penguin Books, 1994).

[4] S. Khilnani, "The Development of Civil Society," in S. Kaviraj and S. Khilnani (eds.), *Civil Society: History and Possibilities* (Cambridge: Cambridge University Press, 2001) 24. From a similarly critical perspective, Krishan Kumar proposed that we do away with civil society as a historical and analytical concept. See his "Civil Society: An Inquiry into the Usefulness of a Historical Term," *British Journal of Sociology* 44:3 (1993) 375–95. Also see C. G. A. Bryant's defense of the concept in the same issue, "Social Self-Organization, Civility, and Sociology: A Comment on Kumar's 'Civil Society'," 397–401.

promised. Despite much talk of reform, the public still sees government as an alien, intrusive, and unresponsive power that is controlled
by special interests, leaving even the regular voters feeling shut out,
ill-informed, unrepresented, and manipulated. The consequent civic
distress, apathy, and alienation show little sign of abating in Europe
and North America; in fact, they are spreading to the newly democratized countries, where many greet them, along with the mass con-
sumerism that accompanies them, as the *cognito ultima* of "progress"
and "modernity." Politics seems as dysfunctional as ever. The civic
virtues, mutual trust, and civility or, to be precise, the lack thereof
continue to be sources of complaints everywhere and an occasion for
the conservative (and liberal) jeremiad, especially in the United States
and increasingly in Europe. Weaker family ties and fraying neighbor-
hoods are loathed universally as the root cause for the evaporation
of mutual trust and erosion of common identity, without which civic
solidarity cannot be sustained. In much of the rest of the world, in
fact, the similar apprehension about the disintegration of traditional
cultural, religious, and communal values is growing more acute, even
taking, in some places, a violent turn in a renewed anticolonial and
antimodernist direction. Social disintegration is feared more than ever.
The market, in the name of globalization, the new economy, and financial capitalism, has become unshackled, rapidly penetrating our lives
to an extent hitherto unimagined. Refashioning society in the image
of the market has so far generated only an unprecedented level of so-
cioeconomic inequality, insecurity, and anxiety, both domestically and
internationally.[5]

Under these circumstances, the simple presence of local voluntary associational life, no matter how autonomously instituted, and a laissez-
faire politics of the soul, for all its implicit concern with good citizenship, do not seem to do much to ameliorate political dysfunction,
social disintegration, and economic anxiety. Furthermore, civil society
sometimes does more harm than good. Organized special interests and
their vigorous activities are only deepening the general public's sense of

---

[5] W. Galston, "Political Economy and the Politics of Virtue: U.S. Public Philosophy
at Century's End," in A. L. Allen and M. C. Regan, Jr. (eds.), *Debating Democracy's
Discontents: Essays on American Politics, Law, and Public Philosophy* (Oxford: Oxford
University Press, 1998) 65–9.

alienation from and mistrust of the political process; the neighborhood groups organized for gated communities can hardly be seen as making a positive contribution to the reinstatement of public commitment, mutual trust, and civic solidarity; economic globalization requires a new global regime for a better coordinated regulation of capital and trade flows, and yet an attempt to build such a regime is often frustrated for domestic political reasons that have to do with powerful workers' unions. In order to jump-start the benign cycle of public engagement, efficacious government, and individual agency, then, a one-sidedly institutional approach does not seem sufficient; instead, we need to pay closer attention to the more substantive side of what civil society can and cannot do. In other words, the question to be raised about civil society seems less about the institutional maturity and autonomy of voluntary associational life than about the variegated civic educational effects that different voluntary associations exert on their individual members' moral makeup. Civil society is in need of a reconceptualization that can allow it to address the question of citizenship and morality more directly. Nancy Rosenblum, one of the prominent theorists of contemporary civil society, observes that

[t]he orthodox preoccupation with associations as buffers against government and avenues to political participation, and with freedom of association as an aspect of personal liberty has been eclipsed. Today, the dominant perspective is moral: civil society is seen as a school of virtue where men and women develop the dispositions essential to liberal democracy.[6]

Theoretically at issue in this recent reorientation is a more profound and troubling question about the self-sustainability of procedural liberalism on its own terms. That is to say, can a liberal democratic regime sustain itself in a robust form while remaining neutral to the moral dispositions and civic virtues of its citizens? What is the role of civil society with regard to the continuing viability of a liberal democratic regime (statecraft) and the self-constitution of its citizens (soulcraft)? Cutting across the vast array of liberal-communitarian interlocutions, an increasing number of contemporary theorists of Tocquevillean persuasions converge on the following points: first, a liberal

---

[6] N. Rosenblum, *Membership and Morals: The Personal Uses of Pluralism in America* (Princeton, NJ: Princeton University Press, 1998) 26.

democratic regime cannot be sustained in a robust form without certain kinds of virtues and characters in its citizens that can capacitate
and motivate their active public engagement[7]; second, these types of
agency are cultivated, reproduced, and reinforced through a local, voluntary associational life in a pluralistically organized civil society[8];
third, American civil society is in serious decline, which has prompted
these neo-Tocquevilleans to call for a "softening," if not a complete
abandonment, of the liberal doctrine of neutrality and to encourage
a stronger form of political and civic education of liberal citizens via
a formative intervention in the organization and structure of civil society.[9] Criticizing the liberal reaffirmation of the strict separation of
statecraft and soulcraft, in short, the neo-Tocquevillean position suggests a politics of civil society in which statecraft and soulcraft are
combined to sustain a more robust liberal democratic regime.

Against this background, my book makes two claims about Weber's
political thought: one pertains to its affinity with the neo-Tocquevillean
politics of civil society; the other, to its crucial distance. First, Weber
agrees that the cultivation of a certain type of moral agent he called
the "person of vocation" (*Berufsmensch*) is critical for the continuing
vitality of the modern liberal democratic regime; that its virtues, dispositions, and characters can be fostered only in a peculiar context of
civil society he called "sectlike society" (*Sektengesellschaft*); and that
the decline of civil society and the concomitant degeneration of the liberal self must be restored as one of the central agendas for late modern

---

[7] P. Berkowitz, *Virtues and the Making of Modern Liberalism* (Princeton, NJ: Princeton
University Press, 1999); R. Dagger, *Civic Virtues: Rights, Citizenship, and Republican
Liberalism* (Oxford: Oxford University Press, 1997); W. Galston, *Liberal Purposes:
Goods, Virtues, and Diversity in the Liberal State* (Cambridge: Cambridge University
Press, 1991); S. Macedo, *Liberal Virtues: Citizenship, Virtue, and Community in Liberal
Constitutionalism* (Oxford: Oxford University Press, 1990).

[8] A. Gutman (ed.), *Freedom of Association* (Princeton, NJ: Princeton University Perss,
1998); E. Shils, *The Virtue of Civility: Selected Essays on Liberalism, Tradition, and Civil Society* (Indianapolis: Liberty Press, 1997); S. Macedo, "Community, Diversity, and Civic
Education: Toward a Liberal Political Science of Group Life" in E. F. Paul, F. Miller,
and J. Paul (eds.), *Communitarian Challenge to Liberalism* (Cambridge: Cambridge University Press, 1996).

[9] B. Barber, "The Discourse of Civility" in S. Elkin and K. Soltan (eds.), *Citizen Compe-
tence and Democratic Institutions* (Philadelphia: Penn State University Press, 1999); M.
Sandel, *Democracy's Discontent: America in Search of a Public Philosophy* (Cambridge,
MA: Harvard University Press, 1996); J. B. Elshtain, *Democracy on Trial* (New York:
Basic Books, 1995).

politics. Statecraft and soulcraft are not separated in Weber's politics of civil society, nor can they or should they be separated.

Second, however, Weber maintains that not just any "revivification of civil society" would be conducive to the empowerment of the modern liberal agency. For he is more sensitive than some contemporary Tocquevilleans to the fact that the simple presence of a vibrant associational life does not offer a coherent guarantee against what John Keane calls the problem of "uncivil society" or "bad civil society."[10] Not all forms of civil society are conducive to a robust liberal democratic regime; some are in fact detrimental to it. Through a genealogical reconstruction, instead, Weber seeks to resuscitate a peculiar mode of civil society as the site where his liberal politics of voluntary associational life and the unique ontology of modern self intersect and interact. It is this theoretically elaborated ideal type of civil society, cutting across his larger reflections on modernity and modernization, that stabilizes the critical vista from which Weber substantiates the morphology of civil society for a vibrant liberal democratic citizenship.

From this perspective, then, it need not surprise anyone that, when questioned in November 1918 about the liberal democratic reform of postwar defeated Germany, Weber replied in the following unambiguous terms:

Foremost among these, too, is the restoration of that prosaic moral "decency" [*Anständigkeit*] which, on the whole, we had and which we lost in the war – our most grievous loss. Massive problems of education, then. The method: only the "club" in the American sense [*amerikanische Klubwesen*] (and associations of every kind based on *selective* choice of members), starting with childhood and youth, no matter for what purpose.[11]

---

[10] J. Keane, *Civil Society: Old Images, New Visions* (Stanford, CA: Stanford University Press, 1998), 114ff, and S. Chambers and J. Kopstein, "Bad Civil Society," *Political Theory* 29:6 (2001) 837–65. An instructive historical example of bad civil society is analyzed in S. Berman, "Civil Society and the Collapse of the Weimar Republic," *World Politics* 49:3 (1997) 401–29.

[11] Letter to Friedrich Crusius as quoted in W. Mommsen, *Max Weber and German Politics, 1890–1920* (Chicago: University of Chicago Press, 1984) 323. A complete letter is in Biography 647/636; E. Baumgarten (ed.), *Max Weber: Werk und Person* (Tübingen: J. C. B. Mohr/Paul Siebeck, 1964) 536ff; and GPS (1st ed.) 482ff, all of which Mommsen claims to be mistranscribed. Material enclosed in parentheses in the quote is based on Mommsen's claims. English rendering was altered to provide a more literal translation.

My book can be summarized as an attempt to understand these somewhat unexpected references by Weber to a robust associational life,
ethical characterology, and America, and to draw their implications
for the contemporary politics of civil society.

READING WEBER: BETWEEN POLITICS AND SCIENCE

As an interpretation of Max Weber's political thought, my book argues
that Weber's reflections on liberal modernity, once adequately recon-
strued, disclose an "immanentist" critique anchored in the logic and
promises of the liberal modern project itself rather than an authoritarian challenge to it. For this purpose, I aim to topically and genealog-
ically reconstruct Weber's political thought. First, this reconstruction
is topical since various elements in Weber's political thought will be
reconfigured in such a way as to highlight a sustained contemplation
of the two questions of the modern self and civil society. Second, it
is genealogical since the main narrative thread will be propelled by
examinations in successive order of early and late modes of modernity that are embedded in Weber's social imagination. Obviously, this
narrative order as well as the subject questions are conceptual artifices. They are artifices because Weber did not organize his ideas on
modernity in such a genealogical order, even if one presumes an overarching architectonic and narrative unity in his vast opus. Nor did
he explicitly privilege the self and civil society as his main themes.
In fact, Weber's main theme is still far from settled, and I do not intend to engage in this highly philological contention among Weber
scholars.[12]

---

[12] For more on this debate, see F. H. Tenbruck, "The Problem of Thematic Unity in
the Works of Max Weber," *British Journal of Sociology* 31:3 (1980), 316–51; idem,
"Das Webers Werk: Methodologie und Sozialwissenschaften," *Kölner Zeitschrift für
Soziologie und Sozialpsychologie* 38:1 (1986), 663–702; W. Schluchter, "Die Paradoxie
der Rationalisierung," *Zeitschrift für Soziologie* 5 (1976) 256–84 (trans. Guether Roth
in W. Schluchter and G. Roth, *Max Weber's Vision of History* [Berkeley: University of
California Press, 1979]); and W. Hennis, "Max Webers Thema: "Die Persönlichkeit
und die Lebensordnungen," *Zeitschrift für Politik* 31:1 (1984) 11–52 (trans. Keith
Tribe in S. Whimster and S. Lash [eds.], *Max Weber, Rationality and Modernity*
[London: Allen & Unwin, 1987]). For Anglophone contributions to this discussion,
see B. Nelson, "Max Weber's 'Author's Introduction' (1920): A Master Clue to His
Main Aims," *Sociological Inquiry* 44:4 (1974) 269–78. For a general overview, see

My book aims instead at an ideal typical reconstruction. It is an ideal type in the sense that any interpretative reconstruction unavoidably entails a hermeneutic accentuation predicated on the investigator's subjective commitments, prejudices, and problematics, shutting down one avenue of interpretation while opening up another. Thus, for example, my examination does not intend to exhaustively follow up the crucial distinction Weber makes between different forms of rationality that can be instrumental in accounting for the problematic nature of the charismatic-caesarist leadership ideal in his political thought.[13] Weber's morphology of rationality certainly figures importantly in my investigation as well – yet in a rather different context of constitution of the modern self and empowerment of its agency. To that extent, my investigation relies on a one-sided reconstruction of Weber's political thought. As Weber maintains that the unavoidable "one-sidedness" (*Einseitigkeit*) can be justified only by means of a clear elaboration and announcement of the subjective values (*Wertideen*) behind any ideal typical construction, then, I am certainly obliged to promulgate the subtexts in light of which my choice of strategy seemed expedient.

The most immediate subtext concerns Weber scholarship proper and, in particular, the continuing controversy among Weber scholars that was initiated by the publication of Wolfgang Mommsen's now classic study *Max Weber und die deutsche Politik* (1959).[14] Through meticulous analyses of Weber's political writings, partisan speeches, and private letters, Mommsen exposed a side of Weber little known until then – a figure whose political ideas epitomize the illiberal nationalism of Wilhelmine Germany and foreshadow at least in part the

S. Kalberg, "The Search for Thematic Orientations in a Fragmented Oeuvre: The Discussion of Max Weber in Recent German Sociological Literature," *Sociology* 13:1 (1979) 127–39.

[13] R. Brubaker, *The Limits of Rationality: An Essay on the Social and Moral Thought of Max Weber* (London: Allen & Unwin, 1984), is still a valuable study for those interested in this direction.

[14] W. Mommsen, *Max Weber und die deutsche Politik* (Tübingen: J. C. B. Mohr/Paul Siebeck, 1959). The revised edition of 1974 was translated by Michael Steinberg as *Max Weber and the German Politics, 1890–1920* (Chicago: University of Chicago Press, 1984); Mommsen's study was foreshadowed by J. P. Mayer's criticism of Weber's political ideas in which he likens Weber to Machiavelli. See J. P. Mayer, *Max Weber and German Politics: A Study in Political Sociology* (London: Faber & Faber, 1944) 90.

totalitarian dictatorship reminiscent of Hitler. Mommsen is essentially
in agreement with Jürgen Habermas when the latter proclaims that
Carl Schmitt, the crown jurist of National Socialism, is the "legitimate
pupil" of Weber's political thought.[15]

In brief, Mommsen's critical examination consists of three points.
First, Weber regarded traditional liberal democratic values as all but
obsolete. Especially the natural rights theory had become, for Weber,
outdated in the modern world, which enabled Mommsen to assert
that Weber "de-normatized" liberal democracy. This was a critical
revision of the liberal credo for Mommsen, since he believed that it
prepared a way for Weber to discuss liberal political values and institutions solely in terms of "rational expediency."[16] Second, expediency for Weber was measured by serviceability to the enhancement of
German national power. National imperialism was the ultimate political value Weber subscribed to consistently throughout his career,
and all other values and institutional commitments were subject to
it.[17] Third, therefore, it should not be taken as a surprise or an aber-
ration that Weber shifted the focus in his proposal for the German
political reform from a liberal parliamentarianism to a charismatic
caesarism. The new focus, if not its inevitable outcome, falls within
the parameters of Weber's political thought, which were delimited by
the abandonment of liberal modernity and sanctification of irrational
nationalism.

According to Mommsen, then, Weber signified a failure of German
bourgeois liberalism, which was too willing to succumb to authoritarian politics in the face of the immanent threat from the working class –
an illustrative piece of evidence, in short, for the *Sonderweg* paradigm
of postwar German historiography.[18] Worse still, Weber paved the way

---

[15] Habermas's discussion of Talcott Parsons's "Value-Freedom and Objectivity" in O.
Stammer (ed.), *Max Weber and Sociology Today* (Oxford: Blackwell, 1971) 66. For
more details, see J. Habermas, *Toward a Rational Society*, trans. J. Shapiro (London:
Heinemann, 1971), chapter V. Cf. Mommsen's agreement with Habermas in Stammer
(1971) 113.
[16] For the clearest statement of this position, see Mommsen (1984) 392–5, 396, 404.
[17] Ibid. 322, 327, 395–6.
[18] Mommsen's revisionism indeed forms a part of generational rebellion in West German
historiography that rejected the previous generation's conservative paradigm (of
Gerhart Ritter et al.). Spearheaded by Fritz Fischer and Hans-Ulrich Wehler, the new
paradigm problematized modern German history in terms of structurally determined

for the demise of the Weimar Republic and ushered in the rise of National Socialism by first formulating and endorsing irrational mass politics capped by charismatic dictatorship as an antidote to the overblown fear of bureaucratic petrification.[19]

defects that are rooted in the discrepancy between economic modernity and political and social backwardness. Seen this way, modern German history is marked by the profound difference, or an aberrational path of development (*Sonderweg*), that sets it apart from the Anglophone experiences of modernization. One of the more salient features of this *Sonderweg* paradigm was the thesis of bourgeois recapitulation by the Junker establishment in which popular and illiberal national imperialism during the Wilhelmine period tends to be held responsible. It is natural that Mommsen's iconoclastic reading of the representative bourgeois thinker of Wilhelmine politics, Weber, was also based on the dichotomy between liberalism and nationalism. For a contextualization of Mommsen's contribution, see G. Eley, "Liberalism, Europe and the Bourgeoisie, 1860–1914," in D. Blackbourne and R. Evans (eds.), *The German Bourgeoisie: Essays on the Social History of the German Middle Class from the Late Eighteenth to the Early Twentieth Century* (London: Routlege, 1991) 295. For the discursive context of West German historiography, see R. Evans, *Rethinking German History: Nineteenth-Century Germany and the Origins of the Third Reich* (London: Allen & Unwin, 1987). For the programmatic critique of the *Sonderweg* paradigm, see G. Eley and D. Blackbourn, *The Peculiarities of German History* (Oxford: Oxford University Press, 1984).

[19] In fact, Mommsen's criticism vacillates between these two different innuendos – that is, between Weber as a symptom of liberal crisis (i.e., the "liberal in despair" thesis) and as a root of its problems (i.e., the "pre-Schmitt" thesis). The second view is more pronounced in the 1959 study. Mommsen, however, gradually toned down his criticism as he turned more attention to Weber's theoretical writings, veering in his subsequent works more toward the first position. See his *Age of Bureaucracy* (Oxford: Blackwell, 1974) and *The Political and Social Theory of Max Weber* (Chicago: University of Chicago Press, 1989). The second position was also reinforced by Raymond Aron and Herbert Marcuse, albeit from their different perspectives. Aron aimed criticism less at national imperialism than at the idolatry of power that brought Weber's political thinking dangerously close to the worship of the state itself. Aron's argument maintained that Weber's obsession with nation cannot be accounted for apart from his belief that the state represents nation in the international power struggle. Embedded in a Nietzschean aestheticization of power and a Darwinian theory of struggle, Weber's political ideas in fact celebrated the modern nation-states as effective media for the continuation of human struggle – a value in and of itself. According to Aron, in short, Weber was a profoundly illiberal thinker who posed a problem "to" modern liberalism. See R. Aron, "Max Weber and Power Politics," in Stammer (1971). Continuing the line of Marxist critique of Weber first promulgated by Georg Lukács, Marcuse confirmed all this and concluded that Weber represented the perversion of capitalist rationality and liberal modernity. Weber's genius and intellectual integrity were apparent to Marcuse, since his idea crystallized the historic turn by which the earlier Enlightenment formal rationality degenerated into a substantive irrationality that attended the authoritarian politics, exploitive economy, and refeudalized society of late capitalism. For Marcuse, Weber was a bourgeois liberal thinker par excellence, and to that extent, the problematic nature of Weber's political ideas was the

The Mommsen thesis constitutes a subtext for my reconstruction not primarily because my aim is to refute Mommsen's reading – that is, to write a liberal apologia for Weber. Although I will critically and substantively engage with it on a number of occasions, the awareness of Mommsen's contribution is valuable to my project insofar as it contributes to the identification of pitfalls in examining Weber's political thought. The virtues of the Mommsen thesis notwithstanding, its value lies more in the methodological weaknesses of his approach than in the strength of its contents and conclusions. In particular, I aim to expose two weak premises of the Mommsen thesis against which I will identify my approach. They are, first, an inconsistency between Weber's political and scholarly writings, and second, Mommsen's understanding of liberalism.

The first problem results from an exclusive attention to the political writings of Weber (mostly public speeches and partisan journalism) without systematically incorporating Weber's more theoretical contributions. Weber's comparative sociology of religion is all but completely ignored, and so is his analysis of rationalization. The sociological concepts of bureaucracy, charisma, and nation, key concepts that are potentially critical for Mommsen's projects, are given only a sketchy elaboration in isolation from the Weber scholarship in general. Thus, contrary comments notwithstanding, Mommsen's Weber appears in the end, in the absence of satisfactory incorporation of his theoretical views, to be schizophrenic in his political thinking – betraying an important inconsistency between the universal "scientific" value of the historical, sociological, and methodological contributions and the political ideas that were

culmination of the problem "of" modern liberalism. See H. Marcuse, "Industrialization and Capitalism," in Stammer (1971). For Lukács's criticism of Weber, see G. Lukács, "Max Weber and German Sociology," *Economy and Society* 1:4 (1972) 386–98. David Beetham managed to chart a middle course by arguing that Weber's political thought represents one problematic aspect of bourgeois liberalism that overemphasizes the defiant, aristocratic, and elitist side of liberal individualism or "tendencies toward elective dictatorship that exist within liberal democracy" ("Introduction" to the second ed., 7). See D. Beetham, *Max Weber and the Theory of Modern Politics* (London: Allen & Unwin, 1974). For a more succinct statement, see his "Max Weber and the Liberal Political Tradition," *European Journal of Sociology* 30 (1989) 313–23. For the best example of recent scholarship on Weber's politics, see P. Breiner, *Max Weber and Democratic Politics* (Ithaca, NY: Cornell University Press, 1997).

steeped in the particularistic considerations of Wilhelmine politics and society.[20]

Not only was Weber's political thought, however, shaped by his passionate political involvements, but also the reverse: his studies in universal history and comparative historical sociology decisively informed his own political ideas, choices, and commitments. This can be argued with more persuasiveness in Weber's case, for he was a politically driven thinker throughout his career; "His thinking," observed Karl Jaspers, "was the reality of a man who was political in every fiber of his being."[21] Thus, for example, Weber's association with a prominent left-liberal politician, Friedrich Naumann, and his *National-sozialer Verein* was based on their shared criticism of the political role of the Junker class, a theme Weber first formulated in the East Elbian studies. His ad hoc studies of the Russian Revolution of 1905 clearly reveal his understanding of the Russian situation in terms contrastive to earlier revolutions of comparable magnitude, that is, the Reformation, the English Civil War, and the American Revolution. These events clearly constitute part of the historical background for the main subject of Weber's most famous scholarly contribution, the Protestant ethic thesis. The sociological concepts of charisma and bureaucracy are, needless to say, inseparably linked with Weber's postwar writings on the reconstruction and democratization of Germany, in which criticism of omnipotent bureaucracy and the plebiscitary presidency as its antidote figure prominently. Without going into further detail, suffice it to say that Weber was a profoundly political thinker, if not a thinker exclusively of the political, whose political thought cannot be convincingly accounted for in isolation from his sociological and historical ideas, and vice versa.

---

[20] This "Jekyll and Hyde" approach to Weber has been no less pronounced among some of the staunchest defenders of Weber's liberal credentials. See, for example, G. Roth, "Weber's Political Failure," *Telos* 78 (1989) 136–49, and F. Blum, "Max Weber: The Man of Politics and the Man Dedicated to Objectivity and Rationality," *Ethics* 70:1 (1959), 1–20.

[21] K. Jaspers, *On Max Weber* (New York: Paragon House, 1989), 39; cf. Gerth and Mills, who say that Weber's political convictions "make up a theme inextricably interwoven with Weber the man and the intellectual" ("Introduction" in *From Max Weber: Essays in Sociology* [Oxford: Oxford University Press, 1946], 32). Also see V. K. Dibble, "Social Science and Political Commitments in the Young Max Weber," *European Journal of Sociology* 9:1 (1968), 92–110.

The second weakness of Mommsen's interpretation lies in his implicit understanding of liberal democracy. Mommsen's premise is that liberal democracy depends on a substantive value orientation that is predicated on inalienable rights issuing from universal natural law as opposed to positive laws. According to Mommsen, for example, stripped of a firm normative foundation rooted in universal values, the Weimar "value-neutral democracy" was predestined to collapse.[22] It is this criticism of formalism predicated on a fundamentalist understanding of liberal democracy that Mommsen shares with Leo Strauss's well-known critique of Weber's methodological distinction between value and fact.[23] According to Strauss, the post-Nietzschean and Weberian transfiguration of virtue into value and the attendant dissociation from truth claims lead only to a radical form of nihilism and existentialist decisionism. Lacking the anchoring foundation of moral virtues that only philosophy, as understood by Strauss's esoteric definition, can identify, the modern political society tends to plunge into a nihilistic maelstrom of amoral self-assertion and self-expression of the unreflective masses – an image curiously reminiscent of the last years of the Weimar Republic, to which Weber and his like gave birth and in which Strauss spent his formative years.[24]

Aside from the theoretical problems associated with the fundamentalist understanding of liberalism per se, which fall beyond the scope

---

[22] Mommsen admits his unique value position in placing his own study in the immediate postwar milieu in German academia. Mommsen (1984) vii. In another review of German historiography since the Second World War, Mommsen still explains the denormatization of liberal democracy in Weberian terms of the displacement of "value-oriented" by "value-free" liberalism, to which he attributes the collapse of the Weimar republic. See W. Mommsen, "The Return to the Western Tradition: German Historiography since 1945," Occasional Paper #4 (Washington, DC: German Historical Institute, 1991), 13.

[23] See L. Strauss, "Natural Right and the Distinction between Facts and Values," in his *Natural Right and History* (Chicago: University of Chicago Press, 1950). Also in agreement is Eric Voegelin in *The New Science of Politics* (Chicago: University of Chicago Press, 1952) 13–23.

[24] For more details on the problem of Strauss's reading of Weber, see R. Titunik, "Understanding the Devil: Max Weber's Political Thought" (Ph.D. dissertation, Department of Political Science, University of Chicago, 1991) 257–74, and K. Löwith, "Max Webers Stellung zur Wissenschaft," in his *Vorträger und Abhandlungen: zur Kritik der christlichen Überlieferung* (Stuttgart: Verlag W. Kohlhammer, 1966) 228ff. For a critical discussion of the Straussian denigration of value-free liberalism, see S. Holmes, *The Anatomy of Antiliberalism* (Chicago: University of Chicago Press, 1993) 61–87.

of my investigation, Mommsen's application of this approach poses two problems in understanding Weber's political thought. The first problem is that Mommsen's fundamentalist presupposition makes it difficult for him to investigate the question of Weber's liberalism on a hermeneutically adequate level. For Weber, value fragmentation and pluralism constitute a starting point to which his political ideas are conceived as a response, not an end of his political thinking. Mommsen's strike at this premise tends to misfire, since it cannot be properly accounted for in the context of political writings; rather, it requires a systematic inquiry into Weber's methodological writings and sociology of religions, the lack of which constituted a loophole identified earlier as the first weakness of Mommsen's argument. In this light, Strauss's criticism is more sustained and consistent, since he at least focuses on Weber's methodological premises. Also, although Mommsen can be justified insofar as his point is to criticize Weber's misunderstanding or overblown fear of the discontents of modernity, such a recognition can hardly justify his subsequent claim that Weber's value-neutral premises lead his political ideas directly to, or foreshadow, authoritarian conclusions. That is to say, the alleged transition from a value-free liberalism to the authoritarian conclusion in Weber's political thinking cannot be made to appear so unmitigated as Mommsen posits.[25]

The second problem pertains more to the practice of drawing a laundry-list-like portrait of liberalism itself. Whether fundamentalist or not, this approach is predicated on identifying and enumerating premises, values, and institutions that in combination more or less exhaust our understanding of liberalism, against which to juxtapose, compare, contrast, or assimilate Weber's political ideas.[26]

---

[25] Needless to say, the sea of change that separates our time and Mommsen's is so great that Mommsen's kind of natural right liberalism is seen by some as ironically contributing to the demise of individual freedom and rights. From this perspective, a mild form of value relativism has been and should be an integral part of the contemporary liberal agenda. See, for example, R. Rorty, "Postmodernist Bourgeois Liberalism," in his *Objectivity, Relativism and Truth: Philosophical Papers*, Vol. 1 (Cambridge: Cambridge University Press, 1991). A useful discussion of this issue is contained in C. Larmore, "Political Liberalism," in his *The Morals of Modernity* (Cambridge: Cambridge University Press, 1996).

[26] See, for example, Regina Titunik's liberal reading of Weber and critique of the Mommsen thesis, which nonetheless takes an ontological approach similar to that

Aside from my methodological suspicion of this kind of acontextual approach, such a project would inevitably draw on a more or less self-contained portrait of liberalism that falls outside the scope of Weber research.[27] Unless one is prepared to discuss substantive problems in liberalism per se as Weber has relevance to them, it tends to result in a dubious caricature that can neither be falsified nor ascertained within the scope of Weber exegesis. And, of course, whether Weber appears liberal or not depends on how one draws liberalism.

In short, Mommsen's reading reveals an odd mixture of highly contextualized analyses of Weber's political writings grounded in Wilhelmine politics, on the one hand, and an acontextual, almost antihistorical evaluation of Weber's political ideas in light of the fundamentalist understanding of liberalism, on the other. Missing between these two extreme poles is an examination of Weber's political thought that is based on a careful analysis of the connection Weber draws between his comparative sociology and universal history, and political and partisan essays. My reexamination attempts to get around these two problems by putting Weber's political ideas in the context of his own theoretical writings, thus avoiding a presumptuous value judgment based on a dubious characterization of liberalism as well as a reductionism to the

---

of Mommsen. R. Titunik, "Status, Vanity, and Equal Dignity in Max Weber's Political Thought," *Economy and Society* 24:1 (1995) 101–21.

[27] Some recent works on liberalism have attempted to get around the problem of definition by arguing that there is no one thing to define. In this view, liberalism is a "family of ideas" (à la Wittgenstein), movements and institutions, changing over time and place, rather than any given laundry list of characteristics. This methodological difficulty involved in defining liberalism led others to call for an inductive, historical, and typological investigation rather than a deductive and ontological one. Those who share this view are, for example, A. Kahan, *Aristocratic Liberalism: The Social and Political Thought of Jacob Buckhardt, John Stuart Mill, and Alexis de Tocqueville* (Chicago: University of Chicago Press, 1992); R. Bellamy (ed.), *Victorian Liberalism: Nineteenth Century Political Thought and Practice* (London: Routledge, 1990); J. Gray, *Liberalism* (Minneapolis: University of Minnesota Press, 1986); J. Sheehan, "Some Reflections on Liberalism in Comparative Perspective," in H. Köhler (ed.), *Deutschland und der Westen* (Berlin: Colloquium Verlag, 1984); and J. Sheehan, *German Liberalism in the Nineteenth Century* (Chicago: University of Chicago Press, 1978). These various authors all find inspiration from H. Rosenberg, "Theologischer Rationalismus und vormärzlicher Vulgärliberalismus," *Histrischer Zeitschrift* 141 (1930) 497–541.

particularistic context of Wilhelmine politics. In short, I aim to account for Weber's political ideas primarily in the intertextual context.[28]

In spite of clear allusions scattered throughout his political writings, however, this task is not always easy, since Weber never left behind a systematic treatise on his political sociology, not to mention one on political philosophy.[29] We have essays on, for example, bureaucracy, legitimacy, nation, and so on, which were published posthumously as *Economy and Society*, yet the conceptual ordering of these essays has not been established beyond doubt.[30] This problem means that a relatively large-scale examination of Weber's political ideas would involve imagining the *unfinished* project that can account for his political, sociological, historical, and epistemological writings with certain coherence. In establishing this kind of artificially coherent interpretative framework for an intertextual reading of Weber's political thought, I

[28] For a good example of the intertextual reading of Weber, see D. Chalcraft, "Bringing the Text Back In," in L. J. Ray and M. Reed (eds.), *Organizing Modernity: New Weberian Perspective on Works, Organization, and Society* (London: Routledge, 1994). Also see B. S. Green, *Literary Methods and Sociological Theory: Case Studies of Simmel and Weber* (Chicago: University of Chicago Press, 1988), especially 179–282. For the hermeneutical issues involved in the stabilization of meaning through intertextual reading, such as the author's intention, extratextual contexts, and the reader's situatedness and response, see J. Kristeva, "Word, Dialogue, and Novel," in T. Moi (ed.), *The Kristeva Reader* (New York: Columbia University Press, 1986); D. LaCapra, *Rethinking Intellectual History: Text, Contexts, and Language* (Ithaca, NY: Cornell University Press, 1983) 23–71; and Q. Skinner, "Meaning and Understanding in the History of Ideas" and "Motives, Intensions, and the Interpretation of Texts," in J. Tully (ed.), *Meaning and Context: Quentin Skinner and His Critics* (Princeton, NJ: Princeton University Press, 1988).

[29] It was for this reason that Johannes Winckelmann's chapter heading of *Staatssoziologie* in the German original was omitted from the English edition. See Guenther Roth's editor's introduction to Weber's *Economy and Society* (Berkeley: University of California Press, 1978), cvii–cix. Winckelmann, who was, along with Marianne Weber, primarily responsible for editing Weber's posthumous works, admits the problems and difficulties associated with his editorship. For example, the ordering of *Economy and Society* was dictated largely by the logic of a larger collective encyclopedia, *Grundriss der Sozialökonomik*, of which Weber's contributions are a part. J. Winckelmann, *Max Webers hintergelassenes Hauptwerk: Die Wirtschaft und gesellschaftliche Ordnungen und Mächte. Entstechung und gedanklicher Aufbau* (Tübingen: J. C. B. Mohr/Paul Siebeck, 1986).

[30] For more philological details, see W. Schluchter, "Wirtschaft und Gesellschaft: Das Ende eines Mythos," in his *Religion und Lebensführung*, Bd. 2 (Frankfurt a. M.: Suhrkamp, 1988) and the editors' introduction by W. J. Mommsen with M. Meyer in MWG I/22-1, 1–65.

proceed from Weber's own model, which can be extracted from the Protestant ethic thesis.

IN SEARCH OF THE PROTESTANT ETHIC THESIS

The meaning of the Protestant ethic thesis has been subject to debate ever since Weber's own time. One of the most immediate responses to the publication of *The Protestant Ethic* came from historians and economists. This controversy revolved around the historical validity of Weber's attribution of the origin of capitalism to certain kinds of Protestant denominations, Calvinist doctrines, and sectarian lifestyles. Weber's attribution was discussed from every imaginable perspective, from a Catholic criticism to a Whiggish applause. In this historiographical context, Weber's Protestant ethic thesis is first of all about the historical origin of modern capitalism.[31] At issue in a more sociological context was, second, the idealist understanding of historical and social changes, as opposed to the Marxian historical materialism. Weber's study was seen less as an empirical statement on the historical origin of capitalism than as an illustrative example of a non-Marxist methodology that puts more emphasis on suprastructure. Seen this way, Weber could be juxtaposed to Marx and, to a lesser extent, to Durkheim, who were collectively rendered as the canonical founding

---

[31] The most immediate responses from German and later discussion in English academic circles centered on this historical question. See, for example, the critique of Weber by Felix Rachfall and Karl Fischer collected and edited by J. Winckelmann in *Die protestantische Ethik II – Max Weber: Kritiken und Antikritiken* (Gütersloh: Gütersloher Verlag, 1978). Some of the more important of these exchanges have recently been translated and edited by Peter Baehr and Gordon Wells in *The Protestant Ethic and the "Spirit" of Capitalism and Other Writings* (London: Penguin Books, 2002). Their introduction is particularly helpful in understanding the various meanings that have been attributed to the Protestant ethic thesis. For Anglophone critiques, see H. M. Robertson, *Aspects of the Rise of Economic Individualism* (Cambridge: Cambridge University Press, 1933); K. Samuelson, *Religion and Economic Action* (Stockholm: Svenska Bokförlaget, 1961); R. H. Tawney, *Religion and the Rise of Capitalism* (New York: Harcourt & Brace, 1952); and R. Trevor-Roper, *Religion, Reformation and Social Change* (London: Macmillan, 1972). This mainly historiographical controversy still continues in, for example, M. H. MacKinnon, "Part I: Calvinism and the Infallible Assurance of Grace," and "Part II: Weber's Exploration of Calvinism," *British Journal of Sociology* 39:2 (1988) 143–210.

fathers of sociology.[32] Reinvigorated in part by the poststructuralist challenge, the third perspective renders the Protestant ethic thesis as a genealogical account of modernity that was a uniquely Occidental product of the metahistorical process of rationalization. Numerous arguments have been made that Weber's fundamental problematic and governing theme are the nature and advance of rationalization and its contribution to the uniqueness of Occidental modernity.[33] Refashioned recently as a theorist of modernity, Weber and his rationalization thesis are understood in relation to a new axis that runs from Nietzsche to Foucault.[34]

Largely overlapping with the third perspective, yet still a different appropriation, is the renewed focus on the self in understanding the meaning of Weber's Protestant ethic thesis.[35] This perspective shares

[32] This agenda was central to the earlier generation of American Weber scholars. See R. Bendix, *Max Weber: An Intellectual Portrait* (New York: Doubleday, 1960), and T. Parsons, *The Structure of Social Action* (New York: McGraw-Hill, 1937). Albeit from a different perspective, this canonical reading persists, for example, in A. Giddens, *Capitalism and Modern Social Theory: An Analysis of the Writing of Marx, Durkheim and Max Weber* (Cambridge: Cambridge University Press, 1971), and J. Alexander, *Theoretical Logic in Sociology, Vol. III, The Classical Attempt at Theoretical Synthesis: Max Weber* (Berkeley: University of California Press, 1983).

[33] There are readings along this line too numerous to list here. Wolfgang Schluchter's *The Rise of Western Rationalism: Max Weber's Developmental History*, trans./intro. G. Roth (Berkeley: University of California Press, 1981), gives one of the more systematic and elaborate versions of this reading. Especially see chapter VI, "The Role of the Reformation in the Transition to Modernity." Also see his more recent *Rationalism, Religion, and Domination: A Weberian Perspective*, trans. N. Solomon (Berkeley: University of California Press, 1989).

[34] For a programmatic reading of Weber along this axis, see the various contributions edited by S. Whimster and S. Lash (ed.), *Max Weber, Rationality, and Modernity* (London: Allen & Unwin, 1987) and A. Horowitz and T. Malley (eds.), *The Barbarism of Reason: Max Weber and the Twilight of Enlightenment* (Toronto: University of Toronto Press, 1994). Also see S. H. Rudolph, "From Weber to Weber (via Foucault)," *World Politics* 48:1 (1995) 21–8; D. Owen, *Maturity and Modernity: Nietzsche, Weber, and Foucault and the Ambivalence of Reason* (London: Routledge, 1994); P. Neunhaus, *Max Weber und Michel Foucault: Über Macht und Herrschaft in der Moderne* (Pfaffenweiler: Centaurus-Verlagsgesellschaft, 1993); C. Turner, *Modernity and Politics in the Work of Max Weber* (London: Routledge, 1992); and B. Turner, *Max Weber: From History to Modernity* (London: Routledge, 1992).

[35] Despite the all too apparent centrality of the self in Weber's research agenda, it has received less attention than it deserves. Despite a few scattered exceptions (see, for instance, A. Eisen, "Called to Order: The Role of the Puritan *Berufsmensch* in Weberian Sociology," *Sociology* 13:2 [1979] 203–18, and E. Portis, "Max Weber's Theory of

with the previous approach the assertion that the central theme in Weber, especially in the sociology of religion, was rationalization understood as the rise of a peculiarly Occidental modernity. As opposed to the macrosociological foci of the third approach, however, the uniqueness of this new approach lies in a more microsociological claim that Weber's religious writings, and the Protestant ethic essays in particular, center on the genealogy of the modern self.[36] Once formulated this way, rationalization is rendered as the logic of (dis)empowerment of the self that poses the most fundamental problem to Weber. His central concern in his sociological and historical writings was, then, to probe into the sociocultural conditions under which a particular type of self is constituted, and its agency strengthened and undermined, during the course of rationalization – in short, to investigate life conduct (*Lebensführung*), life orders (*Lebensordnungen*), or *Habitus* according to Wilhelm Hennis's reading of Weber.[37]

Personality," *Sociological Inquiry* 48 [1978] 113–20), it was not until Wilhelm Hennis drew attention to this neglected aspect of Weberian scholarship that the earlier tradition of according centrality to Weber's philosophical anthropology was revived. See W. Hennis, *Max Webers Fragestellung*, translated by Keith Tribe as *Max Weber: Essays in Reconstruction* (London: Allen & Unwin, 1988), and his more recent *Max Webers Wissehschaft vom Menschen* (Tübingen: J. C. B. Mohr/Paul Siebeck, 1996); for the earlier tradition, see, for example, K. Jaspers, *Max Weber: Eine Gedenkrede* (Tübingen: J. C. B. Mohr/Paul Siebeck, 1926); D. Henrich, *Die Einheit der Wissenschaftslehre Max Webers* (Tübingen: J. C. B. Mohr/Paul Siebeck, 1952); S. Landshut, "Max Webers geschichtliche Bedeutung," in his *Kritik der Soziologie und Schriften zur Politik* (Berlin: Hermann Luchterhand Verlag, 1969); and K. Löwith, *Max Weber und Karl Marx* (Sttutgart: Verlag W. Kohlhammer, 1960). Also see the various essays by early German scholars of Weber compiled in P. Lassman and I. Velody (eds.), *Max Weber's "Science as a Vocation"* (London: Allen & Unwin, 1989). For recent Anglo-American literature on this subject, see, for instance, D. Owen, "Autonomy and 'Inner Distance': A Trace of Nietzsche in Weber," *History of the Human Sciences* 4:1 (1991) 79–91, and R. Schroeder, "'Personality' and 'Inner Distance': The Conception of the Individual in Max Weber's Sociology," ibid. Although it does not explicitly state this theme, Lawrence Scaff's *Fleeing the Iron Cage: Culture, Politics, and Modernity in the Thought of Max Weber* (Berkeley: University of California Press, 1989) also echoes it, insofar as he identifies Weber's central question as a cultural logic of the modern fragmentation of selfhood. Probably the most comprehensive study is Harvey Goldman's pioneering monograph, *Max Weber and Thomas Mann: Calling and the Shaping of the Self* (Berkeley: University of California Press, 1988), and his companion volume, *Politics, Death, and the Devil: Self and Power in Max Weber and Thomas Mann* (Berkeley: University of California Press, 1992).

[36] Goldman (1992) 2–10.

[37] See "Personality and Life Orders: Max Weber's Theme," in Whimster and Lash (1987).

Not always represented in this reading of Weber's Protestant ethic thesis is, nevertheless, Weber's substantial discussion of the "sect" as the social foundation of the Puritan *Berufsmensch*. Harvey Goldman, for example, proclaims that, since Weber's conception of self is deliberately resistant to the influences of others and is instead formed solely from "within," it is a "countersocialized self."[38] This assertion contains only half of the picture, though. Weber in *The Protestant Ethic* was certainly preoccupied with isolating the process of self-constitution that resembles what Charles Taylor now calls a subjective "inward turn."[39] As Weber deduced the highly objectified work ethic ironically from the subjective inner isolation of individuals, however, he did not simply proceed from the subjective self to the conclusion of an antisocial self. This is a misunderstanding that tends to stem from the characteristic ignorance of sect essays among Weber scholars, in which Weber, for example, concludes that

[i]n the time of its heroic youth, this [Protestant-inspired] individualism conjointly produced an eminent power to form communities. . . . On the one hand, the idea that the religious qualifications bestowed on the individual by God are alone decisive for his salvation, that no form of sacramental magic is of use to him here, that only his practical conduct, his "probation [*Bewährung*]," can take him as a symptom absolutely on his own in the matter most important to him. On the other hand, this qualification through self-probation is viewed exclusively as the foundation for the social union of the congregation [*sozialen Zusammenschlußes der Gemeinde*].[40]

---

[38] Goldman (1992) 9. Also see his "Weber's Ascetic Practices of the Self" in H. Lehmann and G. Roth (eds.), *Weber's Protestant Ethic: Origins, Evidence, Contexts* (Cambridge: Cambridge University Press, 1987) 171. Harry Liebersohn is in agreement when he criticizes Weber's ideal type of the Puritan self as being too individual-centered, especially in comparison with Ernst Troeltsch's analysis in the *Social Teachings of the Christian Churches*, trans. O. Wyon (London: Allen & Unwin, 1931). See *Fate and Utopia in German Sociology, 1870–1923* (Cambridge, MA: MIT Press, 1988) 103.

[39] See C. Taylor, *Sources of the Self: The Making of Modern Identity* (Cambridge, MA: Harvard University Press, 1989) and *The Ethic of Authenticity* (Cambridge, MA: Harvard University Press, 1991). For a succinct statement, see "Aims of a New Epoch" in his *Hegel* (Cambridge: Cambridge University Press, 1975).

[40] *Nordamerika* 579–80. For a criticism of this negligence, see B. Nelson, "Max Weber, Ernst Troeltsch, Georg Jellinek as Comparative Historical Sociologists" *Sociological Analysis* 36:3 (1979) 229–40, and S. Berger, "The Sects and the Breakthrough into the Modern World: On the Centrality of the Sects in Weber's Protestant Ethic Thesis" *Sociological Inquiry* 12 (Autumn 1971) 486–99. A relatively recent exception is J. Alexander, "Cultural Grounds of Rationalization: Sect Democracy versus the

Weber makes clear in his sect essays that it is a misunderstanding of his thesis to attribute antisocial nature to his conception of the modern self. And it is in the form of the sect that he formulated his understanding of "the connection of the internal isolation of the individual . . . with his ability to form social groups having the most stable cohesion and maximum impact."[41] In the Protestant ethic thesis, Weber appears as a finely tuned dialectician who charts the irony of social cohesion that is predicated on a subjective self-constitution, avoiding the vulgar dichotomy of *Gemeinschaft* versus *Gesellschaft*.[42]

Taken together, then, the Protestant ethic and sect essays can be read as forming a relatively systematic whole in which Weber's social imagination centers on the anthropology of the modern self and the ontology of his or her social existence, or in short, an inquiry into the ironical compound Weber called "sect man" (*Sektenmensch*).[43] This reformulation facilitates shedding theoretical light on his political ideas, since it leaves wide open two interpretative avenues – one pertaining to the self and civil society and the other to early and late modernity.

This theme of associational pluralism and ethical characterology that figures prominently especially in Weber's postwar political writings has been understood mostly as an antidote to the monolithic bureaucratic state, a polemical apologia for the capitalist system of unfettered competition in opposition to the socialist regimentation, or an expression of the Nietzschean–Darwinian metaphor of struggle. Although these understandings capture various aspects of associational pluralism that Weber imagined in his political writings, they make it difficult to assess the significance of this theme in Weber's overall political thinking. Thus, associational pluralism for Weber tends to be read as of secondary importance to and consequently overshadowed by charismatic leadership in controlling bureaucracy, by market dynamism in fighting off socialism, or by international political struggles in preserving

Iron Cage," in his *Structure and Meaning: Rethinking Classical Sociology* (New York: Columbia University Press, 1989).

[41] Nordamerika 581.

[42] Compare Talcott Parsons's almost opposite schema of interpretation: "When one comes to isolate the main logical outline of Weber's analysis, the prominence of the pattern of dichotomization is striking." T. Parsons, "Introduction" in *Sociology of Religion* (Boston: Beacon, 1963) xxxix, n. 11.

[43] Letter to Adolf von Harnack (5 February 1906) in MWG II/5, 33.

elitist individualism.[44] As opposed to these readings, my reexamination restores the thematic centrality of associational pluralism to Weber's political thinking by tracing its root in his Protestant ethic thesis.

The thematic accentuation of self and civil society also facilitates clarification of the meaning of Weber's alleged *Kulturpessimismus* and its ramifications for his political thinking. Albeit varied in its form of expression and implication, cultural pessimism in Wilhelmine and Weimar Germany is often held accountable as the political cultural background for the deep-rooted hostility to liberal democratic values and modern industrialism and thus for the subsequent rise of National Socialism.[45] Weber's rationalization thesis, especially when viewed in the context of the iron cage imagery is often read as corroborating this antimodernist *Weltanschauung*.[46]

Arthur Mitzman holds, for example, that especially Weber's later works reflect a turn in an antiascetic and protomystic direction. Ironically, Mitzman uses Weber's characterization of the sect as a *Gesellschaft* to support his argument that Weber became increasingly taken with acosmic mysticism.[47] Mitzman's error seems to originate from a simple syllogism: the *Gesellschaft* is an iron cage; the Protestant sect is a

---

44 See, for example, Beetham's new introduction to the second edition of Beetham (1974); Hennis (1988) 181–2; and R. Aron, *Main Currents of Sociological Thought, Vol. II: Durkheim, Pareto, Weber* (Baltimore: Penguin Books, 1970) 253–8.

45 See J. Herf, *Reactionary Modernism: Technology, Culture, and Politics in Weimar and the Third Reich* (Cambridge: Cambridge University Press, 1984); F. Ringer, *The Decline of the German Mandarins: The German Academic Community, 1890–1933* (Cambridge, MA: Harvard University Press, 1969); G. Mosse, *The Crisis of German Ideology* (New York: Grosset & Dunlap, 1964); F. Stern, *The Politics of Cultural Despair: A Study in the Rise of the German Ideology* (Berkeley: University of California Press, 1961); and S. Kalberg, "The Origin and Explanation of *Kulturpessimismus*: The Relationship between Public and Private Spheres in Early Twentieth Century Germany," *Sociological Theory* 5 (1987) 150–65.

46 See, for example, J. Freund, *The Sociology of Max Weber* (New York: Vintage, 1969); F. Stern, *Failure of Illiberalism* (New York: Knopf, 1972); and A. Mitzman, *The Iron Cage: An Historical Interpretation of Max Weber* (New York: Knopf, 1969). Recently, John Patrick Diggins has confirmed this reading with a new twist that celebrates Weber's thought precisely because of its dark pessimism. J. P. Diggins, *Max Weber: The Politics and Spirit of Tragedy* (New York: Basic Books, 1996) 10–11. Also see his *The Promise of Pragmatism: Modernism and the Crisis of Knowledge and Authority* (Chicago: University of Chicago Press, 1994) 22–54, in which he denigrates American pragmatism for being optimistic about modernity compared to Weber.

47 Mitzman (1970) 194–201. In agreement with my critique is J. Alexander (1989) 105–6.

Gesellschaft; thus, the Protestant sect is an iron cage. Albeit with more theoretical underpinning, Habermas agrees with Mitzman's conclusion that Weber's critique of the iron cage reflects a principled rejection of the modern project. Weber analytically overlooked the other side of rationalization, which builds on what Habermas later conceptualized as "communicative rationality" and, as a consequence, wrongly identified the discontents of the iron cage with the problems of modernity per se. Given the selective understanding of rationalization, then, Weber failed to develop an immanent critique of modernity, a critique rooted in the modern discourse of reason, which provides an alibi for the alleged turn, in the face of a seemingly inevitable and unshakable iron cage, in a pessimistic, irrational, and mystic direction that culminates in the nihilist decisionism of his political thinking.[48] As for Mitzman, also prominent in Habermas's critique is the permeation of instrumental rationality by Puritan sects and their secularized heirs.

As opposed to this attribution of antimodernism to Weber, my interpretation brings forth the conceptual schema of Weber's political thinking by dividing it into early and late modes of modernity.[49] Taking the modern self and civil society as two topical foci of analysis, I aim to underscore that Weber's genealogical narrative of degeneration (*Verfallsgeschichte*) does not lead to the rejection of the modern project and to a simple celebration of irrationality. It cannot be equated with antimodernism, because Weber believed that sectlike associations do not serve only as media for the social institutionalization and penetration of means–end rationality, as Habermas insists. More prominently, they function as an ethical disciplinary mechanism that maintains the substantive-rational core of the modern self. In other words, Weber saw the Puritan self and the sectlike associations less as the precursor or institutionalized forms of instrumental rationality than as an educational mechanism for a uniquely modern symbiosis of subjective value and objective rationality that issues in principled, moral conduct

[48] J. Habermas, *The Theory of Communicative Action, Vol. 1: Reason and the Rationalizaiton of Society*, trans. T. McCarthy (Boston: Beacon, 1984) 216–71.

[49] Frederic Jameson's effort to establish the Protestant ethic thesis as an independent historical category cramped between traditionalism and late modernity in Weber's conceptual schema has been curiously ignored by mainstream Weber scholarship. See F. Jameson, "The Vanishing Mediator: The Narrative Structure in Max Weber," *New German Critique* 1:1 (1972) 52–89.

of an autonomous agency. In short, Weber's political ideas were predicated on the recognition of the different possibilities of the modern project and were committed to its reinvigoration under late modern circumstances.

OUTLINE OF THE ARGUMENT

In summary, avoiding both reductionism to a particular context of Wilhelmine Germany and explicit value judgment based on liberal fundamentalism, I aim to put Weber's controversial political ideas in the context of his theoretical contributions – that is, intertextually. I focus on the Protestant ethic thesis first because it offers entry into the two themes of the modern self and civil society in Weber's thought. Taking the modern self and civil society as thematic threads that run through the Protestant ethic thesis and the later political writings, then, I examine Weber's political thought, in which his advocation of individual autonomy and freedom, voluntary associational life in a dynamic civil society, liberal nationalism, and staunch modernism will be highlighted. In the end, I portray Weber as siding firmly with the modern project in his political thinking, because it was the early modern forms of self and civil society that he saw in jeopardy and thus wanted to empower under the late modern conditions of the iron cage. I argue that, in the form of the politician and scientist with a vocation and pluralized group life, Weber strove to preserve the core of political modernity he identified earlier in the Protestant ethic thesis, albeit in a secularized form.

After the brief introduction in this chapter, I reexamine *The Protestant Ethic* and other relevant readings in the sociology of religion in Chapter 2 in order to reconstruct them as Weber's genealogical account of the modern self. Here I argue that in the Protestant ethic thesis Weber aimed to isolate an ontology of the self in which subjective value and objective rationality are willfully brought together to form a systematic whole, thereby enabling modern individuals to act in accordance with the principled sense of moral duty – a view that is distinguishable from both Enlightenment naturalistic anthropology and Victorian liberal characterology and rather resembles the Kantian ideal of the self-legislating self. Although this type of modern self, which Weber called *Berufsmensch*, is constituted in inward, subjective isolation, I argue in

Chapter 3 that it does not usher in an atomized social realm of individual rights in Weber's social imagination. On the contrary, Weber held that a novel mode of sociability results from the modern empowerment of the individual agency, which is institutionalized as a sectlike society. Weber saw that the *Berufsmensch* can be maintained only in a rigorous social mechanism of ethical discipline, which demands a small-scale, pluralized, and voluntary associational life in opposition to state intervention. The result is a permeation of small voluntary associations into modern political society, and I reconstruct the nature and mechanism of sectlike society in Weber's essays on Puritan sects. It is in light of this reconstructed Protestant ethic thesis that I account for Weber's political ideas in subsequent chapters. In Chapter 4, I revisit the theme of the modern self and analyze Weber's understanding of "late modernity" and rationalization, which works as a force of self-disempowerment as opposed to its positive effect in earlier times. The question in this chapter is what Weber proposed to do about disempowerment and what strategies he called for to reempower the modern agency. I argue that Weber's ethical project suggesting the symbiosis of conviction and responsibility continues in his understanding of power politics and ideal type methodology, which aims to provide different practices of the self yet was ultimately meant to reinvigorate the *Berufsmensch* in a secularized version. In Chapter 5, I examine Weber's writings on nationalism, associations, and corporatism in order to show that Weber's empowerment strategy demands the pluralistic organization of civil society, which can function as the main antidote to bureaucratic petrification. I argue that Weber's preoccupation with nationalism reveals, contra Mommsen's reading, his value conviction in liberal individualism via a reinforcement of societal pluralism in late modern circumstances. It will be revealed in these two chapters (4 and 5) on Weber's political writings that, in the face of the erosion of individual freedom and autonomy under the late modern circumstances, Weber wanted to revive a secularized form of Protestant individualism and associational pluralism that underpins the earlier modernity he called "that last of our heroisms."

2

The Protestant Ethic and the Spirit of Individualism

That I may rise and stand, o'erthrow mee, and bend
Your force, to break, blowe, burn, and make me new...
Take me to you, imprison me, for I
Except you'enthrall mee, never shall be free,
Nor ever chast, except you ravish me.

John Donne[1]

INTRODUCTION: "THE LAST OF OUR HEROISMS"

The historical constitution of a certain type of self and the empowerment of its agency through a complex interplay with political, social, and economic conditions always remain close to the heart of Weber's research agenda. Throughout his vast unorganized opus, Weber appears to be occupied with a distinctive ontology and genealogy of the modern self, which he calls the "Occidental self" in the essays on world religions, the "charismatic individual" in the studies of economy and society, personality (*Persönlichkeit*) in the methodological essays as well as in his later writings on politics and science, and the "person of vocation" (*Berufsmensch*) in *The Protestant Ethic*. These ideal-typical individuals share such characteristics as asceticism, methodical self-discipline, a regimented way of life, and an instrumental stance toward this world

[1] "Holy Sonnet XIV" in *John Donne: Selected Poems* (New York: St. Martin's, 1993) 116.

(and even toward one's own self) – all culminating in a fanatic zeal for secular activism. From this perspective, Harvey Goldman claims that Weber's study of the "spirit of capitalism" shows more than the appearance of something new in business life.[2] It shows the emergence of a new kind of person and a new kind of power, a new kind of character, a new attitude toward work, or simply a new self. According to Weber, they have "an unusually strong character," "highly developed ethical qualities," and "temperate self-control," which have saved them from "moral and economic shipwreck," enabled them to win "absolutely indispensable confidence," and given them "strength to overcome the innumerable obstacles."[3] Weber contends with Thomas Carlyle that it is these types of individuals, "raised in the hard school of life, simultaneously calculating and daring but above all *dispassionate, steady*, shrewd, devoted fully to their cause,"[4] who have made it possible to generate "the last of our heroisms."[5]

More than simply establishing a causal link between religion and capitalism, then, Weber's main theme in *The Protestant Ethic* can be formulated as the ontology and genealogy of the distinctively modern self, first constituted in its ideal-typical form during the Calvinist Reformation. Feeling that this main theme was utterly misunderstood, Weber, in his last rejoinder to the controversy triggered by the publication of *The Protestant Ethic*, says that "The advancement of an expanding capitalism was not my *central* interest; rather it was the development of *humankind* [*Menschentum*] as it was produced through the confluence of religiously and economically determined factors."[6] This statement

[2] See Goldman's programmatic statement in "The Problem of the Person in Weberian Social Theory" in M. Milgate and C. B. Welch (eds.), *Critical Issues in Social Thought* (London: Academic Press, 1989) 60–1.
[3] Protestant Ethic 58/69.
[4] Ibid.
[5] Ibid. 31/37.
[6] Schlußwort 303: This essay, "Antikritisches Schlußwort zum Geist des Kapitalismus" (originally published in *Archiv für Sozialwissenschaft und Sozialpolitik* in 1910), was intended to be a rebuttal to Felix Rachfal's criticism of *The Protestant Ethic* as it appeared in 1904–5. Indeed, they had already had a series of vehement and polemical, and sometimes even personal, exchanges, and "Schlußwort" was supposed to be and indeed was Weber's final reply to Rachfal. For this exchange between Weber and Rachfal, as well as the controversy in general that also involved Karl Fischer, Lujo Brentano, and Werner Sombart, see Johannes Winckelmann's collection and edition of major articles that appeared in the controversy in *Die Protestantische Ethik II – Max Weber: Kritiker*

echoes his earlier one in the same reply: "My arguments were *explicitly and intentionally limited* to the theme of 'the development of *Berufsmenschentum*' in its significance as a component of the capitalist 'spirit'."[7]

The questions to be raised are, then: How is Weber's *Berufsmenschentum* psychologically constituted and socially reproduced, and in what way is its political and moral as well as economic agency empowered? My answer will be sought in terms of rationality and freedom, two of the essential elements in any account of the modern self. In this regard, Weber's view seems relatively straightforward:

> The "freer" the actor's "decision"– the more it results from his or her "own considerations," undistorted by "outer" compulsion or irresistible "affects" – the more motivation itself, *ceteris paribus*, falls remorselessly within the categories of "means" and "end.". . . Moreover, the "freer" the "action" is in the sense described here, i.e., the less it bears the character of a "natural event," the more the concept of "personality" comes into play. This concept of personality finds its "essence" in the constancy of its inner relation to certain ultimate "values" and life-"meanings."[8]

This statement, however, might appear puzzling for those familiar with the so-called iron cage imagery of Weber.[9] In one version of this vision, individual freedom and autonomy are viewed as antagonistic to rationality, especially its means–end variety. C. Wright Mills and Hans Gerth go further and claim that "the quest for freedom is identified [by Weber] with irrational sentiment."[10] As opposed to such a

---

und Antikritiken (Gütersloh: Gütersloher Verlag, 1978). The editors' introduction by P. Baehr and G. Wells in M. Weber, *The Protestant Ethic and the "Spirit" of Capitalism and Other Writings* (New York: Penguin Books, 2002), contains a masterful exercise in Weber philology, as they carefully examine the meaning of this controversy for the development of Weber's so-called Protestant ethic thesis and its posthumous reception. Also see E. Baumgarten (ed.), *Max Weber: Werk und Person* (Tübingen: J. C. B. Mohr/Paul Siebeck, 1964) 445–8.

[7] Schlußwort 173; also see 324.
[8] Roscher and Knies 131–2/191–2.
[9] The term "iron cage" is, of course, an inaccurate English rendering of *stalhardes Gehäuse* (literally, "shell as hard as steel") by Talcott Parsons. I still use this term, nevertheless, because it has acquired such a wide currency in academic English with certain connotations and images that might be lost in an alternative translation. For an insightful discussion of this metaphor, see P. Baehr, "The 'Iron Cage' and the 'Shell as Hard as Steel': Parsons, Weber, and the *stahlhardes Gehäuse* Metaphor in *The Protestant Ethic and the Spirit of Capitalism*," *History and Theory* 40:2 (2001) 153–69.
[10] C. W. Mills and H. Gerth, "Introduction" in *From Max Weber: Essays in Sociology* (Oxford: Oxford University Press, 1946) 73. For more agreement on this

reading, Weber here says that individual freedom and autonomy are defined in terms of rationality, and especially of means–end calculability. Even more puzzling is that individual freedom thus defined draws its essence from a commitment to ultimate values and life meanings, which cannot be accounted for in terms of means–end rationality – an *irrational* element from the means–end viewpoint. It appears that what Weber calls *Persönlichkeit* here and its possibility for free-cum-rational action are riddled with inconsistencies.

The immediate purpose of this chapter is to account for these apparent contradictions. I will argue that Weber strove to transcend this contradiction by resuscitating a peculiar character that can bring subjective value and objective rationality together to form a systematic total personality (*Gesamtpersönlichkeit*) under the supremacy of will. This willful combination of value and rationality, I will further argue, enables the modern self to gain a moral, political, and economic agency in the form of worldly activism that is to revolutionize the subsequent course of modern history. In his Protestant ethic thesis, evidently, Weber wanted to isolate this paradoxical compound, a theme that kept on informing his critical evaluation of his contemporary politics and society as a degeneration of this early modern ideal. The story of degeneration (*Verfallsgeschichte*) belongs to the later chapters; this chapter traces the psychological foundation that enables this agency as Weber articulated in *The Protestant Ethic* and other relevant religious writings.

"A RATIONALIZATION TOWARD AN IRRATIONAL CONDUCT OF LIFE"

The Protestant Ethic, the central text for Weber's genealogical ontology of the modern self, was published in two installments in the *Archiv für Sozialwissenschaft und Sozialpolitik*; the first part appeared in late 1904 (although not officially printed until January 1905), followed

interpretation, see L. Coser, *Masters of Sociological Thought* (New York: Harcourt Brace Jovanovich, 1971) 233, and A. Mitzman, *The Iron Cage: An Historical Interpretation of Max Weber* (New York : Knopf, 1970) 168. For an examination of Weber on rationality and freedom, see D. Levine, *Flight from Ambiguity: Essays in Social and Cultural Theory* (Chicago: University of Chicago Press, 1985). For a general overview, see K. Palonen, "Max Weber's Reconceptualization of Freedom," *Political Theory* 27:4 (1999) 523–44.

by the second part in June 1905.[11] The bulk of the first installment, especially its first two chapters, aims mostly at clarifying the central question in his account of the modern self. According to Weber, the familiar Catholic reproach of Protestantism that "'materialism'... has arisen from a [Protestant] secularization of the very meaning of life" is utterly misleading.[12] On the contrary, Protestantism for Weber represents an intensification of the religious ethic in the form of asceticism to an extent hitherto unprecedented in history. Thus, he believes that the modern self he is about to trace back to Protestantism "must not be understood as implying a natural and uncomplicated 'enjoyment of life's pleasures', nor is this 'spirit of work', furthermore, to be understood as otherwise somehow involving 'Enlightenment' as many today now believe.... To whole central aspects of modern life which even the most fundamentalist believer would not wish to banish today, their [Luther's, Calvin's, Knox's, and Voët's] Protestantism stood directly antagonistic." He then quickly identifies his question as somewhat akin to Montesquieu's question of the close relationship between freedom, commerce, and piety in England.[13] The Protestant ethic cannot be equated with the utilitarian affirmation of this world as expressed in Enlightenment naturalism, and in fact it comes rather closer to renouncing the secular world as the medieval monastic life ethic had done, a point that Weber repeats tirelessly throughout *The Protestant Ethic*. Thus he feels it

necessary to note, what is today so often forgotten, that the Reformation of the sixteenth century meant not the *elimination* of the Catholic church's domination [*Herrschaft*] over the believer's life in its entirety, but rather the substitution of one form of control by *another*. A highly agreeable domination that had become a mere formality, one that was scarcely felt in a practical manner, was replaced by an infinitely burdensome and severe regimentation of the entire life conduct [*Reglimentierung der ganzen Lebensführung*]. Religion now penetrated all private and public spheres in the most comprehensive sense imaginable.[14]

---

[11] For an authoritative publishing history of *The Protestant Ethic* and how this text compares to the 1920 edition, see the Editors' Introduction in Baehr and Wells (2002).

[12] Protestant Ethic 34/40.

[13] Ibid. 37-8/44-5.

[14] Ibid. 30-1/37.

Weber maintains, however, that the Protestant ethic still differs from the monastic life ethic in one central aspect: its inner-worldly attitude that prevents the Puritans from escaping into their own enclaves away from the mundane world, encouraging active participation in this world through secular means.[15] For this new attitude to come into being, argues Weber, the old religious end has to be measured in terms of worldly means so that the more religious one becomes, the more one becomes enmeshed in this world. Thus Weber holds that "the entire contrast between the estrangement from this world [*Weltfremdkeit*], asceticism, and ecclesiastical piety on the one hand, and earning of one's living under capitalism on the other, [could] be understood as actually implying an inner affinity [*innere Verwandtschaft*];"[16] and later in the essay, pace Lujo Brentano, "I here expressly maintain the internal continuity between otherworldly asceticism of monks and the thisworldly asceticism of the calling... [which] is (as anyone can see) a fundamental assumption of my whole thesis: the Reformation carried rational Christian asceticism and the methodicalness of life out of the monastery and into the life of work in a calling."[17] For Weber, in short, this paradoxical combination of intense religionization of the end and radical secularization of the means constitutes the central problematic of the account of the rise of the modern self.

Naturally, Weber rejects the view of Werner Sombart – another, and possibly more eminent, economic historian than Weber in their time – on the genealogy of modern capitalism. According to Weber, Sombart simply regarded the spirit of capitalism as part of an overall rationalization in the field of technique and economic organization, that is, a drive toward secularization of means in more Weberian terminology.[18] Sombart's theory depended on a monotonic and unilinear account of rationalization that presumed a symbiotic relationship

---

[15] Schlußwort 315.

[16] Protestant Ethic 35/44.

[17] Ibid. 215/235.

[18] See, for instance, W. Sombart, *The Quintessence of Capitalism: A Study of the History and Psychology of the Modern Business Man*, trans. M. Epstein (New York: Howard Fertig, 1967), especially 324 and 182. For more details on Weber's critical discussion of Sombart's concept of *Technik*, see "Technik und Kultur" (1910) in Sozialpolitik 453–5. Their relationship is discussed in more detail in L. Scaff, *Fleeing the Iron Cage: Culture, Politics, and Modernity in the Thought of Max Waber* (Berkeley: University of California Press, 1989) 202–7.

among its various domains. Such a view would allow Protestantism, with its intense religiosity, at best a transitory or passing stage "prior to the development of a purely rationalistic philosophy." This assertion could not be further from the truth for Weber, who held a view that "the history of rationalism *by no means* charts out a progressive unfolding, according to which all the separate realms of life follow a *parallel* developmental line."[19] Here Weber highlights again that it was rather an intense religionization that the Puritan ethic demanded in everyday life, an *"irrational* element"[20] from the perspective of means–end rationality, that was decisive for what can be called the "spirit of capitalism." Weber sums up this modern paradox, this time following Brentano, as "a 'rationalization' toward an 'irrational' conduct of life [*Lebensführung*]."[21] This unique combination of rational and irrational elements in the constitution of the modern self seems what propels Weber to explore the religious and ethical doctrines of Protestantism and its impact on the practical life conduct in the modern world.

CALLING: SANCTIFICATION AND REGIMENTATION OF EVERYDAY LIFE

Having made clear his central question, Weber moves on to search for the source of this *irrational* element in the Puritan self. He first calls attention to the concept of "calling" [*Beruf*] in Luther, which is defined as "a notion of duty that individuals ought to experience, and do, toward the content of their 'vocational' activity"[22] – in short, defined as a sense of ethical obligation. Here too Weber, as if he is

---

[19] Protestant Ethic 65/77: A better known statement of this view is in his general introduction to the GARS: "There is, for example, rationalization of mystical contemplation, that is, of an attitude which, viewed from other departments of life, is specifically irrational, just as much as there are rationalizations of economic life, of technique, of scientific research, of military training, of law and administration. Furthermore, each one these fields may be rationalized in terms of very different ultimate values and ends, and what is rational from one point of view may well be irrational from another. Hence rationalizations of the most varied character have existed in various departments of life and in all areas of culture.... [The question is] what departments are rationalized and in what direction" (Protestant Ethic 20/26).

[20] Ibid. 65/78.

[21] Ibid. 84/194.

[22] Ibid. 45/54.

afraid of readers being mistaken about the central thesis, repeats the preceding argument about intensification of religion, rather than its elimination, by means of an extensive note on the etymological origin of Luther's translation and indeed virtual invention of the word *Beruf*.[23] In brief, the word appeared in the Greek Bible, especially in the Old Testament, as referring to a divine calling of a prophet, monk, or clergy member only. Before Luther's translation and extensive use of the word in his writings, according to Weber, it never possessed a meaningful implication for purely secular professions, nor did the word *Ruf* in medieval German and Dutch. The fact that Luther chose to extend the meaning of *Beruf* to incorporate the mundane domain of everyday life has tremendous significance for Weber.

Implicated in Luther's notion of calling was that mundane daily labor came to be ordained by God, thus constituting a part of Divine Providence. Early on, Luther justified calling and the attendant division of worldly labor on the ground that it served the public good. This anti-Smithian idea, or "an almost grotesque contrast to Adam Smith's well-known statements on the same subject,"[24] centered on his emphasis on brotherly love: by devoting oneself to a calling, one in fact worked for others. Luther, however, soon abandoned this essentially Scholastic justification, turning to Providence as the sole source for a calling. Central to this shift was, according to Weber, that the sanctity of calling depended on the will of God only and nothing else. Potentially this turn gave a new meaning to the ordinary life; now the ordinary life was elevated to a meaningful level that it had never attained before, which, of course, has been much commented on as one of the central contributions made by Puritanism to modern political and social thought.[25] In premodern times, only the extraordinary life, such as that of a heroic warrior, was supposed to possess meaning, and especially in religion, only the God-ordained works of the priest or saint were viewed as bringing one closer to divinity. Now, being a part of Providence, everyday life could lead to salvation. It was only a

---

[23] Ibid. 100/209–10.

[24] Ibid. 68/81.

[25] For the Puritan contribution to this modern turn in political thought, see Charles Taylor, "God Loveth Adverbs," in his *Sources of the Self: The Making of the Modern Identity* (Cambridge, MA: Harvard University Press, 1989).

matter of time before the ordinary life became elevated over aristocratic, intellectual, or sacred works as a truer path to salvation.

For Weber, furthermore, the Lutheran doctrine of calling has the
effect of putting an individual in a *constant* encounter with God. Now
mundane inner-worldly affairs are not simply designated as belonging
to a realm of sin that should be sanctified through sacraments by the
spiritual power of the church. Now I encounter God not only in the
church or during religious practices, but also in my everyday life in a
calling. Not only has ordinary life attained sacred meaning, but also,
or rather precisely because it is so, everyday life has to be led ethico-
religiously. Thus, Weber claims that in effect Luther had turned the
whole world into a monastery: "under the influence of this dogma,
work in a this-worldly calling came for Luther to have the same con-
notation," which comes from "the monastic translation."[26]

All this, however, still remained only a promise in Luther's doctrine
of calling. Weber says that it was impossible for Luther to usher in
"a new or in any way fundamental connection between worldly activity and religious principles."[27] The problem for Weber is that Luther
fell short of incorporating this doctrine of calling into the inner core of
self, thereby failing to create "psychological rewards" (*psychologischen-
Prämien*)[28] for the formation of self-discipline oriented to worldly asceticism. By relying exclusively on the divine order external to the self
as the ultimate justification for calling, Luther in fact put more emphasis on passive obedience to one's calling than the performance and
outcome of the work itself. Being a part of God's Providence, Lutheran
calling is something to be obeyed rather than performed. This attitude may generate a pious, humble, and even ascetic lifestyle, but it
can never create an active participation in worldly affairs with a zeal
for transforming them, an attitude Weber believed to be the central
characteristics of the modern agency. Lacking this kind of pathos, the
Lutheran idea of calling remained traditionalistic and even fatalistic.[29]

In this light, the importance of Luther, still an essentially medieval
figure for Weber, lies not in his having brought new content to theology,

[26] Protestant Ethic 104/210.
[27] Ibid. 71/85.
[28] Schlußwort 307.
[29] Protestant Ethic 70/85.

as Calvin would, but rather in his having thematized what was already implicit in the medieval monasticism. Indeed, this is the moment to re-call, once again, Weber's view of the medieval monastery as an enclave of rationalization within a traditional world: "In that epoch the monk is the first human being who lives rationally, who works methodically and by rational means toward a goal, namely the future life. Only for him did the clock strike, only for him were the hours of the day divided – for prayer."[30]

From Weber's perspective, it is because Luther represents a con-scious and indeed agonized renewal of the traditional religious think-ing of the Middle Ages that he strikes down the artificial isolation of monastic life. Luther's aim was thus a regeneration of religious value or end orientation; but in doing so, without realizing it, he liberated the nascent rationalism of the monasteries, which was able to pene-trate all domains of life. To use a set of Weberian dichotomies, we may describe the medieval situation before Luther found himself as one in which "outer-worldly otherworldliness" (the institutional sanction of otherworldliness, or in short, the monasteries) and "inner-worldly this-worldliness" (ordinary daily secular life in general) coexisted. Luther did not bring anything new to this situation; yet by destroying the insti-tutional possibility of an outer-worldly practice of otherworldliness, he prepared the way for Calvin's more decisive formulation, which gave birth to a new inner-worldly otherworldliness, or in Weber's term, a "worldly asceticism" (*innerwertliche Askese*).[31] For such a paradoxical compound to come into being, what was only promised in Luther's idea of calling had to be incorporated into the very psychological core of the selfhood in the Protestant theology. And to identify such a psy-chological mechanism, we need to turn to the second irrational element Weber isolated: the Calvinist doctrine of predestination.

---

[30] General Economic History 311/365.
[31] For the conceptual distinction among other-, this-, outer-, and innerworldly orienta-tions and their relationship to the formation of modern individualism, see L. Dumont, "A Modified View of Our Origins: The Christian Beginnings of Modern Individual-ism," *Religion* 12:1 (1982), 1–27, and S. Eisenstadt's comment on the paper in "Tran-scendental Visions, Otherworldliness and Its Transformation: Some More Comments on L. Dumont," Religion 13:1 (1983), 1–17. Briefly, the outer-/inner- distinction has to do with an individual's attitude toward the secular world, which results in passive escape from or active participation in the secular world; the other-/this- distinction is drawn by one's fundamental value orientation.

PREDESTINATION: OBJECTIFICATION OF THE WORLD AND
DISEMPOWERMENT OF THE SELF

The idea of predestination was, of course, not uniquely of Calvinist origin; Luther also believed in predestination. What distinguishes the doctrine in Luther's and Calvin's hands is, however, its practical implication for individual moral psychology. For Luther, predestination indicates an assurance by graceful God that a true believer will be granted salvation in the end, a sign of God's grace rendering a sense of certainty in this world. In effect, the Lutheran idea of predestination relieves the tremendous pressure of the believer's sense of sin, for God's grace is revocable and regainable by means of good faith and obedience to one's calling. His doctrine of predestination provides at best an emotional assurance with which to live in this world.[32] For Calvin, the doctrine of predestination is exactly the opposite: it is a doctrine of uncertainty, inscrutability, and mystery.

According to Weber, behind the Calvinist predestination of mystery lies the absolutization of God and disempowerment of the human agency, which generates "an unimaginably great ethical chasm between the transcendental God and the human being continuously enmeshed in the toils of new sin."[33] God's Providence is so absolutely transcendental and His will so inscrutable that they lie completely beyond the reach of human comprehension. Trying to make sense of God itself indicates an insufficient faith, and, at best, only a fragment of God's will can be known through revelation. The Calvinist God is, thus Weber says, "the Jehovah of the Old Testament" as against "the Heavenly Father of the New,"[34] or simply, God as portrayed in the Book of Job. The idea of predestination in this light comes to imply the opposite of what it entails in Lutheranism; now all that can be known is that a few who are predestined shall be saved in the end and the rest damned eternally. Most important, I do not know if *my* soul shall be saved.

To make this already precarious psychological state even more anxious is that predestination can never be affected by human conduct – another difference from the Lutheran counterpart. It is simply logically

---

[32] Protestant Ethic 120–1/101–2.
[33] Economy and Society 317/522.
[34] Protestant Ethic 196/221.

inconsistent for a pious Calvinist to believe that, given God's absolute freedom and omnipotence, His Providence and decision are dependent in any way on what humans do, including the religious practices of the church. From such a standpoint, no amount of good work and no sincerity of religious practice can guarantee salvation, and, as long as I dwell in this world, any hope for a "regular 'discharge' of an emotional consciousness of guilt was now done away with."[35] Giving no emotional assurance of salvation (*certitude salutis*), the Calvinist doctrine of predestination in effect throws the individual, so completely disempowered and psychologically tormented, on the unconditional mercy of God, so completely absolutized and enigmatized. According to Weber, it amounts to the "greatest tension between world and God, between the actually existent and the ideal."[36]

In fact, it is not only humanity but also the whole of this world that is completely devalued in Calvinism. Weber calls it an "objectification" of the world vis-à-vis the absolute God that culminates in its complete loss of meaning. It is the world objectified in the sense that the natural world is now regarded as a hermeneutically vacuous vessel as opposed to what Weber calls "magical cosmology." According to magical cosmology, nature is understood as a "grand garden of magic" and society as a magical or animistic sib relationship. This cosmology can be summarized, according to Weber, as "magical symbolism."[37] It is centered on the organically given natural and social relationship and piety toward the concrete person, as in Confucianism, whether living or dead.[38] This reverence for the intrinsic value of nature and the human being is, however, shattered by the demagification (*Entzauberung*) process that reaches its apotheosis in Protestantism, in which the intrinsic value of this world, including the naturalistic existence of humanity, becomes completely destroyed. "The idea of the 'worthlessness of the flesh' was an indigenous, true product of the Calvinist spirit, and this notion directed Calvinism out of Protestantism's normal path of development only in those instances where the 'worthlessness of the human desires' led to an actual flight from the world."[39] Indeed, the physical

35 Ibid. 124/106.
36 Economy and Society 317/523.
37 Ibid. 248-9/405.
38 China 522-3/236.
39 Protestant Ethic 222/240.

existence in this world is not only worthless but also sinful, constituting a "natural vessel of sin."[40] In this light, the frequent Calvinist
accusation of "the idolatry of the flesh" becomes more sensible once it
is set against the Puritan objectification of the world.

Remarkable in such a cosmology, or rather "acosmism"[41] à la
Weber, is that everything belonging to this world ceases to provide
an intrinsic source of meaning, especially with regard to the salvation
of *my* soul. Now I cannot and should not expect any spiritual assis-
tance from any source that this world can provide when it comes to the
existential question of the meaning of life and death as well as what
lies beyond my death. In this light, both the church and even familial
relationships fall under suspicion. The consequence is, says Weber, that
"the Calvinist's interaction with his God took place in deep spiritual
isolation."[42]

This spiritual inner isolation and "the complete elimination of salvation through the Church and the sacraments," according to Weber,
form the "decisive difference from Catholicism."[43] Obviously, the
whole notion of the Catholic Church as the mediator between God and
laymen and, more important, its function of sacrament lose their theoretical ground in the Calvinist doctrine of predestination. The practice
of sacrament is predicated on a belief in religious rituals as a magical
means of exorcizing demonic elements in the past or redeeming ethical
sin in a more demagified religion, a view Weber contends is incompatible in principle with the monotheistic theodicy of Protestantism. Thus,
although Catholic "trinitarianism appears to have a monotheistic trend
when contrasted with" other forms of religion, Weber still holds that
"in practice, the Roman Catholic cult of masses and saints actually
comes fairly close to polytheism."[44] The Catholic belief in sacrament
is seen as indicating its insufficient demagification as a world religion.
For Weber, monotheism reaches its apex only with the emergence of
Protestantism:

That overarching process in the history of religion – *demagification*
[*Entzauberung*] of the world – found here, with the development of the

---

[40] Economy and Society 329/543.
[41] Rejections 545/331.
[42] Protestant Ethic 124/106–7.
[43] Ibid. 123/104–5.
[44] Economy and Society 314/518.

[Calvinist] doctrine of predestination its final stage. This development, which began with the prophecy of ancient Judaism in the Old Testament, rejected, in conjunction with Hellenistic scientific thought, all *magical* means to the quest for salvation as superstition and sacrilege.[45]

Nor can secular social relationships be of any help in this regard. In the Protestant rejection of salvation through the institutionalized sacraments, it is already implied that the Calvinist would deny participation in any social relationship as a means of salvation. Indeed, social organization is meaningless with regard to salvation. Nor does benevolent work toward the public good ensure my salvation, nor can I learn from other members of society an exemplary path toward salvation. In a world in which everybody is equally uncertain, I cannot know who is elected and who is not and thus cannot determine from whom to learn.[46] A good person measured by this-worldly standards does not yield any information about one's status of predestination, and such pretension, furthermore, is vulnerable to an idolatry of the flesh. Thus, Weber believes, for example, that the proud civic republicans of Machiavelli's time, who place "the love of their native city above their fear for the salvation of their souls," are merely followers of "sinful idolatry of the flesh" in the eyes of the Calvinists.[47] This explains why it is important to Weber that the departure from a family signifies the commencement of the long journey to salvation in Bunyan's *Pilgrim's Progress*.[48] My own salvation should come second to nothing, and it cannot be aided in any manner by the this-worldly, including church, family, brotherhood, or any emotional loyalty to social groups; moreover, "any excess of emotional feeling for one's fellow men is prohibited as being a deification of the creaturely, which denies the unique value of the divine gift of grace."[49]

---

[45] Protestant Ethic 123/105.
[46] Ibid. 127/110.
[47] Ibid. 86/195.
[48] Ibid. 124–5/107.
[49] Economy and Society 329/543; Thus, for instance, even missionary work for the Calvinist is not in principle motivated by any sort of brotherly love; "Whether these heathen should be converted to Christianity and thus attain salvation, even whether they could understand the language in which the missionary preached, was a matter of small importance and could be left to God, Who alone could control such things.... The end was not the salvation of those subject to it, which was the affair of God alone (in practice their own) and could not be in any way influenced by the means

Weber's point here becomes clearer when it is juxtaposed to another source of solipsism. The Victorian liberal attitude of "defiant solitude," for instance, as expressed eloquently by E. M. Forster, as well as any kind of liberal belief in the private realm over the public as a genuine source of meaning for individuals, can be traced to a similar source of skepticism toward extraindividual sources of meaning and knowledge.[50] Appearance to the contrary, however, there exists a crucial difference between the Calvinist solipsism and that of Victorian liberalism, and it derives from their almost opposite view of the self. The Calvinist solipsism comes from a complete disempowerment of the self vis-à-vis God, an anthropology predicated on the renunciation of any worldly source of meaning but God. The Calvinist individuals have no privileged private realm as a depository of meaning to turn to in this world; Forster, and Victorian liberals in general, on the other hand, believed that meaning could dwell only in the private relationships and aesthetic taste of an individual. Their solipsism presumes an empowered self who does not and need not rely on the nonprivate sphere for the source of genuine meaning in life. Weber's Calvinist, by contrast, does not have such a privileged inner sanctum in this world. The Victorian liberal attitude would certainly be condemned as the idolatry of the flesh by Weber's Calvinists.

In the worldliness of its anthropology, the Enlightenment account also comes into sharp contradiction with its counterpart in Weber. The Calvinist anxiety amounts to a disillusioned and pessimistically inclined individualism, according to Weber, as opposed to Enlightenment individualism, which is predicated on a utilitarian and hedonist anthropology – the kind of individualism both Rousseau and Kant criticized as too simple or too thin. Compared to Enlightenment naturalism, which presumes an *I* whose action is "self-transparent"

at the disposal of the Church, but simply the increase of God's glory.... Calvin himself [even] denied the duty of sending missions to the heathen since a further expansion of the Church is *unius Dei opus*.... [T]he duty to love one's neighbor is satisfied by fulfilling God's commandments to increase his glory.... Humanity in relation to one's neighbor has, so to speak, died out" (Protestant Ethic 100–1/ 225–6).

50 See A. Arblaster, *The Rise and Fall of Western Liberalism* (Cambridge: Cambridge University Press, 1984) 301–4; also see R. Bellamy (ed.), *Victorian Liberalism: Nineteenth-Century Political Thought and Practice* (Cambridge: Cambridge University Press, 1990).

once understood against the utilitarian maxim of "increase happiness; decrease pain," Weber's Puritan self portrayed here seems predicated on a different account of an individual whose main existential question is not easily resolvable with the utilitarian calculus. What we see here in the Weberian self is a person of Augustinian ambiguity whose fundamental reason for action depends on one's own interpretation of the meaning of this world, most importantly of life and death.

In short, one of the critical psychological consequences of the absolutization of God, objectification of the world, disempowerment of the agency, or, simply put, the complete devaluation of this world is the radically solipsistic soteriology of Calvinism. For Weber, what is central to the Calvinist doctrine of predestination is "a feeling of unprecedented inner loneliness of the single individual."[51] In this regard, neither any institutional grace such as sacraments nor social relationships help, and this point forms the decisive difference between Calvinism and Lutheranism:

the individual confronts his God in an immensely harsher manner than in that of Lutheranism, thrown back solely upon himself and his state of grace, as it can only be recognized in the *totality* of his conduct of life.[52]

Note again that the Calvinist self à la Weber constitutes an empty vacuum riddled with anxiety coming from existential meaninglessness and helplessness, without any possibility for relief in this world. This fall from grace as a human being should be borne in mind when accounting for the Calvinist's psychological drive to an active participation in this world. In other words, for Weber, the most significant outcome of this radically individualistic soteriology of Calvinism and the enormous psychological trauma it inflicts on each individual is that it generates what can be least expected from such a worldview. Ironically, this psychological disempowerment of the self generates a relentless impulse toward active participation in this world via a willful reempowerment of the agency.

---

[51] Protestant Ethic 122/104.
[52] Schlußwort 308.

EMPOWERING THE INDIVIDUAL AGENCY: SELF-MASTERY
AND DISCIPLINE

Weber indeed views it as rather ironic that the Calvinist doctrine of predestination did not usher in passive fatalism, which might be the more logical conclusion that he observes in the Islamic doctrine of predetermination.[53] He attributes this irony to the *"psychological effect"* that "cut off the fatalistic consequences of logic,"[54] drawing from Nietzsche's well-known fable of eternal recurrence, which ironically provides the benchmark of an autonomous and responsible agency for Nietzsche.[55] Here, by psychological effect, Weber means a need to repossess a self-confidence or conviction, or, as opposed to eternal anxiety, "the conscious possession of a lasting, integrated foundation for the conduct of life."[56] This need, we recall, arises exactly because the modern self is forced to give up any such hope in this world. And the Calvinist doctrine meets this need by reinvigorating the doctrine of calling in this world.

One way of gaining self-conviction is naturally an assumption; that is, by assuming that I am chosen, I can devote myself to my calling in this world. Obviously, this does not suffice for Weber's Puritan self, for the act of assumption itself involves or is grounded in the interpretation of the world, and Weber's *Berufsmensch* is disempowered precisely on the ground of the interpretation imposed by the Calvinist doctrine of

[53] Protestant Ethic 203–4/227.
[54] Ibid. 211/232.
[55] "What if some day or night a demon were to steal after you into your loneliest loneliness and say to you: 'This life as you now live it and have lived it, you will have to live once more and innumerable times more; and there will be nothing new in it, but every pain and every joy and every thought and sigh and everything unutterably small or great in your life will have to return to you, all in the same succession and sequence'" (F. Nietzsche, *The Gay Science*, trans. W. Kaufmann [New York: Random House, 1974] 273); what, then, can an individual do in the face of such a grave fate? Nietzsche precepted that only the individual who is determined to accept and live through it with an affirmative attitude can achieve genuine autonomy, thus turning the self into a genuine personality. (For the centrality of the idea of recurrence in Nietzsche's thought, see A. Nehamas, *Nietzsche: Life as Literature* [Cambridge, MA: Harvard University Press, 1985], esp. 141– 69.) It seems more than coincidental that Weber takes note of the idea of eternal recurrence in Nietzsche; indeed, Wilhelm Hennis suggests that Weber's ideal type of Puritan self is taken over entirely from Nietzsche's idea of self-discipline (W. Hennis, *Max Weber: Essays in Reconstruction*, trans. K. Tribe [London: Routledge, 1988] 146–62).
[56] Economy and Society 326/538.

predestination. Also, an assumption of my salvation includes an assurance coming from my good faith or benevolent works, which would constitute the human arrogance of denying the absolute inscrutability of Providence – the kind of attitude Calvin would condemn as an idolatry of the flesh. No assumption, faith, or simply any sort of spiritual belief, not to mention worldly philanthropy, can yield assurance of my salvation. At the most, it can play an instrumental role for such *certitude salutis*.

To attain the necessary self-conviction, the Puritan self needs proof, indeed, more than proof, tangible proof; "faith had to be proved by its objective results in order to provide a firm ground for the *certitude salutis*."[57] The outcome of my labor in calling becomes the only sign of my salvation in this world. Of course, this does not imply that I can alter my predetermined status through my performance of worldly works. Indeed, such an endeavor is useless. However, it is still "indispensable as signs of election. They are technical means, but not ones that can be used to purchase salvation; rather, good works serve to banish the anxiety about one's salvation."[58] Worldly labor in one's calling yields the *sign* of salvation, in other words, rather than salvation itself. It constitutes merely the means by which to escape from the existential fear and trembling. My worldly activity is free from existential concern, which is unimaginable if it is believed to relate to my salvation directly. I need not be concerned with the ethical criteria of my everyday life; they are already determined (e.g., the Ten Commandments), and only the outcome of my action is my prerogative. Of course, this does not mean that my everyday life is finally free from any restrictions: Quite the contrary. Now my life should be conducted in strict accordance with means–end rationality that guarantees the best output of my labor and thus renders more proof of my salvation. This is what Weber means when he says that the Calvinist doctrine of worldly labor enables us to eliminate any ethical dilemma; "The conflict between the individual and the 'ethic' (in Søren Kierkegaard's sense) did not exist for Calvinism."[59] To be more precise, the existential question of ethics has been removed and replaced by a new ethic of a practical kind.

[57] Protestant Ethic 130–1/114.
[58] Ibid. 131/115.
[59] Ibid. 126–7/109.

In order to maintain the necessary self-conviction through the worldly life in accordance with this practical ethic, then, I need an affirmative attitude toward the world, even though it is a meaningless entity. This seems to run counter to the complete devaluation of the world vis-à-vis God, as explained earlier. Yet it is not necessarily so, for here, according to Weber, "asceticism showed its Janus-face [*Doppelgesicht*]."[60]

Indeed, it is time to recall Luther's idea of calling, which in effect sanctifies this world as God's divine creation. More important in the Puritan objectification of the world for Weber is that it does not lead to a renunciation of this world as such. The ground on which this world is affirmed is that it is created by God; the world is useless as a source of meaning, yet it is not valueless, for it is also God's creation. In this light, the world is not only meaningless, worthless, and sinful, but, to be more exact, *imperfect*. It is precisely because this world is imperfect that it is sinful. Thus, I should not only abstain from worldly happiness and pleasure, but also transform this world according to God's will in order to bring it closer to perfection; "the 'world' is viewed as material to be fashioned ethically according to the norm."[61] My calling and *certitude salutis*, then, come from the belief that I am the elect instrument of God for the divine mission of bringing this world closer to God's will. Once stripped of intrinsic meaning, the world for the Puritan self becomes the object of transformation according to God's will and for the sake of His glory. In so doing, I can affirm my sense of election and the resulting psychological assurance.

This instrumental view of the human being, as opposed to that of the human being as a vessel of divine will, is decisive for Weber, since the latter promotes a harmonious disposition among various spheres within the self, leading to a pietistic and world-rejecting attitude, which he found in Lutheran Pietism. This instrumentalization of ourselves makes it easier to understand Weber's emphasis that important for the self-constitution of the Puritan self is, rather than a harmony, the domination and conquest of the natural self by the higher self. That is, the instrument of God's will does not include my whole self; there exists a higher self within me that, according to God's will,

---

[60] Rejections 540/327.
[61] China 521/235.

methodically and rationally transforms the world, including my natural self.

Even more so than Lutheranism, Weber's counterexample is the Catholic anthropology. According to Weber, it is predicated on a view of individual personality as "*not* an absolutely and clearly defined unity to be valued as such; rather people's moral lives were viewed as (normally) influenced by conflicting motives and often by contradictory modes of behaviour."[62] A good illustration for Weber is again the Catholic doctrine of sacrament. For Weber, a sacrament presumes a possibility of salvation through redemption in this world. That is to say, my life is disorganized in such a way that one domain of my life riddled with sin can be redeemed by a different part of more sacred nature. Thus, the concrete intention and content of a particular action come to gain decisive importance; "The *intentio*, according to the ethical evaluation of behavior in Catholicism, is not really a uniform quality of personality, of which conduct is the expression. Rather it is the concrete intent... behind a concrete action.... A result is that the conduct of life remains, from the viewpoint of ethics, an unmethodical and miscellaneous succession of discrete actions."[63] In this view, I constitute less a systematic unity with a consistent principle that runs through various facets of my life than a sandpile of different life spheres put together by chance. To use Scholastic terms, the divine (*status gratiæ*) and the natural (*status naturæ*) simply coexist within myself without a coherent order.

By contrast, the Calvinist anthropology emphasizes a systematic whole conduct that is an expression not of a particular intention but of an "ethical total personality."[64] It also embraced the Scholastic dualism of *status naturæ* and *status gratiæ*, two opposing strands of the human soul, yet here the relationship between the two has become different from that in the original doctrine. Now the natural element within myself, that is, the part of my self that depends on the psychophysical laws of nature, should be subject to a constant supervision by a higher self within me, that is, *status gratiæ*; "for only by a fundamental change in the meaning of one's entire life – every moment and every

[62] Protestant Ethic 133/116.
[63] Economy and Society 324/533.
[64] Ibid.

action – could the effects of grace, namely transforming a man from *status naturæ* to *status gratiæ*, be proved through action."[65] For such a refashioning to be completed, says Weber, the most decisive quality is the capacity for self-control and self-discipline under "the primacy of the will."[66]

The Calvinist transvaluation of the Scholastic dualism in effect means that in no domain of life am I allowed to take a lax attitude toward the content of my action, expecting that a sinful action can be redeemed by the church or more piety in a different domain of my life; "he [a Calvinist] could not hope to atone for hours of weakness and frivolity by intensified good will at other times, as could Catholics and Lutherans. The Calvinist God demanded of his believers not isolate 'good works', but, if salvation were to occur, an intensification of good works into a *system*."[67] Such a psychological state induces a systematic unity within me by which I can organize my everyday life in my calling with the sole purpose of refashioning myself as an elect instrument of God. A systematic order must be created between various, and even conflicting, spheres of life.

This subjection of the natural elements to the constant supervision of reason is what Weber meant by self-control, which is moreover elevated to the state of categorical imperative. Naturally, a constant evaluation of my life and a deep self-reflection – what Weber calls "inner light"[68] or "the ethic of conviction [*Gesinnungsethik*]"[69] – become integrated into everyday life. Thus, says Weber, drawing from a Puritan theologian, Charnock, "Reflection and knowledge of self is a prerogative of a rational nature.... *Cogito ergo sum* is the first principle of the new philosophy."[70]

[E]verything is *sinful* which is contrary to the reason. Reason is created in us by God and given by him as a norm for our action. In other words, not simply passions, because of their content as such. Rather all meaningless or unrestrained affects as such are sinful – because they destroy the "countenance" [in English]. Moreover, as processes purely of the realm of physical desires, they

[65] Protestant Ethic 134/118.
[66] Ibid. 215/235.
[67] Ibid. 133/117.
[68] Ibid. 159/147.
[69] Economy and Society 324/534.
[70] Protestant Ethic 134/235.

turn us away from the rational relationship with God that all of our activity and sensibility should cultivate.[71]

This sober self-discipline based on reason and will Weber discovers in the attitude of the Puritan soldiers during the English Civil War; "Cromwell's Ironsides, with cocked pistols in their hands, and approaching the enemy at a brisk trot without shooting, were not the superiors of the Cavaliers by virtue of their fierce passion, but on the contrary through their cool self-control, which enabled their leaders always to keep them well in hand. The knightly storm-attack of the Cavaliers, on the other hand, always resulted in dissolving their troops into atoms."[72] In cool self-control even in the face of death on a battleground Weber finds an exemplar of Puritan self-control based on the primacy of reason.[73] Reason as the fundamental and indeed the only principle of action should be obstructed by nothing but my concern with proving myself and the increase of God's glory in this world. Both of these tasks have to be done in this world and, more important, through the transformation of this world as well as the natural self. Now I should live in calling "within the institutions of the world but in opposition to them."[74]

What Weber tried to isolate, then, in the formation of the Puritan character traits amounts to the newly empowered self he called *Berufsmensch*, who was strong, goal-oriented, confident, controlled, methodical, ethical, and yet free from debilitating angsts. And key to Weber's genealogical account of this type of modern self was a series of paradoxical compounds in its historical emergence.

---

[71] Ibid. 216/236.

[72] Ibid. 215–16/235–6.

[73] Indeed, war and death form one of Weber's favorite metaphors. For instance, Weber says that, for the soldier in war, the ultimate existential anxiety over the meaning of death ceases to exist by believing in "death for a just cause" or simply a "calling"; "in war, and in this massiveness *only* in war, the individual can *believe* that he knows he is dying 'for' something. The why and the wherefore of his facing death can, as a rule, be so indubitable to him that the problem of the 'meaning' of death does not even occur to him.... Only those who perish 'in their callings' are in the same situation as the soldier who faces death on the battlefield" (Rejections 548/335). Harvey Goldman sees here a "militarization of the self" in Weber's ideas (Goldman [1989] 67–70). His preoccupation with struggle and choice in the face of death will be given more attention in Chapter 4, especially in his account of the polytheistic nature of the modern value sphere.

[74] Economy and Society 329/542.

First, the fundamental question for Weber was never a unilinear account of rationalization. Weber's modern self was grounded in the intense religionization of life, a traditional or irrational element, which was carried out via secular means, a rational element. To put it otherwise, secular means were justified only in terms of an unequivocal commitment to an absolute value. As he said, the historical formation of the modern self reflected "a rationalization toward an irrational conduct of life."

Second, the world was simultaneously sanctified and objectified in the Puritan cosmology, and in this paradoxical compound Weber discovered the possibility of what he called "worldly asceticism." On the one hand, intense religionization in the Puritan doctrine of predestination was predicated on the absolute theodicy of the transcendental God and the complete loss of meaning of this world. On the other hand, to the extent that God was elevated to an unprecedented level, so were His creations of this world. Now ordinary life in this world was also elevated to a meaningful level as providing the only means by which to ascertain salvation. This-worldly activity gained religious value, however, precisely because the world ceased to exist as an independent source of meaning and became an object of transformation in accordance with God's will. Succinctly put, this world was objectified on the level of end, yet sanctified on the level of means.

Third, the empowerment of our agency for Weber was predicated on the complete disempowerment of the self. As the world lost its innate meaning, so did the self. The resulting existential uncertainty and powerlessness that were not avoidable in this meaningless world generated a relentless search for self-conviction. It could be formed only by means of the divine duty of transforming this imperfect world. As an elect instrument of God, or rather to prove that election, a pious Puritan had to lead life in a calling with the sole purpose of the methodical and rational transformation of the world. And self-transformation was the prerequisite to such an endeavor as well as a part of it, for it was achieved through the willful subjugation of the natural self by the higher self based on reason.

To summarize: the more I am uncertain, the more I search for certainty; the more I search for certainty, the harder I work in my worldly calling. In the end, I can eliminate my existential anxiety by measuring my uncertain otherworldly salvation in terms of the tangible performance of my inner-worldly work in calling. This constitutes the chain of psychological effects Weber attempted to isolate in his account of the empowerment of the modern self – a dialectical process of intense religionization that ends in deethicalization of everyday life; the accentuated existential angst, in regained certainty through active participation in this world; or, succinctly put, a psychological transformation from the disempowerment of the self to the empowerment of its agency. The modern self, thus empowered, is an artificial product of a willful self-mastery of the natural self by reason, fashioning itself "into a life in the world, but neither of nor for this world."[75]

CONCLUSION: VALUE, RATIONALITY, AND FREEDOM

In Weber's discussions of the Puritan *Berufsmensch*, we see a reflection of the origin of one of the great paradoxes of modern philosophy. The philosophy of engagement and objectification has helped to create a picture of a human being, at its most extreme in certain forms of materialism, from which the last vestiges of subjectivity seem to have been expelled. It is a picture of a human being completely from a third-person perspective. The paradox is that this severe outlook is connected with – indeed, based on – attributing a central place to the first-person stance. Radical objectivity is intelligible and accessible only through radical subjectivity, which has been, of course, much commented on by Heidegger and Merleau-Ponty. Such a paradox is salient especially in the Enlightenment package of rationality, discipline, and freedom. For instance, holding the package of Locke's moral horizon together is an ideal of freedom and autonomy, backed by a conception of disengagement, procedural reason, and rational self-discipline. This Enlightenment picture of the moral agency – that is, inwardness/radical self-reflexivity and instrumental rationality/objectification of the world – also reflects in the paradoxical nature of Weber's Puritan self.

A word of caution. It should be borne in mind that the Enlightenment package contains an element integral to its core belief which Weber categorically rejected. It was a "thin" account of human being,

[75] Protestant Ethic 165/153–4.

an idea that views the individual as an agent motivated by desire and need, an essentially hedonistic and utilitarian anthropology, also known as "Enlightenment naturalism." It was based on the leveling of human will, too simple a view of the human will, as intent on happiness in a utilitarian sense. It pushed further the denial of any qualitative distinction in the will; all was desire – in the more radical variants such as that of Hobbes, even physical desire. Weber was, of course, vigorously opposed to any strand of utilitarian and hedonist anthropology, which in his view accounts for the degeneration of modern humanity from *Berufsmensch* to *Fachmensch*. But so was Kant, and this is why the Kantian formula of the moral agency comes closest to that of Weber.

Kant rebels against the leveling tendency of the modern self inherent in Enlightenment naturalism and utilitarianism, which in his view leaves no place for a moral dimension at all. For Kant this means leaving no place for freedom, for freedom has to entail a moral dimension. The linkage that bridges freedom and morality is the natural law of universal and rational nature. For Kant the decision to act morally is the decision to act with the ultimate purpose of conforming my action to universal law; this amounts to the determination to act according to my true nature as a rational being. And acting according to the demands of what I truly am, of my reason, is freedom. This is why merely following natural desire and needs is in principle a kind of heteronomy for Kant. Thus, in order to gain genuine freedom, I must repress or subject natural impulses to the instrumental control of the autonomous will drawn from reason. Herein, moreover, lies the essence of human dignity, which differentiates a human being from animal. "Everything in nature works according to laws. Only a rational being has the capacity of acting according to the conception of laws, i.e., according to principles. This capacity is will."[76] Everything else in nature, in other words, follows laws blindly. Only rational creatures conform to laws that they themselves formulate by means of rational appropriation. Everything else in the universe can be treated as a mere means to our goal, for these things have no unconditional worth. Their value is only instrumental,

---

[76] I. Kant, *Foundations of the Metaphysics of Morals*, trans. L. W. Beck (Indianapolis: Bobbs-Merrill, 1969), 412. My reference is to the page number in the standard text of the Berlin Academy edition, which is also noted on the margin of Beck's translation.

and as Kant put it later, other things have a price; only rational agents have dignity.[77] In a sense, our obedience to moral law is simply the respect that this dignity commands from us.

Here, Kant gives a firm but quite new basis to the subjectification or internalization of the sources of normativity that Rousseau inaugurated with his ethic of authenticity. The moral law is what comes from within; it can no longer be defined by any external material order. It is not defined by the impulse of nature in me either, but only by virtue of reasoning, by, one might say, the procedures of practical reasoning, which demand that one act by general principles. Kant thus follows Rousseau in condemning utilitarianism; instrumental-rational control of the world in the service of our desires and needs just degenerates into organized egoism. In order to prevent it, mere freedom of choice based on elective will (*Willkür*) must be replaced by the exercise of purely rational will (*Wille*). Also, this project of self-transformation is for Kant a matter of will that should precede moral education or enlightenment of the Lockean sort.[78] Instrumental transformation of the self and the world thus becomes the crucial benchmark of freedom and moral agency for Kant as well as for Locke, but its basis has been fundamentally altered in Kant; now it should be done with the purpose of serving a higher end, that is, the natural law of reason. A willful transformation is demanded now in the service of a higher law based on reason or, one might say, of an ultimate value.[79]

This Kantian package of value, rationality, and freedom as the foundation of moral agency, in my view, can be construed as a philosophical

---

[77] Ibid., 434.

[78] Compare, for instance, "education can develop it, sharpen it, give it practical substance, but it cannot create it [the faculty for making moral distinctions]" in Weber's undated letter to his cousin (Biography 167/157).

[79] For a reading of the Kantian project of individual freedom in terms of subjective value and objective rationality, see Taylor (1989), especially 363ff. Also see his *Hegel* (Cambridge: Cambridge University Press, 1975) 29–36 and "Kant's Theory of Freedom" in his *Philosophy and the Human Sciences: Philosophical Papers II* (Cambridge: Cambridge University Press, 1993). The precarious nature of this balance between conviction (*Gesinnung*) and moral-cum-rational action is well explored in Henry Allison's examination of Kant's philosophical anthropology. See H. Allison, *Kant's Theory of Freedom* (Cambridge: Cambridge University Press, 1991) 136–45. Daniel O'Connor reads this as a critical inconsistency in Kant's philosophical anthropology that constitutes a large void in his theory of individual autonomy. See D. O'Connor, "Good and Evil Disposition," *Kant-Studien* 76:3 (1985), 288–302.

counterpart to Weber's notion of the Puritan *Berufsmensch*.[80] This cannot, of course, be a mere coincidence, which Weber also acknowledges in passing.

[L]oveless fulfillment of duty stands higher ethically than sentimental philanthropy. The Puritan ethics would accept that in essentials. Kant in effect also comes close to it in the end, being part of Scotch ancestry and strongly influenced by Pietism in his bringing up. Many of his formulations are closely tied to ideas of ascetic Protestantism.[81]

What I notice is the series of elements in the account of the modern self in both Kant and Weber: an instrumental control of the self and the world (objectification) according to the law formulated solely from within (subjectification) wherein both Kant and Weber discovered the source of moral agency and individual freedom. Also, for Weber as well as for Kant, such a radical subjectification is made possible by an internalization or willful acceptance of an ultimate value, a transcendental rational principle, or what Weber called "a belief in absolute values." Indeed, this element saves them from falling into

---

[80] Weber's place in the German idealist tradition is a neglected area in Weber scholarship. It was not until the past decade that, for example, the all too apparent influence Nietzsche exerted on Weber received systematic attention. The exception is E. Fleischman, "De Weber à la Nietzsche," *European Journal of Sociology* 5 (1964) 190–238. See, for example, T. Strong, "'What Have We to Do with Morals?' – Nietzsche and Weber on History and Ethics," *History of the Human Sciences* 5: 3 (1992) 9–18; M. Warren, "Max Weber's Nietzschean Conception of Power," ibid. 19–37; and R. Eden, *Political Leadership and Nihilism: A Study of Weber and Nietzsche* (Philadelphia: Temple University Press, 1983). Equally apparent, yet even less investigated, is the Kantian link. Except for the interest in the neo-Kantian epistemology of Weber's time (via such figures as Rickert and Windelband), Kant has been all but completely left out in contextualizing Weber's thought. For the neo-Kantian traces in Weber's epistemology, see G. Oakes, *Weber and Rickert: Concept Formation in the Cultural Sciences* (Cambridge, MA: MIT Press, 1988). For a brief yet strong argument for the Kantian nature of Weber's examination of modernity, see Ernest Gellner, who claims, "Thus the preoccupations of Kant and of Weber are really the same. One was a philosopher and the other a sociologist, but there, one might say, the difference ends. It is of course a very significant distinction. They saw the same problem, but Kant saw it as a universal one, which concerned man as such; Weber saw it as a differential problem – concerning why some men, but some men only, saw the world in a certain way and acted in a certain manner." See his *Legitimation of Belief* (Cambridge: Cambridge University Press, 1974) 184–95.

[81] Protestant Ethic 260/270.

the hedonist justification of subjectification they both detested.[82] For Weber, the subjectification of value by no means implies a subjection to the natural desire and impulses that one can find in the Enlightenment or utilitarian formula of subjectification. The inward turn in Weber is brought into being by means of the absolute commitment to ultimate value that transcends this-worldly existence of the modern individual. From such a standpoint, the part of the self that is dependent on the external world has to be conquered by the more rational part of the self. In the formation of a higher rational self and the attendant willful self-transformation Weber finds the modernity of modern individual and a genuine possibility of autonomous freedom.

As the loss of a transcendental justification of our instrumental rationality obscures the crucial mark of human dignity for Kant, it indicates for Weber the degeneration of the *Berufsmensch*. In the conclusion of *The Protestant Ethic*, thus, Weber promises that his next researches will follow the "dissolution" of the this-worldly asceticism "into pure

---

[82] In this light, it is quite illuminating to observe Weber's attitude toward the increasingly popular Freudian theory of his time, as revealed in his letter of 3 September 1907 to Else Jaffé about the paper written by the notorious Freudian disciple in their contemporary Germany, Otto Gross. Weber says in the letter, filled with his characteristic eruption of volcanic temper: "They are 'diapers.' For what else shall one call an 'ethics' which, ... is too 'cowardly' to admit to itself that its 'ideal' ought to be the wholly banal, healthy *nerve-proud person* [*Nervenprotz*], an ethics which believes that it can discredit some 'norms' by proving that their observance is not 'beneficial' to the dear nerves? ... *this* is the only *ethical* content of the new doctrine. There is nothing, nothing *whatever*, concrete behind it other than this philistinism: If *every* suppression of emotion-laden desires and drives leads to 'repression' ... and if the 'repression' as such is the absolute evil (allegedly because it leads to inward untruthfulness, to 'error and cowardice,' but in reality because from the viewpoint of a *specialist in nervous hygiene* it involves the danger of hysteria, compulsive neurosis, phobias, etc.), *then* this nerve ethics would, for instance, have to give this message to a Boer fighting for his freedom: Take to your heels, for otherwise you will 'repress' your feelings of anxiety and might get the 'red laugh' of L. Andreyev. ... In other words, I am believed capable of being shabby enough to ask, 'How much does it cost?' before I act the way I think I owe it to my human dignity to act. ... I most definitely doubt that Dr. Gross has any idea of what 'a belief in *absolute* values' really means" (Biography 380–1/377–8). It should not be shocking to see such hostility toward the "ethical" content of the Freudian theory in Weber, who describes the absolute commitment to the ultimate value as leading the Puritan *Berufsmensch* to a "hysteria-producing [*hysterisierenden*]" state of mind! (China 518/232). For more on Weber and Gross, see H. J. Helle, "Max Weber über Otto Gross: Ein Brief an Else Jaffé vom September 1907," *Zietschrift für Politik* 41:2 (1994) 214–23.

utilitarianism."[83] The meaning of this dissolution is more explicit in *Schlußwort*: "what is most decisive [for the *Berufsmencsh*] is that the vocation and the inner ethical core of the personality formed one unbroken whole.... And in the present,... the *subjective dissolution* of this unity [*die* innere Lösung *jener Einheit*] – the denigration [*Verfehmung*] of the *Berufsmenschen* – is obvious."[84] Unfortunately, Weber failed to keep this promise, which is quite characteristic of his fragmentary style of investigation, and the process of dissolution that he refers to here has to be glimpsed from his other and later writings, especially, in politics, ethics, and epistemology. This reconstruction will occupy much of Chapter 4. For now, we turn in Chapter 3 to an exploration of the other side of this seemingly solipsistic self – its sociability, that is – to deepen our understanding of Weber's *Berufsmensch* and to investigate his account of modern civil society.

[83] Protestant Ethic 189/183.
[84] Schlußwort 319.

3

The Protestant Sects and the Spirit of Civil Society

> But with the member of a Nonconforming or self-made religious com-
> munity, how different! The sectary's *eigene grosse Erfindungen*, as Goethe
> calls them, – the precious discoveries of himself and his friends for ex-
> pressing the inexpressible and defining the undefinable in peculiar forms
> of their own, – cannot but, as he has voluntarily chosen them and is
> personally responsible for them, fill his whole mind. He is zealous to do
> battle for them and affirm them; for in affirming them he affirms himself,
> and that is what we all like.
>
> Matthew Arnold[1]

INTRODUCTION: SOCIABILITY OF THE PURITAN *BERUFSMENSCH*

Weber's modern self was predicated on the existential meaninglessness
of this world; and yet the attendant psychological anxiety generated
a most active sort of this-wordly agent he called the *Berufsmensch*. It
reflected an attitude that sought with fanatical zeal to renounce and,
moreover, to transform this world for the sake of the other world. In
this light, the most remarkable fact in Weber's genealogical account of
the *Berufsmensch* was that a natural self of unhindered impulses and
desires was seen as a part of this world to be conquered and transformed by means of reason and will. For the sociability of such a self,

[1] *Culture and Anarchy*, ed. S. Collini (Cambridge: Cambridge University Press, 1993)
195–6.

the existing mode of association also constituted a part of this world to be renounced. Thus, the proud civic patriotism of Machiavelli's time was regarded as the deification of the creaturely. Christian's departure from his family and native community – appropriately named the "City of Destruction" – left its most enduring impression in Weber's reading of *The Pilgrim's Progress*.[2] Thus, Weber wryly proclaimed, "'Humanity' in relation to one's 'neighbor' has, so to speak, died out."[3] Given the radically solipsistic and even antisocial nature of Weber's *Berufsmensch*, it seems hardly probable that such individuals can form any stable and lasting social association. We seem to have a clear case for what Michael Sandel attacked as "unencumbered self" – a modern liberal self being "empowered" through "decontextualization."[4]

Surprisingly, though, Weber categorically denied any antisocial reading of the Puritan *Berufsmensch*. This type of modern self has an immense power to form a cohesive social life, albeit of a novel and unique kind, and this social life in turn sustains the reproduction of one's own kind.

> *In the time of its heroic youth, this individualism conjointly produced an eminent power to form communities....* On [the] one hand, the idea that the religious qualifications bestowed on the individual by God are alone decisive for his salvation, that no form of sacramental magic is of use to him here, that only his practical conduct, his "probation," can be for him a *symptom* that he is on his way to salvation, places the individual absolutely on his own in the matter most important to him. *On the other hand, this qualification through self-probation is viewed exclusively as the foundation for the social union of the congregation.*[5]

Furthermore, he even claimed

that connection of the internal isolation of the individual (which means that most of his energy is deployed externally) with his ability to form social groups

---

[2] Protestant Ethic 124–5/107.

[3] Ibid. 203/226.

[4] M. Sandel, "The Procedural Republic and the Unencumbered Self," *Political Theory* 12:1 (1984) 81–96. The modern decontextualization of self has a larger implication for Stephen Toulmin, who attributes its root to the Cartesian form of modernity. *Cosmopolis: The Hidden Agenda of Modernity* (Chicago: University of Chicago Press, 1990).

[5] Nordamerika 579–80 (italics mine).

having the most stable cohesion and maximum impact at first was realized most
fully in the climate of the formation of the sects.[6]

For Weber, one of the most interesting aspects of the rise of modern
individualism is that it accompanies a unique and peculiar principle of
association that is not readily accounted for by identifying the characteristics of modern selfhood.[7] Weber's mind here seems almost as
dialectical as when he explained the emergence of worldly activism
in terms of the world-rejecting attitude that would have had passive
fatalism as a more logical outcome. Likewise, the Puritan *Berufsmensch*
has to be "socialized" to become "personality."[8] What is interesting
is that this type of self is cultivated in a society predicated on recalcitrant individuality that does not necessarily negate, and in fact actively
promotes, social bonding. Here, in other words, Weber envisions a
social mechanism by which individuation and integration reinforced
each other via public participation. This chapter aims to articulate
this unique "social imagination" of Weber, to see its peculiarity by
juxtaposing it to his own formal typology of social organizations as
well as other social imaginations of his time, and to explore its implication for what can be called "civil society." But first, we take a
small digression into Weber's personal life for reasons to be made clear
shortly.

[6] Ibid. 581.
[7] Weber's Protestant ethic thesis has been criticized for being too centered on the individual, especially compared to Troeltsch's more sociological approach to the same
question. For such a critique, see H. Liebersohn, *Fate and Utopia in German Sociology,
1870–1923* (Cambridge, MA: MIT Press, 1988), esp. 103. Also in agreement is Harvey
Goldman, who characterizes Weber's *Berufsmensch* as a "countersocialized self." See
his "Weber's Ascetic Practices of the Self" in H. Lehmann and G. Roth (eds.), *Weber's
Protestant Ethic: Origins, Evidence, Contexts* (Cambridge: Cambridge University Press,
1995) 171. On numerous occasions, however, Weber makes clear his agreement with
Troeltsch's studies, and there is abundant evidence of Troeltsch's debt to Weber for
the well-known tripartite schema of sect, church, and mysticism. See M. D. Chapman,
"Polytheism and Personality: Aspects of the Intellectual Relationship between Weber
and Troeltsch," *History of the Human Sciences* 6:2 (1993) 1–33. I believe that this misunderstanding originates in part from the characteristic ignorance of sects and America
in Weber scholarship. For the centrality of the concept of sect in Weber's Protestant
Ethics, see footnote 26.
[8] Protestant Ethic 135/119.

GEMEINSCHAFT, GESELLSCHAFT, AND AMERIKANISMUS

Weber's long and arduous journey of complete psychological breakdown, which started in 1897 following his showdown with and the
death of Max Weber Senior, came largely to an end by late 1904,
when he took over the coeditorship of the Archiv für Sozialwissenschaft
und Sozialpolitik. This period has been subjected to much speculation
and interest among Weber scholars. The cause and start of the breakdown do not constitute the immediate concern here. Its outcome and
end do.[9]

By 1902 at the latest, Weber managed to resume his scholarly writings, finished by 1903 the first part of a methodological essay to be
known later as "Roscher and Knies," and, most important, started to
work on The Protestant Ethic. The first part of "Roscher and Knies"
indeed seems to reflect his deep torment; his arguments appear neither
organized nor systematic, bordering on a nearly impenetrable mono-
logue. Although Weber was neither before nor after the breakdown
known for clarity of the style of exposition, his stylistic density was
mostly attributed to the fact that his encyclopedic scope of knowledge
could hardly find a suitable mode of written expression, not to confu-
sion and inarticulateness, which characterize the first essay in "Roscher
and Knies."[10] Then Weber's brilliance suddenly came back in 1904 in
"Objectivity" and The Protestant Ethic (the first installment), two of his

[9] It was Friedrich Meinecke who first noted the potential importance of this psychological crisis in understanding Weber's ideas. See F. Meinecke, "Max Weber"
(1927), in R. König and J. Winckelmann (eds.), Max Weber zum Gedächtnis
(Köln: Westdeutschen Verlag, 1964). Also see E. Baumgarten (ed.), Max Weber:
Werk und Person (Tübingen: J. C. B. Mohr/Paul Siebeck, 1964) 635–52. For
more on Weber's psychological crisis examined from a Freudian perspective,
see A. Mitzman, The Iron Cage: An Historical Interpretation of Max Weber
(New York: Knopf, 1970). For a decidedly anti-Freudian investigation, see
E. Portis, Max Weber and Political Commitments: Science, Politics, and Personality
(Philadelphia: Temple University Press) 49–67, and J. Frommer and S. Frommer,
"Max Webers Krankheit: Rechercher zur Krankheits – und Behandlungsgeschichte
um die Jahrhundertwende," Fortschritte der Neurologie, Psychiatrie 66:5 (1998)
193–200.

[10] See, for instance, Marianne Weber's apologia: "Weber did not care about the systematic presentation of his thinking. . . . Once he got going, so much material flowed
from the storehouse of his mind that it was often hard to force it into a lucid sentence
structure. And yet he wanted to be done with it quickly and express himself as briefly
as possible, because new problems from the realm of reality constantly crowded in
upon him" (Biography 322/309).

most important contributions, which also signal an escape from his personal iron cage. What happened?

What led him out of this serious psychological breakdown is subject to as much speculation as what brought him to it in the beginning. What is certainly known to us is, however, that if the beginning is marked by Weber's confrontation with his father and the latter's death, the end almost coincides with Weber's extensive trip to America in 1904. Marianne Weber, who accompanied her husband throughout the trip, recalled her thrill and delight in attending his public lecture at the St. Louis Exposition – "the first time in six and a half years !"[11] She recalled that "He looked back with gratitude to the country where he had been granted such happy days. Marianne sometimes had the feeling that she was bringing home a man restored to health, a man who had again become conscious of the reserves of energy that had slowly accumulated."[12] Weber himself agreed with his wife on the positive effect of the American trip on his recovery: "the trip can be justified in our present situation only from the general point of view of a widening of my scholarly horizon (*and* improving my state of health)."[13] Whether this trip to America was a decisive turning point in his recovery or simply another of the journeys that Weber took on numerous occasions during his illness is not our concern.[14] The remarkable fact is that Weber himself seized on the occasion as an experience of "widening" of his scholarly horizon and "recovery" of his mental health. Weber's claim is well attested to by the outpouring of his works on his return to Germany, especially in the formulation of the Protestant ethic thesis. And in all this,

---

[11] Biography 303/290.

[12] Ibid. 317/304.

[13] Ibid.

[14] Even after the American trip, in fact, Weber complained of sporadic headaches and insomnia well into 1908, and it is now believed that he had never fully recovered from the illness. Still, it is strange to discover that Mitzman in his psychoanalytical study of Weber pays no attention to Weber's American trip and his subsequent publication of articles on American sectlike society. One possible explanation is that Weber's positive observations on American sects and the timing do not seem to fit into Mitzman's overall claim that postbreakdown Weber turned from Protestant asceticism to romantic mysticism as a way out of the modern iron cage. I disagree with this direction of Mitzman's interpretation, and to that extent I accord more importance to Weber's American and sect writings. For more critique of Mitzman, see footnote 64.

America always remained an important reference of comparison in Weber's mind.[15]

Weber's enthusiasm for the New World is well documented in his biography. Marianne Weber underscored the contrast of her husband's enthusiasm with the critical contempt for America shared by most of the other German academic luminaries who were invited along with the Webers.[16] Certainly Weber was overwhelmed by the spectacle of the New World: he saw in the skyscrapers dominating Manhattan a superb expression of modern aesthetics that defied any Old World notion of beauty, "the most appropriate symbol . . . of what goes on here [in the New World]," which stands "beyond both [beauty and ugliness by traditional measure];"[17] he discovered another supreme symbol in Chicago, "the monstrous city which even more than New York was

---

[15] For the importance of America in Weber's Protestant ethic thesis, as well as for his political thought in general, see W. Mommsen, "Die Vereinigten Staaten von Amerika im politischen Denken Max Webers," *Historische Zeitschrift* 213 (1971) (later reprinted in W. Mommsen, *Max Weber: Gesellschaft, Politik, und Geschichte* [Frankfurt a. M.: Suhrkamp, 1974], to which the page numbers will refer). Also see J. Alexander, "The Cultural Grounds of Rationalization: Sect Democracy versus the Iron Cage," in his *Structure and Meaning: Relinking Classical Sociology* (New York: Columbia University Press, 1989); J. P. Diggins, *Max Weber: Politics and the Spirit of Tragedy* (New York: Free Press, 1996); S. Kalberg, "Tocqueville and Weber on the Sociological Origin of Citizenship: The Political Culture of American Democracy," *Citizenship Studies* 1:2 (1997) 199–222; and L. Scaff, "The 'Cool Objectivity of Sociation': Max Weber and Marianne Weber in History," *History of the Human Sciences* 11:2 (1998), 61–82. Discussing the meaning of America to Weber, P. Baehr and G. Wells even dub Weber the "German Tocqueville" (Weber [2002] xiv). For the historical details surrounding Weber's American trip, see H. Rollman, "'Meet Me in St. Louis': Troeltsch and Weber in America" in Lehmann and Roth (1995). Written from an American perspective with a particular interest in so-called American Exceptionalism, one will also find interesting G. Roth, "Marx and Weber on the United States – Today," in R. Antonio and R. Glassman (eds.), *A Weber–Marx Dialogue* (Lawrence: University of Kansas Press, 1985).

[16] Biography 294/281; also see Troeltsch's letter to Marta, his wife (14–16 September 1904), quoted in Rollman (1995) 373 and P. Honigsheim, *On Max Weber* (New York: Free Press, 1968) 11; The German academic luminaries included, among others, E. Troeltsch, A. von Harnack, W. Sombart, F. Tönnies, and W. Windelband.

[17] Biography 295/282–3: Compare this observation with that of Le Courbusier, the founder and most energetic propagandist of architectural modernism: "New York is exciting and upsetting. So are the Alps; so is a tempest; so is a battle." Note especially Le Courbusier's characterization of New York as defying traditional aesthetics, as well as his frequent reference, as in this quotation, to war and battle in connection with New York. Quoted in M. Berman, *All That Is Solid Melts into Air: The Experience of Modernity* (New York: Penguin, 1982) 297.

the crystallization of the American spirit," "an endless human desert," which was likened to "a man whose skin has been peeled off and whose intestines are seen at work," and the ultimate "modern reality."[18] In other words, Weber appears here to isolate the two almost opposite signs of "America" to European intellectuals – one based on a deep attraction to the youth, vibrancy, enterprise, movement, and magnanimity that leads to the description of America as the "ultimate modern reality" and the other on repulsion from the harshness, vulgarity, instability, alienation, and sheer materialism this ultimate modern reality called America had come to symbolize. If the latter attitude found wide sympathy among highbrow intellectuals of Weber's generation like his companions during the American trip, the former became symptomatic of the next generation of European intellectuals, especially in the postwar youth movement.[19]

For Weber, however, neither aspect of the modernity of America intrigued him; it was rather a premodern aspect that aroused his interest most – that is, *religion* in American society. Thus, he discovered among the new settlers of the frontier – in this case Oklahoma – as well as in the older parts of the country such as North Carolina and Virginia a pervasive sense of religiosity that accompanied a rather strict code of social behavior or civility. During an expedition to an Oklahoma settlement, he said, "It is quite wrong to believe that one can behave as one wishes. In the conversations, which are, to be sure, quite brief, the courtesy lies in the tone and the bearing, and the humor is nothing short of delicious."[20] Even in Chicago, in comparison with which the Oklahoma settlement appeared "a more 'civilized' place,"[21] Weber detected "distinct traces of the organizational strength of the *religious* spirit [*organisatorischen Kräfte religiösen Geistes*]."[22] On sighting a street poster proclaiming "Christ in Chicago," the Webers asked

---

[18] Biography 298–300/285–7. Also see Baumgarten (1964) 450–1.

[19] Mommsen (1974) 72. For the meaning of America to the postwar generation of European modernists, see M. Eksteins, *Rites of Spring: The Great War and the Birth of the Modern Age* (London: Bantam, 1989) 267–71, and D. Peukert, *The Weimar Republic* (London: Hill & Wang, 1993), esp. "'Americanism' and *Kulturkritik*." On the youth movement in postwar Germany in general, see R. Wohl, *The Generation of 1914* (Cambridge, MA: Harvard University Press, 1979) 42–84.

[20] Biography 305–6/293.

[21] Ibid. 305/293.

[22] Ibid. 301/288.

"Was this a brazen mockery?", which they answered with an empathetic "No."[23] It seems redundant to repeat here Weber's keen interest in the religious practices of the Quakers and Baptists in the older parts of America.

Naturally, the essay drafted immediately on his return was called "Kirchen und Sekten in Nordamerika" to be published sixteen months later in the *Frankfurter Zeitung* (15 April 1906) and later, in an enlarged edition, in the *Christliche Welt* (June 1906). The much later and more scholarly elaboration of "The Protestant Sects and the Spirit of Capitalism" in the first volume of *Gesammelte Aufsätze zur Religionssoziologie* (1920) is also based on the same text.[24] This series of essays is remarkable in that, first, they attest to the fact that religion was the most impressive social phenomenon in America to Weber, although he also did not fail to notice the newly emerging power of *secular* modernism there, and, second, Weber was particularly interested in the *social* manifestation of Puritanism in the form of a sectlike constitution of society. That Weber was instantly intrigued more by religious phenomena than secular modernism in America can be readily explained in part by the fact that he had finished the first part of *The Protestant Ethic* shortly before his American trip, followed by the second part written shortly after his trip and published in June 1905, in which he located the source of modernity in the religious Reformation, consciously in preference to the secular Renaissance and Enlightenment. Thus, he confessed that these essays on American sects were meant to "supplement" *The Protestant Ethic*.[25]

What is not self-evident at once is that Weber found the "organizational strength" of religion most interesting in America. According to these essays, Weber was intrigued mainly by two characteristics of the organizational strength of religion: first, these religious associations were of Puritan origin, that is, they consisted of a peculiar

[23] Ibid. 300/287.
[24] "Sect, Church and Democracy," written for the section on *Religionssoziologie* in *Economy and Society*, is also based on the same series of earlier essays, but with more theoretical elaboration. According to Wolfgang Mommsen, this text is an "attempt to give a more comprehensive scope to his empirical observation [from Nordamerika] and to give them a scientific underpinning" (Mommsen [1974] 80). We will come back to this text and its theoretical underpinning shortly.
[25] Protestant Sects 299/450.

type of the modern self he called *Berufsmensch*; and, second, these sect forms of associations, secular as well as religious, permeated and constituted a social sphere clearly distinguishable from and independent of the state, market, and family. What Weber found most intriguing in America was, in other words, that the Puritan *Berufsmenschen*, so self-regarding, angst-ridden, world-renouncing, and even antisocial, formed cohesive communal associations that permeated the social sphere and made possible its distinctiveness and independence. No wonder it was a "horizon-widening" experience![26]

Weber's awe can also be attributed to the fact that these two characteristics of sectlike associations could not easily be identified by the theories of associations readily available in contemporary Germany. This type of association posed a grave problem, for instance, for the uniquely German framework of *Gemeinschaft* versus *Gesellschaft*. This famous dichotomy, given a definitive formulation by Ferdinand Tönnies in 1887, had taken on a life of its own in Germany by the turn of the century and became something of a cliché later in Weimar politics.[27] Regardless of Tönnies's own intention, the vulgarized form of this dichotomy had been usurped mostly by the more conservative flank of the German literati with their all-too-familiar tone of fervent antimodernism. According to the antimodernist-conservative reading, *Gesellschaft* was synonymous with the modern, thus by implication evil, realm of atomized and materialistic individuals lacking a harmonious whole – the source of all malaise associated with the revolutionary social transformation that took place in Wilhelmine Germany. By contrast, *Gemeinschaft* stood for everything not modern in such a

---

[26] The centrality of sect in Weber's Protestant ethic thesis has often been neglected. For exceptions, see S. Berger, "The Sects and the Breakthrough into the Modern World: On the Centrality of the Sects in Weber's Protestant Ethic Thesis," *Sociological Quarterly* 12 (1971) 486–99, and B. Nelson, "Max Weber, Ernst Troeltsch, Georg Jellinek as Comparative Historical Sociologists," *Sociological Analysis* 36:3 (1975) 229–40, as well as Jeffrey Alexander's insightful essay, "Cultural Grounds of Rationalization: Sect Democracy versus the Iron Cage," in Alexander (1989).

[27] See F. Tönnies, *Community and Society* (New Brunswick, NJ: Transaction, 1993); for the acceptance of the Tönniesean paradigm in German Society, see F. Ringer, *The Decline of the German Mandarins: The German Academic Community, 1890–1933* (Cambridge, MA: Harvard University Press, 1969) 265–6/164–71. On the antimodernist usurpation of this dichotomy, especially by Spengler, Jünger, and Sombart, see J. Herf, *Reactionary Modernism: Technology, Culture, and Politics in Weimar and the Third Reich* (Cambridge: Cambridge University Press, 1984), 36,84,136.

reading: family, home, church, neighborhood, fraternity, community, or anything that invoked an illusory emotion of stability, security, and congeniality.

Analytically, these contrasts were reduced to two antinomic modes of associational membership. The natural and spontaneous integration of a *Gemeinschaft* was seen to draw its strength from "particularism" (i.e., that associational membership is in principle limited to those sharing a certain set of particularistic features) and "ascriptivism" (i.e., that defining characteristics of associational members are inherited), which in combination provided the most visible locus for the us–them distinction. By contrast, the modern "voluntarist and universalist principle" of association eroded this distinction, thereby ushering in the modern society of atomized individuals and universal sovereignty of the state. Whenever *Gemeinschaft* was cast in terms of its contrast to *Gesellschaft*, its antinomy was drawn between these two sets of principles – particularist and ascriptive versus universalist and voluntarist modes of association.[28]

There can be no doubt that Weber was familiar with this conceptual dichotomy and its ideological implication. On several occasions, he paid respect to Tönnies and his dualism.[29] The intellectual relationship between Tönnies and Weber notwithstanding,[30] Weber seemed to defy the conceptual dualism of *Gemeinschaft* and *Gesellschaft*, as well as its contemporary conservative, antimodernist bent. That this dualism was unsustainable in light of historical experience was obvious to Weber, for whom the very social forces that most German

[28] See M. Riedel, "Gesellschaft, Gemeinschaft," in O. Brunner, W. Conze, and R. Koselleck (eds.), *Geschichtliche Grundbegriffe: Historische Lexicon zur politische-sozialen Sprache in Deutschland*, Vol. 2 (Stuttgart: Ernst Klett Verlag, 1972) 854ff.

[29] Weber, for example, praised Tönnies's book as "one of the fundamental books of our modern social philosophical orientation" (Sozialpolitik 470).

[30] It remains unclear how close their relationship was. As two of the leading members of the younger generation in the *Verein für Sozialpolitik*, the bastion of left-of-center intellectuals in turn-of-the-century Germany, Tönnies and Weber maintained a relatively close personal relationship throughout their lives. Their mutual intellectual influences, however, remain controversial. See D. Krüger, "Max Weber and the Younger Generation in the *Verein für Sozialpolitik*," in W. Mommsen and J. Osterhammel (eds.), *Max Weber and His Contemporaries* (London: Allen & Unwin, 1987), and W. Cahnman, *Weber and Tönnies: Comparative Sociology in Historical Perspective* (New Brunswick, NJ: Transaction, 1995).

literati of his time saw as the antidote to the modern *Gesellschaft* –
the Protestant religious ideals as embodied in church, the academic
Bildung ideal, the Prussian bureaucratic establishment with its moral
self-glorification, and even the Junkerdom – were in fact the main con-
tributors to the modernization process that was rapidly undermining
the foundations of the alleged *Gemeinschaft* in Germany. Thus, for instance, he isolated the Protestant ethic as the womb of modernity and
bureaucracy as its tomb; the Junker, according to his analysis, provided the main driving force behind the rapid transformation of the
agricultural East Prussia. Under the circumstances, a reestablishment
of the authority of the church and bureaucracy would only deepen the
collective anxiety caused by rapid modernization. Even in Germany,
the Tönniesean dualism would have appeared too thin a framework
to accommodate the modern experience for Weber. One might say
that the alleged tension between *Gemeinschaft* and *Gesellschaft* is seen
by Weber less as a tension between premodern and modern principles of association than that between two different modes of modern
institutions.[31]

In a different way, yet with more clarity, America à la Weber defies
the antinomic structure of a Tönniesean paradigm. In America, he
seems to have discovered or confirmed a different mode of modern society that can be grasped conceptually in terms neither of *Gesellschaft*
nor of *Gemeinschaft* models. What he called sectlike associations in
America were no *Gemeinschaften*, in that *voluntary* consent of individual members formed the constitutive foundation; but neither were they
Gesellschaften, in that they did not simply consist of atomized individuals and the universal sovereignty of the state, lacking the dense cohesion
of a spontaneous civil society. They were *voluntary* associations that
were nevertheless predicated on a *particularistic* principle of membership, permeating the intermediary sphere between the state and individuals. They bore little resemblance to what were called *Gemeinschaft*
and *Gesellschaft* in contemporary Germany, where society was viewed
as either cohesive or fragmentary, organic or mechanistic, holistic or
atomistic, antimodern or modern, yet certainly not both. It was both
in America.

---

[31] In agreement is Alexander (1989) 106.

MODES OF SOCIABILITY: AMERICA VERSUS EUROPE

Most prominent in Weber's observations on the Puritan sects in America is a unique mode of association in which ethical concern and individual autonomy are preserved while not hindering the cohesiveness of social bonding. Weber makes two related points: that individuality and sociability can be compatible and moreover can reinforce each other, and that the source of mutual reinforcement is the fact that they both depend on the shared ethical qualities of the individuals. In the Puritan sects in America, Weber finds a principle of modern society according to which solidarity is enhanced by a shared ethical public sphere that cultivates a defiant and even recalcitrant kind of individualism. For Weber, this mode of sociability is possible only insofar as individuality is defined in terms of transcendental ethical qualities he called *charisma* – and not, for example, of self-interest (Smith), private property (Locke), labor (Marx), or even formal rights (Kant).

Although this mode of modern society was being rapidly displaced even in America, Weber nevertheless says, "for true Yankeedom, this [displacement] is a recent phenomenon, and as far as Anglo-American circles are concerned, 'secularization' [*Säkularisation*] has still not penetrated deeply." It may be a "residuum [*Rückständen*]," yet still "it remains one of the most powerful components of life conduct [*Lebensführung*] as a whole."[32] In order to account for this American "peculiarity," Weber first points to the "immature" legal system and "legal proceedings [that] are anchored in Anglo-Norman formalism,"[33] which can hardly maintain stable social transactions over the vast territory of America with sparse settlement and mobile population. Under the circumstances, Weber holds that "social reputableness" becomes the only alternative to the legal guarantee for stable social transaction, and church membership becomes the only social network to fulfill such a function where no preexisting mode of social bond exists. Thus, for instance, a traveling salesperson can gain the necessary trust and credit for a business transaction in a new place only if he or she proves a stable membership in a reputable denomination or sect at home. It is important to note, however, that it is not only the role of credit union that

---

[32] Nordamerika 559.
[33] Ibid. 560.

sectarian groups assume; "the religious congregation embraces almost all 'social' interests in which the individual participates beyond his own doorstep."[34] Weber in fact considers the social sphere in America at once expansive and distinctive.

First, Weber's emphasis is put on the "comprehensiveness" of the sect associations. The sect is not limited to what pertains to the religious activities of the members but attends to "almost all 'social' interests." This observation naturally follows from the Puritan doctrine of calling, which does not exempt any trivial corner of everyday life from constant religious scrutiny. This intense "religionization of everyday life" brings about one effect that Weber does not fail to notice: not only the religious sphere, but also the secular social sphere in general, becomes organized. Insofar as every aspect of secular life falls under the spell of religion, religious sects provide the social sphere with its organizational structure and strength, a process Weber calls "the religious penetration of social life 'from below' [*von unten*]."[35] Especially in America, where no secular associations preceded those of religious origin, the domination of sect associations is more conclusive.[36] This does not mean, nevertheless, that America is a papal state, or a caesarocephalous society à la Weber, for it is sect, and not church, that provides the nuclei of social constitution.[37] The consequence for the society in general is the permeation of voluntary associations.

Another consequence, and probably more important for Weber, is that the scope of the social sphere or what is called civil society can be more clearly demarcated. Weber's emphasis on the *social* seems to mean that any activities not belonging to the political realm, and thus political parties, revolve around religious groups, which become the only medium for "the guarantee of *social* qualities."[38] In other words, Weber recognized the existence of the social realm in America between private lives and the political arena – a *civil society*, in more conventional

---

[34] Ibid.

[35] Ibid. 583

[36] Weber observed in this regard that the organization of religious congregations preceded even the "political societalization [*politischen Vergesellschaftung*]" of the New England colonies (Protestant Sects 217/450).

[37] For the concept of a caesarocephalous society, see Economy and Society 690–2/1159–63.

[38] Nordamerika 560.

terms, posed beyond the individual "doorstep" yet delimited by the "principle of the separation of church and state." This observation is significant since, if a civil society becomes coterminous with the boundaries of religious groups, the separation of church and the state becomes its visible demarcation.

Weber's emphasis on the separation of church and state is understandable given the existence of "*hostility* to the religious communities" among "all 'liberalism' in the broadest sense of the word."[39] According to this view, religious groups and social integration tend to negate each other; thus, Hobbes and Pufendorf, respectively, imagined a political society in which hardly any private associations, likened to "wormes in the entrayles of a naturall man" by Hobbes,[40] exist under one omnipotent sovereignty, and their absolutist vision makes sense only in the context of the religious wars that dominated their time. Especially for Weber's German readers, with a vivid historical memory of religiously motivated national crises – the Thirty Years War as well as the more recent experience of the *Kulturkampf*[41] – religious affiliation that actually promotes solidarity, instead of schism, appeared hard to understand; "the concept of 'membership' [*Zugehörigkeit*] in an ecclesiastical community means something entirely different [in America] than it does for us," Weber thus warns.[42]

On this score, Weber is in agreement with Georg Jellinek, a leading liberal jurist of Weber's time as well as his Heidelberg colleague, that Calvinist doctrine and Puritan sects gave birth to the modern doctrine of separation of church and state.[43] As opposed to a Hobbesean argument for the separation, which is predicated on the fear that religiously motivated sectarianism poses one of the gravest threats to social

---

[39] Ibid. 581.

[40] T. Hobbes, *Leviathan*, ed. R. Tuck (Cambridge: Cambridge University Press, 1991), Part II, Ch. 29, 230. Cf. S. Pufendorf, *On the Duty of Man and Citizen* (Cambridge: Cambridge University Press, 1991), Book II, Ch. 11, §12, 154: "It is therefore the sovereign's task to ensure that factions do not arise; to prevent citizens from forming associations by private agreements."

[41] For the German liberals' critical attitude toward religious schism, especially during and after the *Kulturkampf*, see M. John, *Politics and the Law in Late Nineteenth-Century Germany* (Oxford: Oxford University Press, 1989).

[42] *Nordamerika* 559.

[43] *Economy and Society* 725–6/1209–10. See G. Jellinek, *The Declarations of the Rights of Man and of Citizens: A Contribution to Modern Constitutional History*, trans. M. Farrand (Westport, CT: Hyperion Press, 1901).

integration, and thus in need of restraint, Weber, following Jellinek's and other liberal arguments, proceeds from the idea of freedom of consciousness. In fact, this refocus makes it easier to understand Weber's insistence that Puritanism has a Janus-like face – that is, in this case, Puritanism rejects any glorification of politics per se while creating a deep psychological reservoir for political participation.

On the one hand, Weber maintains that a more psychologically consistent outcome of the Puritan doctrine is less a *political* schism than a complete political *apathy*. In contrast to the ancient republican tradition that views active political participation in the collective self-rule as intrinsic to, indeed, the loftiest ideal of, human virtues, a preoccupation with the political easily falls prey to the idolatry of the creaturely in the eyes of the Puritans and thus needs to be renounced for the sake of one's own spiritual salvation in the other world. For "those oaths of allegiance should be made to God alone and that it is an insult to His majesty to accord them to a person." Weber goes on to declare that

[t]he unconditional rejection of all such demands of the state that go against one's conscience and the demand that the state recognize "freedom of conscience" as the inalienable right of the individual were conceivable from the position of the sect only as a positive *religious* claim.[44]

More important, the Puritan doctrine does not make any universal claim over the society in general, a characteristic that makes it distinct from both the Catholic Church and the political state. According to Weber, the Catholic Church purports to extend its domination outward and thus is eager to incorporate the saved as well as the damned. This universalist claim of the church entails a potential tension with another domination over laypersons with a no less universalist ambition – that of political power. Historically, the competition between the state and the church for the loyalty of the lay population tended to result in compromises in the church's doctrine as well as conflicts and war.[45] By contrast, the Puritan sects do not compete with the state over universal loyalty, for they are simply indifferent to the destiny of those outside

[44] Nordamerika 579.
[45] Economy and Society 699–702/1173–6.

the sects.[46] Their only political demand is neither a division of the loyalty laypersons reserved for the state nor official recognition as the state church, but rather nonintervention by the state in the realm of spiritual salvation and individual conscience – a mutual apathy and indifference in principle. Weber says thus that "the question of church membership . . . corresponds to the Homeric inquiry about homeland and parents."[47]

For Weber, on the other hand, the aversion to politics in the Puritan doctrine does not necessarily mean that it is *apolitical* in practice. Quite the contrary. Despite their principled indifference to mundane politics, Weber's Puritans have a deep reservoir of political activism that can be discharged at crucial moments. As in the English Civil War, especially when a threat is perceived to the basic rights and freedom of conscience, political participation is approached with the same fanatic zeal, methodical discipline, and unflinching sense of duty that govern Puritans' daily conduct. It is in terms not only of economic ethics, but also of their *political* attitudes, for instance, that Weber draws one of the crucial contrasts between German Lutheranism and Anglo-American Puritanism. Lutherans tend to accept the secular political order with a passive obedience, which, according to Weber, made Germans susceptible to the authoritarian state bureaucracy. It was, by contrast, the Puritan readiness for a political recalcitrance and collective action in common defiance that ushered in the first antiauthoritarian democracies in England and America; "the 'inverting' of this principle [Catholic monastic asceticism that emphasizes passive obedience] by Protestant asceticism is the historical foundation for the uniqueness, even today, of the *democracy* among peoples influenced by Puritanism."[48] It is little wonder that the question driving Weber's inquiry into the Protestant ethic is self-confessedly akin to that of Montesquieu, which is not only about piety and commerce in England, but more importantly about piety and *freedom*.[49]

The kind of political activism that Puritanism is prepared to endorse, of course, shares little with the classical republican and civic humanist

---

[46] Ibid. 725/1208.
[47] Nordamerika 559.
[48] Protestant Ethic 241/256.
[49] Ibid. 38/45.

tradition, or what Michael Sandel describes as "the strong version of the republican ideal."[50] Such a republican glorification of politics would surely constitute an idolatry of the creaturely in Puritan eyes. Although political participation does not have an intrinsic value in the Puritan ethical doctrine, however, it can still have a crucial *instrumental* meaning, in the same manner that economic acquisition, while lacking *definitional* value, is absolutely crucial to the constitution of the Puritan *Berufsmensch*. Political activism, especially in pursuit of grandeur and glory, cannot be an end in itself, and yet it is an important means for the Puritans by which to protect their formal rights and individual freedom of conscience, even enabling them to crusade against "evils" for God's glory in what they perceive to be a "just war."[51] One might say that here Weber's Puritanism harbors "more modest" republicanism or an instrumental kind of republicanism that even Benjamin Constant deemed indispensable for the self-sustainability of the modern liberal and counterrepublican regime of private rights and negative liberty.[52] One does not have to affirm the intrinsic value of political participation to value it in the name of republicanism. It is indeed not only our economic agency that Puritanism empowers; so is our political agency enabled through this-worldly asceticism.

Given these political implications of Puritan asceticism, a formal separation of state and church gains all the more importance for Weber, and he reminds the readers that it is in the United States that the principle of separation of church and state is most explicitly

---

[50] For this conceptual distinction between what can be alternatively called an "Athenian-Aristotelean" and a "Roman-Ciceroian" republicanism, see M. Sandel, *Democracy's Discontents: American in Search of a Public Philosophy* (Cambridge, MA: Harvard University Press, 1996) 26. On republicanism in general, see M. Viroli, *Republicanism* (New York: Hill & Wang, 2002); Q. Skinner, *Liberty before Liberalism* (Cambridge: Cambridge University Press, 1998); and P. Pettit, *Republicanism: A Theory of Freedom and Government* (Oxford: Oxford University Press, 1997). Wilhelm Hennis has suggested that Weber's political thought should be understood as belonging to the ancient republican tradition that forces "the individual into the political order, allowing him to participate in the responsibilities and risks of these orders" (Hennis [1988] 50). Peter Baehr has raised doubts, rather persuasively in my view, about this classical republican genealogy (P. Baehr, "An 'Ancient Sense of Politics'?: Weber, Caesarism, and the Republican Tradition," *European Journal of Sociology* 60:2 [1999] 333–50).

[51] Rejections 549–50/336–7.

[52] See, for instance, B. Constant, *Political Writings* ed. trans. B. Fontana (Cambridge: Cambridge University Press, 1988) 323.

promulgated in the constitution. Weber seems to believe that if an expansive civil society, embracing every imaginable social activity that takes place "beyond one's doorstep" exists in America, it owes its dynamism to formal and effective demarcation of its limit by the principle of separation of church and state. Also, conversely, the doctrine could be clearly enumerated only in America due to its Puritan nature. Once the private and public realms are clearly demarcated and their boundaries respected, religious sectarianism need not be elevated automatically into political schism despite its political energy. Puritan sectarianism should not be suspected as being a disintegrating force; Weber asserts that it may provide the most important nuclei for a stronger kind of political integration.

The third and most important point for Weber is, hence, that not only is it possible to prevent sectarianism from escalating into the overall disintegration of political society, but sectlike associations can actively promote the integration. This is achieved only by sectlike associations, for they constitute the form of sociability in which the shared ethical qualities of individuals are paramount. Weber's point depends on the claim that the *social* guarantee of the sects is in fact predicated first and foremost on the individual member's *ethical* discipline. For instance, Weber recalls his student days in Heidelberg, where he enjoyed limitless cash credit from the moneylenders simply because he was a member of a reputable fraternity. The same phenomenon is mentioned as characteristic of the Prussian officer corps.[53] It also provides an example of the mechanism of "social guarantee," that is, that the social existence of an individual rests on his or her membership in a community; yet Weber is not interested in German examples of such a mechanism. Despite the similarity, Weber holds that it is rather the fear of expulsion from the traditional network of society that motivates these German students and officers to comply with the contract they agreed on. Even the regular churchgoers in Germany, Weber mocks, are happy "if they do not have anything more [than paying taxes to the church] to do with the [religious] matter. The only reason they do not leave the church is because the consequences for advancement and for all other possible social prospects [*gesellschaftliche Chancen*]

---

[53] Nordamerika 560.

would be disagreeable."[54] Weber's despair here is directed at the German Lutheran Church's inability to instill religious and ethical concerns in the believers; "it is just this factor (in connection with an absolute indifference, which asks only what is customary and expedient for the 'proper' citizen [*korrekten Staatsbürg*]), in short, the weakness of the religious motives, which is fostered by the 'established' church [of Germany], and not only by it but by the 'church' in general, for the foreseeable future."[55]

The same fear of ostracism is no less important for Americans, but Weber maintains that the source of the fear is rather different: social ostracism in America signifies the flaw in the social outcast's individual *ethical* quality. Thus, for instance, a business transaction is made following an inquiry into the partner's religious affiliation, less because the partner's church is a financial guarantor in case of misconduct in business than because the membership proves his or her ethical quality. That this primary emphasis on the ethical quality of an individual provides the cornerstone of sociability is what Weber holds to distinguish American sociability from its European counterpart.

SECT CONTRA CHURCH: PARTICULARISM AND VOLUNTARISM

In order to sharpen the contour of this contrast between the two meanings of sociability in Germany and America, we need to turn to Weber's church–sect dichotomy. He maintains that the conventional criteria of differentiation, such as the size of congregations and the statutory lack of recognition for the congregation by the state, do not provide a sufficient *causa differentia* between the two forms of religious congregation. Instead, he turns to the ideal typical dichotomy between institution and community:

A "church" wants to be an "institution" [*Anstalt*], a kind of divine foundation [*Fideikomißstiftung*] for the salvation of individual souls who are *born into it* and are the *object* of its efforts, which are bound to the "office" in principle. Conversely, a "sect"... is a voluntary community [*freie Gemeinschaft*] of individuals purely on the basis of their religious *qualification*.[56]

---

[54] Sozialpolitik 469.
[55] Nordamerika 582.
[56] Ibid. 578; cf. "a sect is not an institution [*Anstalt*] like a church, but a community [*Gemeinschaft*] of the religiously qualified" (Sozialpolitik 463).

The most obvious contrast, which Weber seems to want to highlight in the text, is that between institution [*Anstalt*] and community
[*Gemeinschaft*]. It is interesting to find that Weber tries to isolate the nature of sectlike society in terms of its opposition to *Anstalt*, an analytical
concept developed by Otto von Gierke, who put it as an antithesis to
what he called *Genossenschaft*.[57] Gierke's antinomy was drawn chiefly
from the contrasting mode of associational integration by which he
attempted to contrast *Anstalt*'s mechanistic solidarity – either contrac-
tual or bureaucratic – with the organic and spontaneous solidarity of
Genossenschaft. The latter draws its strength, Gierke believed, from the
particularistic social bond among members of an association, a feature
that cannot be made to apply universally in principle. For instance, ethnic, linguistic, or national groups were viewed as more spontaneously
cohesive because the members of the group cast their self-identity in
terms of their *natural* difference from or contrast to others. The *Anstalt*
mode of association, on the other hand, lacks a spontaneous and cohesive integration precisely because it dispels the particularistic elements,
or a visible self–other distinction. Gierke traced the origin of the modern *Anstalt* to the universal, cosmopolitan, or "decontextualized" individualism presumed by the political theories of the Enlightenment in
which social imagination was, according to Gierke, predicated on the
revival of Roman law concepts that failed to posit an appropriate conceptual realm between private individuals and the public state.[58] Gierke
maintained, in short, that group formation depends on the particularistic nature of sociability; that a social imagination with no appropriate
place for it, as in natural rights theories, cannot properly account for
human sociability; inappropriate understanding of sociability cannot
help but turn to an artificial alternative for social integration such as
contractarianism, the market, or bureaucracy – all poor substitutes in
Gierke's view.

---

[57] O. Gierke, *Das deutsche Gennosenschaftsrecht*, Vols. I–III (1868–81). There are several editions of this seminal work in partial English translation, the most famous of
which is *Political Theories of the Middle Age*, intro./trans. F. W. Maitland (Cambridge:
Cambridge University Press, 1901). New selections have been edited by Antony Black
and translated by Mary Fischer as *Community in Historical Perspective* (Cambridge:
Cambridge University Press, 1990). For a recent discussion of Gierke, especially in
association with British pluralism, see David Runciman's *Pluralism and the Personality
of the State* (Cambridge: Cambridge University Press, 1997).

[58] See, for example, Gierke (1901) 94 and 98.

As for Gierke, the important point for Weber when he characterized the sect mode of association in terms of its opposition to *Anstalt* is that it is also based on particularism or exclusivity.[59] Weber alleges, for instance, that the Catholic Church is not particularly interested in the *ethical* qualities of its lay population, because it is vested with a power to redeem their sin periodically. Thus the church members include periodic sinners as well as religiously sincere personalities. This is why, earlier, Weber calls it a "salvation-dispensing foundation" (*Fideikomißstiftung*), an institution based on leveling universalism. By contrast, Puritan sects tend toward a religious elitism or spiritual aristocracy. For Puritans, as their name indicates, only the *pure* can be admitted to the Lord's Supper, and "it is a sin not to purge the sacramental communion of nonbelievers."[60] As opposed to *Anstalt* or institution, a Puritan sect is not a universal organization that embraces everybody and anybody. It is in a sense an elite group of those who have passed the strict test of admission, usually decided by a ballot of members.[61] Those belonging to sects are the new elites and aristocrats by virtue of proven quality, or in short, *charisma*: "The possession of such faculties is a 'charisma,' which to be sure, might be awakened in some but not in all."[62] In this clear-cut self–other distinction lies, one might say, the affinity between Gierke's *Genossenschaften* and Weber's sects.

While distinguishing Puritan sects from the church, this particularistic mode of membership sets them apart from other historical examples of sectlike associations and, especially, from those predicated on mysticism that Weber called "pneumatic sects."[63] Although it was Ernst Troeltsch who first made a formal distinction between sectarian and mystic forms of association, Weber seemed fully aware of the difference between the two. In fact, Weber showed great interest in sectarian

---

[59] For Weber's use of Gierkean categories in general, see M. Riesebrodt, "From Patriarchalism to Capitalism: The Theoretical Context of Max Weber's Agrarian Studies (1892–3)," in K. Tribe (ed.), *Reading Weber* (London: Routledge, 1989). Riesebrodt argues, for example, that Weber's characterization of the estate-based society of East Elbia was heavily influenced by Gierke's concept of *Genossenschaft*.

[60] Sozialpolitik 453.

[61] Protestant Sects 212/307.

[62] Economic Ethics 259/287.

[63] For Weber's characterization of mysticism in general, in opposition to which he defines asceticism, see Rejections 538–42/324–6.

movements based on mysticism, which include not only ancient religious groups but also modern varieties.[64] His avid reading in Russian
literature, especially of Tolstoy and Dostoevsky, can be explained in
part by the fact that he saw them as fully embodying the spirit of
Russian mysticism.

Generally speaking, if you wish to understand Russian literature in its full
greatness, then you must regard the mystical as the substratum upon which
everything is built. When one reads Russian novels like *The Brothers Karamazov*
by Dostoevsky, for example, or Tolstoy's *War and Peace*, one has the impression,
above all, of the total meaninglessness of events, a senseless promiscuity of
passions. This effect is absolutely not accidental . . . the cause lies in the secret
conviction that the political, social, ethical, literary, artistic, and familially
shaped life is really meaningless in contrast to the substratum which extends
beneath it, and which is shown and embodied in the specific forms of Russian
literature. This, however, is extraordinarily difficult for us to grasp because it
rests upon the simple classical Christian idea which Baudelaire calls the "holy
prostitution of the soul," the love of our fellow creature, i.e., anyone at all
no matter who he may be, even the second-best. . . . From this acosmic quality,

---

[64] The modern form of mysticism intrigued Weber greatly since he regarded it as a
consequence of the hermeneutic chaos of the modern world; to be more specific, it
reflects a conscious effort to escape from the meaninglessness of the modern world
by indulging oneself, for example, in "active aestheticism" or in the "erotic sphere,"
in which one can once again become a "vessel" of a meaningful order – an attitude
that reflects what Weber called a "contemplative flight from the world" (Rejections
539/325). For the exploration of this theme in Weber, see L. Scaff, *Fleeing the Iron
Cage: Culture, Politics, and Modernity in the Thought of Max Weber* (Berkeley: University of California Press, 1989), esp. the chapter "Culture and Its Discontents." The
same themes are also discovered – in a greatly exaggerated and misguided form, in
my view – in Mitzman (1969) when he holds that Weber's efforts to escape from the
iron cage were directed entirely in an antiascetic and protomystic direction. Ironically, Mitzman uses Weber's characterization of sects as a *Gesellschaft* to support his
argument that Weber became increasingly taken with acosmic mysticism (Mitzman
194–201). Mitzman's error seems to come from a simple syllogism; the *Gesellschaft*
is an iron cage; the Protestant sect is a *Gesellschaft*; thus, the Protestant sect is an
iron cage. Mitzman fails to take note of Weber's subtle use of the *Gemeinschaft* and
Gesellschaft categories. By contrast, it was Weber's enthusiasm for one form of Protestant asceticism, rather than mystical flight from the world, that provided inspiration.
Thus, for instance, charisma, which Weber attempts to reinvigorate in a secular form
in the modern society, is traced back to the early Puritan idea of the chosen people of religious qualifications rather than to a magician or sage. Likewise, Weber
viewed sectlike associations, one form of *Gesellschaft*, as the social manifestation of
the charismatic Puritan *Berufsmensch*.

characteristic of all Russian religiosity, is derived a specific kind of natural right which is stamped on the Russian sects and also on Tolstoy.[65]

When Weber asserts that Russian religious sensibility and its attendant form of sect organization are deeply enmeshed in mysticism, its most distinctive contrast to Puritan sectarianism is attributed to the former's different mode of membership, that is, "universal brotherhood" as opposed to the Puritan particularism. According to Weber, the mystic sect is in principle open to all; it is based on what Weber called "acosmism of love."[66] He believes that the *causa differentia* for mystic sectarianism is this universalist tendency, which characterizes the Christian humanism of Tolstoy's kind.

By contrast, "As a religion of the virtuoso, Puritanism renounced the universalism of brotherly love."[67] Weber's repeated emphasis on particularistic elements in the Puritan sects reflects the belief that the highest possible sense of duty and methodical life conduct can be achieved only within an organizational environment that constantly probes and reinforces the ethical standard to which individual members should conform; without a particularist principle, the organization loses its most important method of sanction in case of breach. The universalist tendency of mystic sects precludes this method of sanction and, to that extent, its members are not likely to develop the "inner-worldly asceticism" of the Puritan *Berufsmensch*. This contrast accounts in part for Weber's pessimism about the prospect of liberal democratic reform of Russia in 1905.[68] By contrast, liberal democracy could flourish in Anglo-American societies because their social constitution relies on the "aristocratic charismatic principle of predestination and the degradation of office charisma."[69]

Weber does not believe, however, that this aristocratic-particularistic nature of sectlike society necessarily antagonizes one of the integral elements of political modernity – democracy. In his only endnote in "Nordamerika," Weber takes issue with Ernst Troeltsch's characterization of aristocracy and democracy as reflecting heteronomous

[65] Sozialpolitik 467.
[66] Ibid. 470.
[67] Rejections 545/332.
[68] Russia 152–64/65–6.
[69] Economy and Society 722/1205.

principles of society, thus his assertion that Calvinism was, after all, insufficiently modern and too authoritarian to be linked to the modern ideal of democracy.[70] Weber especially opposes Troeltsch's undifferentiated categorization of aristocracy, which is portrayed as based on a social principle of exclusivity and particularism rather than on the democratic principle of universal equality. Instead, Weber introduces a more nuanced characterization by holding that the principles of aristocracy are based on principles of exclusivity *and* ascriptive membership. By doing so, Weber intends to show that the democratic mode of exclusive community formation is in no way self-contradictory, and furthermore, that a genuinely democratic society resembles an aristocracy in its principle of particularism – a crucial point Alexis de Tocqueville had championed.[71] In other words, Weber agrees that democracy and aristocracy can be in tension with each other, and yet they are so not because of the latter's particularism as opposed to the former's alleged universalism, but because of the ascriptive principle of membership that democracy cannot accept in principle. Conversely, particularistic elements in the aristocratic mode of association are indeed an essential part of democracy, Weber insists.[72] Weber says that the total equation of aristocracy with conservative antidemocratic ideas results more from the German peculiarity in which the domination of the Junker establishment still persists.

Weber's understanding of aristocratic particularism and egalitarian democracy brings out interesting points of contrast with Adam Smith

[70] Nordamerika 580–1. Also see Weber's wartime speech, titled "Demokratie und Aristokratie im amerikanischen Leben" and delivered in Heidelberg on 23 March 1918, which seems to repeat essentially the same points. The original draft is not extant; only the newspaper reports are available (MWG I/15 739–49).

[71] Cf. E. Troeltsch, *The Social Teachings of the Christian Churches*, trans. O. Wyon (London: Allen & Unwin, 1931) 617–25. Troeltsch certainly knew this criticism of Weber's, for he cited "Nordamerika" in E. Troeltsch, *Protestantism and Progress: A Historical Study of the Relation of Protestantism to the Modern World* (Boston: Beacon, 1958) 149. In the same book, he responded, without naming Weber, by reemphasizing the tension between the aristocratic nature of the Calvinist doctrine of predestination and modern egalitarian democracy: for example, "This is still, however, an essentially religious and aristocratic idea, sharply distinguished from the pure rationalism of the conception of the Natural Law in the period of Enlightenment, and from the democratic sympathies of Rousseau's teaching. . . . Democracy in the strict sense is everywhere foreign to the Calvinistic spirit" (ibid. 115–16).

[72] For more on what Weber calls "the elective affinity between the sect and democracy," see Economy and Society 724–6/1208.

as well as with Tocqueville. When Smith, like Weber, understood sects as being in opposition to church, his primary focus was on the benefit of the small size of the former in maintaining the constant social surveillance of the individual members' ethical behavior. Smith found a similarity in this sectarian process of moral socialization to the way in which aristocratic status honor was upheld by belonging to a closely knit, small-scale society of its own.[73] Tocqueville's belief that everyday associational life plays the functional equivalent to the quasi-aristocratic ethical regimentation in America is also predicated on the belief in the merits of small scale.[74] In essence, Weber is not in disagreement with Smith's and Tocqueville's belief when he underscores the affinity between aristocracy and democracy – that is, an everyday social life in which "a man must hold his own under the watchful eyes of his peers."[75] Although Weber seems willing to concede importance to the size of a group, he still insists that "but yet it *is* not that essence itself."[76] Weber's point is rather that small scale itself hinges on the exclusivity of the sectlike associations in which he finds its striking affinity to aristocratic social organizations. For different reasons from those offered by Tocqueville, hence, Weber makes the Tocquevillean statement that

[w]hoever presents "democracy" as a mass fragmented into atoms, as our Romantics like to do, is fundamentally mistaken so far as the American democracy is concerned. "Atomization" is usually a consequence not of democracy but of bureaucratic rationalism and therefore it cannot be eliminated through the favored imposition of "organic structures" from above. The genuine American society...was never such a sandpile [*Sandhaufen*]. Nor was it ever a building where everyone who enters, without exception, found open doors. It was and is permeated with "exclusivities" [*Exklusivitäten*] of every kind.[77]

73 See A. Smith, *An Inquiry into the Nature and Causes of the Wealth of Nations* (Chicago: University of Chicago Press, 1976), Vol. II, Book 5, Ch. 1, 309–38. For Smith's ideal type of sect and its secular implication for civil society, see S. Macedo, "Community, Diversity, and Civic Education: Toward a Liberal Political Science of Group Life," in E. F. Paul, F. Miller, and J. Paul (eds.), *Communitarian Challenge to Liberalism* (Cambridge: Cambridge University Press, 1996) 242–52.
74 See, for example, A. de Tocqueville, *Democracy in America* (New York: Harper & Row, 1988), Vol. 2, 604.
75 Economy and Society 723/1206.
76 Nordamerika 578.
77 Ibid. 580; Protestant Sects 215/310; Sozialpolitik 443. For more on the affinity and difference between Tocqueville and Weber, see Kalberg (1997).

Despite the fact that sects are based on particularism, thus being characterized as *Gemeinschaft* earlier, Weber's characterization of sects in terms of *Gemeinschaft* never has a Tönniesean ring. For Weber's sects conspicuously lack an important component that constitutes particularism in Tönnies's *Gemeinschaft*: primordiality. These sects draw their strength from the ascriptive nature of group formation, what Weber calls being "born into it" or sheer "chance."[78] That is why Tönnies viewed them as more stable, natural, authentic than either *Gesellschaft* or *Anstalt*. In this aspect, Tönniesean understanding comes closer to what Weber calls here "churchlike associations." On the contrary, what is remarkable for Weber's characterization of *Gemeinschaft* is its voluntary nature, that is, conscious and free choice and formation by the individuals of the purposive social group. In this respect, Weber's *Gemeinschaft* here is closer to Tönnies's *Gesellschaft*; in fact, later in the essay, Weber concedes that sectlike association is *Gesellschaft* in Tönniesean terms.

The latter [sects] are always "artifacts" of "societies" [*Gesellschaften*] and not communities [*Gemeinschaften*], to use the terminology of Ferdinand Tönnies. In other words, they neither rest on "emotional" needs nor aspire toward "emotional values." The individual seeks to maintain his *own* position by becoming a member of the social group. Missing is that undifferentiated peasant, vegetable-like "geniality" [*Gemütlichkeit*] without which the German can imagine no community. The cool objectivity [*Sachlichkeit*] of the sociation [*Vergesellschaftung*] promotes the precise placement of the individual in the purposive activity [*Zwecktätigkeit*] of the group.[79]

Cutting across the conventional dichotomies by which to account for the modern associational life, whether *Genossenschaft* versus *Anstalt*, *Gemeinschaft* versus *Gesellschaft*, or aristocracy versus democracy, Weber's church–sect dichotomy effectively highlights the latter's voluntarism and particularism – an eclectic combination of associational attributes designed to produce a most rigorous social mechanism of moral discipline of its members. In a sectlike society, associational membership is in principle voluntary, yet the entry and maintenance cost for the individual members is not inconsiderable. To join and remain a sect member, one can rely on no other sources but "proving

[78] Nordamerika 578.
[79] Ibid. 581.

oneself in life."[80] From an individual member's viewpoint, this emphasis on achievement must usher in a terribly insecure social life in which "not objectivized contracts and traditions, but rather the religiously qualified individual is seen as the bearer of revelation, which continues *without ever being completed*." The consequence for the social milieu is not mere communal congeniality, but purposive activities that promote the highest "ethical rigorism" among the members.[81] Despite the powerful mechanism of social sanction and discipline, then, Weber's sectlike society represents "the formation of the social structure" predicated "upon an 'egocentric' base" that is designed to create and sustain *individual* ethical qualities.[82] While maintaining that "this task of 'proving' himself is present more than ever within the group, in the circle of his associates," Weber insists that it is "the individual's need to constantly attend to his self-affirmation [*Selbsbehauptung*]" that binds the group together.[83] In a sectlike society, thus, Weber concludes that individuality and sociability were "mutually complementary and operated in the same direction," and furthermore, that "the ascetic conventicles and sects formed one of the most important historical foundations of modern 'individualism'."[84] Weber's social imagination is clearly distinguished from his contemporary approaches to modern society precisely on account of this emphasis on the possibility of an individual-centered group life.

In Weber's dialectical postulation of individual and group life, in sum, it is important to note that civil society is not a site for the free and open market for associational life in which individuals can freely enter a group and remain members, although they are entitled to establish their own at any time. Nor is it a premodern communal paradise in which the emotive desire for solidarity and identity drawn from shared ascriptive qualities are paramount. It is rather a disciplinary and formative site in which certain moral traits and civic virtues are cultivated via collective emphasis on individual achievement and ethical qualities. The sectarian form of social organization ensures that even in the most modern society, there will be "*ongoing* inquiries about moral and

---

[80] Ibid. 561.
[81] Ibid. 579 (italics mine).
[82] Sozialpolitik 470.
[83] Nordamerika 581.
[84] Protestant Sects 235/321.

social conduct,"[85] which guarantee that the individuals with whom one interacts have the proper "*social* correctness [*Rechtlichkeit*],"[86] qualities linked to individual achievement and ethical probation. While administered according to the voluntary consent of the members, thus, a sectlike association must establish a clear boundary of its identity and a high threshold for entry, combined with a constant threat of expulsion. In Weber's sectlike associations, voluntarism needs to be complemented by what has recently been dubbed "gatekeeping," for otherwise it loses its power of sanction for the ethical disciplining of individual members.[87] It might be said that, for Weber, this gatekeeping function is a precondition for a democratic organization of civil society.

How, then, does or does not this unique vision of civil society fit into Weber's theoretical architectonic? What is the place for this eccentric social imagination within Weber's larger thematic scheme? In what way does his description of sectlike associations in America relate to his better-known tripartite typology of social organizations and their transformation? More important, how do we account for the sectlike society in the context of Weber's overall vision of modernity and modernization?

SECULARIZATION OF CHARISMA: FROM SECT TO STATUS GROUP AND BUREAUCRACY

In accounting for sectlike associations in the terms drawn from Weber's formal typology of social organizations, the key word is clearly "charisma." Indeed, we find a growing emphasis on the concept of charisma as Weber further revised his essays on the American sect, especially in "Sect, Church, and Democracy" written for *Economy and Society*, increasingly disclosing a social imagination dramatically similar *and dissimilar* to what Edward Shils called a "charismatic social order."[88] Here, two preliminary considerations are in order – one of charisma and the other of social organizations.

---

[85] Nordamerika 561.

[86] Ibid.

[87] N. Rosenblum, *Membership and Morals: The Personal Use of Pluralism in America* (Princeton, NJ: Princeton University Press, 1998) 64.

[88] E. Shils, "Charisma, Order and Status," in his *The Constitution of Society* (Chicago: University of Chicago Press, 1982).

According to Weber's original definition, charisma is "applied to a certain quality of an individual personality by virtue of which he is set apart from ordinary men and treated as endowed with supernatural, superhuman, or at least specifically exceptional powers or qualities."[89] According to Weber's minimalist definition, it seems to designate any personal quality that distinguishes the individual from other ordinary people; this definition does not tell us its nature and characteristics but indicates that it is something *personal* and *extraordinary*. His definition notwithstanding, Weber usually uses this concept with more substance drawn from concrete historical examples. Of course, his prime examples are religious prophets and warrior chieftains, especially of the Old Testament. Thus building on Weber's usage, Shils defined charisma as "the quality which is imputed to persons, actions, roles, institutions, symbols and material objects because of their presumed connection with 'ultimate,' 'fundamental,' 'vital,' order-determining powers."[90] This definition substantially broadens *and distorts* Weber's understanding of charisma while bringing it closer to our concern.

Two elements stand out in this revised reading of charisma: the transposition of charisma to institutions and the emphasis on transcendental qualities as the core of charisma. This "weak reading" of charisma, especially by Shils, is concerned mainly with the *weakening* of the *personal* element that looms large in Weber's original conceptualization and the subsequent attribution of the same quality to the collective institutions. This weakening is, however, clearly at odds with Weber's intention.[91] Weber in fact suggested an ideal type of "office charisma (*Amtscharisma*)" that can be understood as a variation of what Shils and other revisionists call "institutional charisma."[92] The difficulty is that, as opposed to the revisionist insistence that charisma need not disappear in its institutional form, Weber's office charisma appears mostly in the context of its antinomy to "personal charisma," which he holds to be the only genuine form of charisma. For example, the concept of office charisma is used to describe the bureaucratic institutions of the Catholic Church in contrast to the personal charismatic principles of medieval monasticism or the Puritan sects; given Weber's church–sect

---

[89] Economy and Society 140/241.

[90] E. Shils, *Center and Periphery* (Chicago: University of Chicago Press, 1975) 127.

[91] For the controversy on the "weak reading" of charisma, see J. G. Merquior, *Rousseau and Weber: Two Studies in the Theory of Legitimacy* (London: Routledge, 1980) 105–6.

[92] Economy and Society 674–5/1139–41 and 693–4/1164–6.

antinomy, it is hardly persuasive that Weber, when mentioning office charisma, believed that charismatic qualities could remain intact even if transposed to institutions.[93] As we will see shortly, office charisma is rather the first step to the evaporation of charisma or to its routinization. Thus, even the "charisma of reason," which Weber calls the last of the charismatic upsurges in history, appears only in the personalized form of Robespierre and is never attributed to the institutions of the French Revolution.[94]

A more important point for us is that the charismatic qualities, whether strictly personal or institutional, are ascertained by successfully claiming the "connection with ultimate, fundamental, vital, order-determining powers," which lends, in Talcott Parsons's words, "teleological 'meaning' to men's acts and events of the world."[95] It was this contact with what Weber calls "supernatural derivations,"[96] which, for him, as for his interpreters, constituted the source of charismatic authority. It was along this line that Weber's notion of charismatic legitimacy or domination was later expanded by Shils and others, such as Shmuel Eisenstadt, to characterize that ultimate or "divine force" that is at the root of all authority and constitutive of all social order.[97]

What this elaboration of Weber's charisma tends to underemphasize is, however, that it is a destructive as well as a conservative force that defines and sustains existing order in everyday life. Weber believes that from charismatic authority spring all forms of social organizations. Thus, traditional and even legal types of domination had a moment of charismatic upsurge in their infant periods, according to this understanding. Also, the charismatic principle of legitimacy poses the most potent threat to the traditional and legal authorities, for it introduces a new mode of life conduct (*Lebensführung*) that has little regard for thisworldly order. In fact, charismatic authority tends to define itself in defiance of any status quo. By claiming an unmitigated contact with the transcendental source of order, one might say that charismatic authority gives birth to thisworldly social organizations and also sometimes

---

93 Ibid. 694–5/1167–8.
94 Ibid. 726/1209.
95 T. Parsons, *The Structure of Social Action* (New York: Free Press, 1968) 668.
96 Economy and Society 691/1162.
97 S. N. Eisenstadt, "Comparative Liminaity, Liminality and the Dynamics of Civilizations," *Religion* 15:3 (1985) 315–38.

brings them to an end. It is a timeless possibility within the genesis and transformation of social organizations – an ahistorical "'creative' revolutionary force of history."[98]

Even less well known than the concept of charisma is that social organizations become sociologically significant to Weber only when a power relationship between the ruler and the ruled is formed for the sake of the continuity of the organization itself. The basis of such an interest in organizational perpetuation, whether cultural, economic, or religious, is not important for Weber; the decisive point is that it is a relationship of power and domination.[99] Thus, leaders and administrative staffs become the hallmark of an *association* (*Verein*) and an *organization* (*Verband*) for Weber; otherwise, it is merely a social *relationship* (*Beziehung*).[100] This does not mean that Weber simply attributes to naked power relationships the origin of social associations. More important for Weber is how this power relationship comes to obtain, maintain, and lose the legitimate authority that the dominated accept as a normative state of affairs: "The merely external fact of the order being obeyed is not sufficient to signify domination in our sense; we cannot overlook the meaning of the fact that the command is accepted as a 'valid' norm."[101] This is why the well-known tripartite ideal type of traditional, legal, and charismatic authorities in Weber pertains not only to political power and its legitimacy, but also to the typology of social organizations in general. For Weber, power, domination, and legitimacy are the first principles of human society, without which social associations are hardly conceivable.

Sectlike society is hardly conceivable from this perspective. Albeit a charismatic community, it represents a peculiar case in that a clear structure of domination is relatively absent; the transcendental connection is seen as widely distributed among individual members of the group, instead of as a more ordinary pattern of monopoly of charismatic qualities by the leader(s). When Weber characterizes the Puritan sects as charismatic social organizations in which charismatic qualities are shared by individual lay members, he seems clearly aware

---

[98] Economy and Society 658/1117.
[99] Ibid. 541/941.
[100] Ibid. 26–7/48–50.
[101] Ibid. 544/946.

of the mechanism Shils called the "dispersion of charisma." It is because Weber recognizes the possibility of a diffuse form of charisma, which does away with the uneven distribution of charisma and hierarchical structure of domination, that his formal understanding of charismatic social organization, especially his emphasis on power and domination, cannot fully account for sectlike associations in America. With the terms drawn from the preceding discussion, then, one can characterize the sectlike association as a peculiar kind of social organization in which authority is legitimated only on the grounds of a consensual order created voluntarily by individuals possessing their own quantum of transcendental order-defining power, or a charismatic legitimating power. In short, the consensual order maintained by the charismatic individual members of the group is a peculiar case of a social organization predicated on charismatic legitimation.

As long as Weber characterizes the sect as a variant of charismatic association, its stability and continuity become acute problems, because Weber sees charisma as an inherently unstable principle of legitimation. It lacks structure and depends on the presence of concrete, irreplaceable personalities. It does not make possible "a lasting institutional structure."[102] The establishment of institutional continuity, however, might be in the interest of the sect members. With the loss of the carriers of charisma, this interest becomes a pressing concern. For this reason, Weber places the problem of the successors and electing new members at the center of his analysis of the process of continuity formation. The designation of the successor, however, results in binding the charismatic mission to external rules. It appears as if not only this, but every transposition of charisma into something institutional, has to lead to its transformation – that is, its routinization. Personal charisma is then either "traditionalized or rationalized (legalized)."[103] No matter how Weber characterizes this process of routinization, whether in terms of traditionalization, legalization, or objectification (*Versachlichung*), they all point to Weber's belief that the charismatic quality is not supposed to provide a lasting foundation for a social organization. Charismatic qualities evaporate in the process of institutionalization that is indispensable for the organization's continuing existence.

---

[102] Economy and Society 656/1113.
[103] Ibid. 143/246.

The self-perpetuation of sectlike associations runs into a similar dilemma, and especially the absence of a relatively visible web of domination further contributes to their destabilization. The clearest example is their transformation into status groups (*Stände*). Weber was convinced that sectlike associations in America, with their syncretic membership principle, were being rapidly displaced, a process he dubbed "secularization" or "Europeanization." His conviction relied on two observations: first, the secular clubs and associations, the heirs to the Puritan sects, were no longer voluntary associations; hence, second, they no longer attended to the ethical discipline of individual members' life conduct. The important criterion for membership is less individual achievement in ethical *life conduct* than a certain *lifestyle*, an exclusivity that cannot be easily shared by the lay population, even by those who can afford it. Thus, Weber says that "these status groups develop...partly in *contrast* to the naked plutocracy."[104] An associational membership tends to be determined by inheritance, mere chance, whether cultural and material, from Weber's perspective. Weber ridicules, for example, the conscious efforts made by American bourgeois to imitate the European aristocratic lifestyle, which he observes in the spread of the Germanic dueling clubs among college students. The loss of charismatic qualities transforms these sect associations and their secular heirs into merely exclusive groups and ethical standards into status honor and prestige. In terms of their organizational principle, these new groups are little different from feudal aristocracy – due not to their particularism but to their lack of voluntarism. If a hierarchical order is imposed on different lifestyles of status groups, they are even seen as castes.[105] Weber was convinced that American society was on the road to Europeanization, in which society would become "refeudalized," unable to maintain the ethical standards that once sustained the social dynamics of American civil society.

Paralleling refeudalization is the overall bureaucratization of civil society. In terms of its mode of membership, Weber's ideal type of

---

[104] Protestant Sects 286/310.
[105] Louis Dumont thus isolates Weber's definition of caste as representing a view that regards it as an extreme case of status and class phenomena, that is, essentially as a continuum. See L. Dumont, *Homo Hierarchicus: The Caste System and Its Implications* (Chicago: University of Chicago Press, 1970) 26–7, 30, 249–50.

bureaucracy also entails sectarian elements; formally, it forms an artificial and purposive organization, admission to which depends on *proving* oneself. For Weber, thus, training and discipline constitute integral elements in his construction of the ideal type of bureaucracy, wherein lies his conviction that bureaucrats regard their job as a vocation. But all this occurs without a shred of charisma; bureaucracy in fact reflects a charismatic organization thoroughly routinized. This contrast originates from Weber's attribution of charismatic qualities to the ideal type of the *Berufsmensch*. Thus, the democratic ballot is decisive for an admission to sects, for each member is seen to possess a quantum of charismatic legitimating power. Bureaucracy replaces this test for charismatic qualification with formal examinations that, with their emphasis on technical knowledge, contribute to the displacement of the transcendental aspect of charismatic individualism.[106] Bureaucracy à la Weber represents a form of organization in which individual charismatic qualities have completely withdrawn. The peculiar lack of bureaucracy in American civil society, Weber appeared convinced, would not last and indeed was undergoing a fundamental transformation in the direction of more bureaucratization – another critical evidence of Europeanization of America. This means the end of a social organization that depends on the shared ethical public sphere and the disappearance of charismatic defiance and consequent dynamism, or in short, the "dissolution" of the *Berufsmensch*, as Weber put it in *The Protestant Ethic*. Thus, Weber loathed the convergence between American and German societies in which religious concerns reflect mere hypocrisy and ethical probing is displaced by mere opportunism:

"Hypocrisy" and conventional opportunism in these matters were hardly more strongly developed in America than in Germany where, after all, an officer or civil servant "without religious affiliation or preference" was also an impossibility. And a Berlin ("Aryan!") Lord Mayor was not confirmed officially because he failed to have one of his children baptized. Only the *direction* in which this conventional "hypocrisy" moved differed: official careers in Germany, business opportunities in the United States.[107]

---

[106] Economy and Society 677–9/1143–5.
[107] Protestant Sects 214/309.

CONCLUSION: THE PUBLIC AND THE PRIVATE

Weber's sect and American writings disclose a unique vision of modern civil society. Its novelty becomes clearer once we recognize that, despite this unambiguous focus on civil society, Weber chose not to use the term *bürgerliche Gesellschaft* in his vast opus, and understand his reason.

German use of the term *bürgerliche Gesellschaft* was heavily overshadowed by its conceptualization by Hegel and Marx.[108] Hegel maintained that civil society, which he located between the private family and the public state, contained, in addition to basic legal institutions, two heteronymous forms – a "system of needs," a purely economic sphere of market activities, and a "system of integration," a social sphere of associations and corporations. While the former was driven by immanent conflict of private interests, Hegel considered the latter responsible for social harmony through the socialization of otherwise recalcitrant individuals.[109] This conceptual tension between two modes of civil society was resolved by Hegel through the invocation of the bureaucratic state. The state for Marx was, however, merely an executive apparatus of civil society under bourgeois class hegemony, and this tension had no easy resolution. He took over from Hegel the concept of civil society with renewed emphasis on its economic aspect with a twist: it was now seen as a depository of false class ideologies perpetuated through constant socialization and dictated in the last instance by the economic logic of market and class interests. The system of integration was now subordinated to the system of needs as a thinly guised veil for class exploitation, making the mediating function of the state hopeless and total revolution all but inevitable.[110]

Evidently, Weber could not have used the term *bürgerliche Gesellschaft* in a Marxian sense lest his vision of civil society be imbued with an unduly economic tone. He was interested in the *social*, that which could not be reduced simply to economic factors and that,

---

[108] For a general conceptual history of civil society, see M. Riedel, "Bügerliche Gesellschaft," in O. Brunner, W. Conze, and R. Koselleck (eds.), *Geschichtliche Grundbegriffe: Historisches Lexicon zur politische-sozialen Sprache in Deutschland*, Vol. 2 (Stuttgart: Ernst Klett Verlag, 1972).

[109] G. F. W. Hegel, *Elements of the Philosophy of Right*, ed. A. Wood/trans. H. B. Nisbet (Cambridge: Cambridge University Press, 1991).

[110] K. Marx, *Critique of Hegel's Philosophy of Right*, ed./trans. J. J. O'Malley (Cambridge: Cambridge University Press, 1970).

inversely, determined the *economic* in some instances. This is exemplified by his frequent use of an anecdote about the social regulation of
creditworthiness in America. In this overwhelming emphasis on the social, Weber could have allowed his vision of civil society to be framed
in Hegelian terms, yet the problem there was no less severe. For the
social aspect of Hegel's civil society was primarily concerned with socialization toward a harmonious integration of society, and yet it was
precisely this Hegelian function of civil society that Weber found most
troubling in Germany. As we will see in Chapter 5, Weber's civil society was to be, on the contrary, a sphere of struggle, competition,
contestation, or simply the *political*. Weber also disagreed with Hegel's
characterization of civil society on another score. The tension within
Hegel's civil society was not only functional but also temporal; the
system of integration was inspired by feudal corporatism and its remnants, while the system of needs was resolutely modern in origin.[III]
By contrast with Hegel's system of integration, Weber's vision of civil
society was firmly modernist in its genealogy. Thus, the archetype of
voluntary association for Weber is the Protestant sect. In other words,
modern civil society was born in the aftermath of the Reformation and
the politico-social upheaval it brought about in social organization. It
had little to do with Germanic feudalism. It was rather predicated on
the voluntary will and reason of individuals and a clear collective purpose agreed on by such individuals. It is little wonder that Weber's
archetypical civil society was America, a society without a feudal
past.

    Although decidedly modernist, Weber's genealogy also contrasts
sharply with an alternative modernist genealogy – for instance, Jürgen
Habermas's Kantian genealogy in which voluntary associations are
imagined after Enlightenment salons and clubs. Put very simply, the
causa differentia can be traced back to the question of discipline versus
communication. For Weber, civil society is *not* a site in which identity is
safely assumed (and set aside), and what matters is a fair adjudication
of different ideas and interests through rational communication and
public deliberation. Clearly, Weber's vision is different. For Weber's
civil society remains sufficiently public without ceasing to be ethical

---

[III] On this internal tension, see J. Cohen and A. Arato, *Civil Society and Political Theory*
(Cambridge, MA: MIT Press, 1992) 91–116.

and private. If Kantian political theory had to establish a formal, juridical principle of social deliberation in order to retain healthy social pluralism (based on ethical conviction) while maintaining necessary social integration (based on formally defined rights), Weber's ideal type of American civil society depends on a shared ethical horizon reinforced by differentiated voluntary associations. If the Kantian formula for the public sphere aimed at formal compromise among presumably irreconcilable private interests and identities, Weber envisions a public sphere of social integration predicated on a certain type of ethical individual he calls *Berufsmensch*, who can be cultivated only by associational pluralism. While for Kant, pluralism and integration were objects to be reconciled in theory, for Weber, they are indispensable to each other.[112] For, in the end, Weber's civil society is a purposefully formative site in which certain moral characters and civic virtues are cultivated through ethical discipline in everyday life.

The remarkable aspect of Weber's social imagination is that social integration depends on individuals sharing a common ethical vision, which in turn sustains a defiant and recalcitrant kind of individualism. The ethical vision is manifested neither as formal rights nor as a theological doctrine, but rather as a certain form of principled life conduct Weber calls "innerworldly asceticism." The irony Weber has successfully isolated is, then, that this social mechanism of discipline and even repression empowers our moral and political as well as economic agency to an extent hitherto unprecedented in history. Small voluntary associations predicated on particularism provide the ideal social setting for forming and sustaining such agency, which is indispensable for a robust pluralism and a vibrant public sphere. As Weber maintained that this unique social mechanism and moral psychology can be explained in terms of charisma, the loss of charismatic individualism for Weber pointed to the end of social pluralism, which constitutes the backbone of his view on modern society. To this story of degeneration (*Verfallsgeschichte*) we now turn.

[112] For more on this contrast between Kant and Weber, see A. Seligman, "The Representation of Society and the Privatization of Charisma," *Praxis International* 13:1 (1993) 68–84.

4

Politics, Science, Ethics

My friend, nature has to be governed and guided, or we'd be drowned in prejudices. Without it there would never be one great man. They say "duty is conscience." Now I have nothing to say against duty and conscience, but let's see, how do we understand them?

Feodor Dostoevsky [1]

Again, back to the modern self. To recall, our journey started from the question: What is Weber's understanding of the modern self and its attendant form of sociability? We attempted, in our previous discussion of the Puritan "person of vocation" (*Berufsmensch*), to reconstruct Weber's concept of the modern self in terms of its possibility for genuine freedom, and the most important categories in this endeavor were his understanding of value and rationality. The reconstruction emphasized that Weber's archetypical modern self reflected one of the central problematics in modern metaphysics – the dichotomy of subjectivity and objectivity. On the one hand, Weber focused on subjective value commitment as the unavoidable and indispensable precondition for the exercise of the modern self's autonomy and freedom. On the other hand, such an expression of subjectivity, in order to avoid the utilitarian-naturalistic danger of arbitrariness, was seen to materialize

[1] *Crime and Punishment* (New York: Literary Guild of America, 1953) 52.

95

in a highly methodical form of life conduct, one based on calm means–
end rationality, or simply life as a "duty." One of the essential preconditions for such a life to come into being was that this world had come
to be stripped of intrinsic value and subsequently to exist as an object
to be reconstructed and mastered, a process Weber called "demagification" (*Entzauberung*). The self also belonged to the world to be
demagified and objectified; it had to be mastered and conquered according to God's Providence. Thus, the irony was that the self became
subjectified and objectified at once.

The preceding argument was further highlighted by the fact that
Weber's picture of the Puritan *Berufsmensch* appears in the final analysis similar to a *certain* aspect of the Kantian self-legislating self. In conscious opposition to the utilitarian-naturalistic justification of modern
individualism, both Kant and Weber wanted to maintain a principled
and self-disciplined moral action that is simultaneously an expression
of genuine freedom and autonomy. They discovered the sources of
normativity and individual freedom in the instrumental control of the
self and the world (objectification) according to the law formulated
solely from within (subjectification). Such a paradoxical compound
was made possible by an internalization or willful acceptance of an ultimate value, a transcendental rational principle, or what Weber simply
calls "a belief in absolute values." Indeed, this element saves them from
falling prey to a hedonistic justification of a subjectification they both
detested. In short, their prescriptions for a modern individual freedom
converged on the precarious balance, or "unbroken unity" in Wilhelm
Hennis's stronger formulation,[2] between subjective value commitment
and rational life conduct based on it.

I will begin the argument of this chapter with a qualification of
this assertion of affinity between Weber and Kant. Weber's project, in
fact, cannot be completely identified with that of the Kantian metaphysics of freedom in one central aspect – the possibility of universal
law on which Kant's moral axioms depended in the end. For Kant,
the rational and subjective can and must conform to universal law, so
that the autonomous will (*Wille*) does not fall into an exercise in sheer
caprice (*Willkür*). Weber cannot accept this requirement. This point is

[2] W. Hennis, *Max Weber: Essays in Reconstruction*, trans. K. Tribe (London: Allen &
Unwin, 1988) 93.

obvious from the outset, for Weber's Puritan *Berufsmensch* is an outcome of temporal and spatial particularity. It is no more or less than a
historical by-product – a "vanishing mediator," according to Frederic
Jameson.[3] After ridiculing those who worry about "*too much* 'democracy' and 'individualism',", thus, Weber admits that "the genesis of
modern 'freedom' presupposed certain unique, never-to-be-repeated
historical constellations."[4]

Weber's historicism is nowhere clearer than in his thesis of rationalization. The problem for Weber is that rationalization does not come
to a grand Hegelian end of history with the rise of the Puritan *Berufsmensch*. It is an ongoing process that varies in its effect. This historical process that brought about the dialectical dichotomy between
subjectivity and objectivity and once made possible the corresponding
strategy for empowerment of our agency is seen by Weber this time as
rapidly eroding the very condition for such an empowerment. In other
words, a drive toward a monotheist and universalist ethical worldview
of, for instance, the Kantian moral project has come to turn against its
own brainchild. Now the rationalization process in "late modernity" –
late in the sense that it is preceded by the earlier modernity expressed
by the Reformation and the Enlightenment for Weber – has extended
its power of demagification to whatever grand metanarrative it once
helped to consolidate. The effect is the fragmentation of a once unified
value sphere – or a clearer self-consciousness that does not allow for
any transcendental belief.

Weber was acutely sensitized to the fact that the Enlightenment linkage between growing self-consciousness, the possibility of a universal
moral law, and a principled and *thus* free action had been broken.
Kant managed to preserve the difficult duo of nonarbitrariness and
self-autonomous freedom by asserting such a linkage, which Weber

---

[3] F. Jameson, "The Vanishing Mediator: The Narrative Structure in Max Weber,"
New German Critique 1:1 (1972) 52–89. Also see E. Gellner, *Legitimation of Belief*
(Cambridge: Cambridge University Press, 1974) 185.

[4] After pointing out the role of science in creating an ideal of "universal personality"
that is essential to the constitution of modern freedom, Weber attributes the genealogy
of such an ideal to the idea that "the specific 'ethical' character and 'cultural values' of
modern man have been molded by certain ideal notions of value which grew out of a
peculiar set of religious ideas rooted in a concrete historical epoch, in conjunction with
numerous other, equally specific, political constellations and the material preconditions
mentioned above" (Russia 64/69–70).

believed to be antiquated in his time of "high modernity." According
to Weber, growing self-consciousness, which he calls "intellectualization," leads only to a radical skepticism that cannot accept not only
any form of religion, but also any metaphysical construction of universally valid metanarrative. It is as if the world has gone back to the
infant period of modernity, when the traditional worldview had been
delegitimated by Cartesian skepticism and a search for a new foundation for autonomy and freedom was underway. Then, as for Weber,
the question was how to secure a thoroughly autonomous and free
individual independently of his or her contingent situatedness – that
is, without endorsing the arbitrary elements contained in the modern
self-legislating agency. Whether thoroughly self-legislating Kantian self
or radically situated Hegelian self, they all in the final analysis relied
on a metaphysical construction of a grand narrative in order to avoid
the arbitrariness of the modern subject's autonomy and freedom. To
some, secular metaphysics simply replaced religion as a solution to this
problematic.

Gianni Vattimo holds that, according to such a genealogical diagnosis of modernity as culminating in the "death of God," the alternative
under the new modern conditions seems to be either a radical self-
assertion and self-creation at the risk of being arbitrary (as in Nietzsche)
or a complete desertion of the modern ideal of self-autonomous freedom (as in Foucault, at least in his early works).[5] If the first approach
leads to a radical divination of humanity, one possible extension of the
essentially modernist strategy of self-empowerment, the second leads to
a "dedivination" of humanity, a postmodernist enlightenment. Weber
nevertheless refuses to follow either a Nietzschean divination or a Fou-
caultian resignation. His project is that of neither a celebration of arbitrary freedom nor a surrender to a grim future in which there is little
hope for individual freedom. In Weber's own formulation, it rather
amounts to the question "How can one save *any remnants* of 'individualist' freedom in any sense?"[6] Put more positively, Weber searches for

[5] See, for example, G. Vattimo, "The Crisis of Humanism," in his *The End of Modernity:
    Nihilism and Hermeneutics in Postmodern Culture*, trans. J. Snyder (Baltimore: Johns
    Hopkins University Press, 1988) 31–47.
[6] Parliament 465–7/159.

an antifoundational yet nonarbitrary form of freedom for the modern self – a reconciliation between subjective value and objective reason minus a foundationalist argument.

In this chapter, I will reconstruct Weber's antifoundationalist strategy for the empowerment of the late modern agency. Following a brief synopsis of Weber's diagnosis of modern value fragmentation, I will first examine Weber's ethical project and argue that, in opposition to Wolfgang Schluchter's reading that highlights sharp distinction, it prescribes the symbiosis of two ethics – an ethic of subjective conviction (i.e., ethical decisionism) and an ethic of objective responsibility (i.e., ethical consequentialism). Then I will investigate Weber's identification of *aporia* of modern politics (i.e., idealism and realism) and science (i.e., value assertion and value freedom) and argue that, for Weber, politics and science under the late modern conditions constitute separate value spheres that nonetheless reflect a single practice of self-empowerment.[7] This Weberian "practice of self" aims to recover the "unbroken unity" between subjective value and objective rationality on which the non-foundational affirmation of individual freedom and autonomy is predicated. Thus reconstructed, the newly empowered late modern agency shall unmistakably point to the Puritan *Berufsmensch* – a person with a sober, matter-of-fact sense of responsibility and a passionate conviction whom Weber sees to have given impetus to the birth of modernity.

DISENCHANTMENT AND REENCHANTMENT

Weber never treated the subject of modernity as such, yet his whole oeuvre can be read as an effort to make sense of modernity in every aspect of culture and society, as a lifelong endeavor to "grow old to understand

---

[7] In agreement with regard to the anthropological meaning of Weber's ideal type of methodology is Karl Löwith, who maintains that "the ideal-type construct is motivated by the stand taken by a person who has lost his illusions, who finds himself in a world that has become objectively meaningless and very sober, and who, thrown back on himself, is forced to conceive the meaning of things and even man's relationship to reality as basically, his own problem, and to 'create' meaning, both practical and theoretical." K. Löwith, "Die Entzauberung der Welt durch Wissenschaft: Zu MaxWebers 100.Geburtstag," *Merkur* 18 (1964) 513.

the devil himself."[8] In his later speeches and writings in particular, Weber wants to make clear that the loss of meaning is the dominant issue of the present. Insofar as the most significant intellectual events of modern history have been the disenchantment, intellectualization, and rationalization of the world, the question of the role of science and politics affects the question of the modern world's meaning. Because it was scientific knowledge that broke the monopoly of the salvation religions, Weber treats science as not only symptomatic of modernity as such, but also as the source of the modern problem of meaning. The uniquely modern dilemma for Weber is that the late modern progress of knowledge dispels any sort of metaphysical teleology; nevertheless, without a teleology, science cannot render meaningful justification for its own practice, let alone for other spheres of value.

This dilemma is likened by Weber to Tolstoy's metaphor of life and death. Tolstoy à la Weber detected a similar dilemma when he raised the question of whether or not death is a meaningful occurrence.[9] Tolstoy believed that due to the nature of modern life conditions, one can never be satiated with life on one's deathbed. Without conclusion, life is a mere part of a random chaos, something provisional, never final; thus death becomes a meaningless occurrence. More important, since death is meaningless, according to Weber's Tolstoy, so is life.[10] And so is a science without teleology, Weber adds: "Every scientific 'fulfillment' means new 'questions'; it asks to be 'surpassed' and made obsolete.... Such progress is in principle infinite, and here we come to the *problem of the meaning* of science."[11] In other words, without a vision of a teleological conclusion, which modern science has helped disintegrate, it also loses its own ability to produce meaningful accounts of human action. Thus, Weber says:

And today? Who... still believes today that a knowledge of astronomy or biology or physics or chemistry could teach us anything at all about the *meaning* of the world? How could one find clues about such a "meaning,"

---

[8] Politics 248–50/367.
[9] Cf. L. Tolstoy, "My Confession" and "What Shall We Do Then?" in *Complete Works* (New York: AMS Press, 1968), Vols. 13 and 14.
[10] Science 87–9/14.
[11] Ibid. 84–6/12.

if there is such a thing? If anything, the natural sciences tend to make the belief that there is something like a meaning of the world die out at its very roots.... After Nietzsche's devastating criticism of those "last men" who "have invented happiness," I may completely ignore the fact that science – that is, the techniques of mastering life based on science – has been celebrated with naive optimism as the way to *happiness*. Who believes that other than some overgrown children [*großen Kindern*] among the professoriat or in editorial offices?[12]

This hermeneutic need has been met traditionally by religion. Weber notes that, as Nietzsche correctly observed, the origin of religion has to do with the ethical irregularity and instability of the empirical world. The meaning of fortune and luck as well as suffering, pain, and death cannot be accepted empirically. We as hermeneutic beings require them to be given a coherent meaning, according to Weber; "all religions have demanded as a specific presupposition that the course of the world be somehow *meaningful*, at least in so far as it touches upon the interests of men.... From here, the claim has tended to progress step by step towards an ever-increasing devaluation of the world [*Entwertung der Welt*]."[13]

Weber maintains that this existential and hermeneutic interest lies in the roots of any rational religion, and that economic and social conditions, no matter how significantly they might influence the actual formulation of dogma in a specific case, are rather secondary. From this perspective, Weber even rejects the Nietzschean moral psychology of *ressentiment*, not to mention Marxist materialism, on the ground that it is too class-deterministic. According to Nietzsche, Weber says, "The ethic of 'duty' is thus considered a product of 'repressed' sentiments for vengeance on the part of banausic men who 'displace' their sentiments because they are powerless, and condemned to work and money-making. They resent the way of life of the lordly stratum who

---

[12] Ibid. 90–2/17.
[13] Rejections 567/353. Apparently, Weber is referring to Nietzsche in the third essay of the *Genealogy of Morality*, in which Nietzsche locates the source of moral asceticism ("devaluation of the world" in his own words) in the interpretation of the meaning of life and existence. F. Nietzsche, *On the Genealogy of Morality*, ed. K. Ansell-Pearson/trans. C. Diethe (Cambridge: Cambridge University Press, 1994) III: 20. For more on religion and interpretation, see, for example, F. Nietzsche, *The Gay Science*, trans. W. Kaufmann (New York: Random House, 1974) 353.

live free of duties."[14] Weber warns against such a genealogical account of the ethical worldview: "Resentment has not been required as a leverage; the rational interest in material and ideal compensations as such has been perfectly sufficient."[15] In Weber's view, a moral psychology has less to do with *ressentiment* or material conditions than with the existential need for *legitimation* of life in general. As a hermeneutic being, Weber says, even "The fortunate is seldom satisfied with the fact of being fortunate. Beyond this, he needs to know that he deserves it, and above all, that he deserves it in comparison with others.... Good fortune thus wants to be 'legitimate' fortune. Religion provides the theodicy of good fortune [*Theodizee des Glückes*] for those who are fortunate."[16]

With more urgency, on the other hand, the unfortunate also need a meaningful justification of their sufferings. The theodicy of misfortune [*Theodizee des Leidens*], Weber notes, tends to develop a unique strategy to cope with this psychological need, and it is expressed most ideal-typically in what he calls a "salvation religion." Weber focuses on the salvation religion because it creates a conceptual otherworld by which the ethical limitations of the empirical world are exposed, wherein he finds the seed for rationalization: "The rational conception of the world is contained in germ within the myth of the redeemer. A rational theodicy of misfortune has ... been a development of this conception of the world."[17] In a salvation religion, the otherworld usually takes the form of a mirror image of the empirical world, except that it is devoid of the ethical irregularities of this world; as opposed to the empirical world, it constitutes a rational and systematic totality of a meaningful cosmos. It is a strategy of generating meanings in this world by juxtaposing it to the otherworld; as the otherworld becomes rational, so does this world. That is, it might become an imperfect impression of the otherworld, yet

[14] World Religions 241/270.
[15] Ibid. 248/277.
[16] Ibid. 242/271. Weber's interpretation here is in direct opposition to that of Nietzsche, who held that the fortunate ("the blond beasts") do not feel compelled to justify their fortune, but simply enjoy their supremacy over the less fortunate, wherein lies the defining feature of the *Übermensch*. For example, see *Genealogy of Morality* I: 22–3.
[17] Ibid. 245/274.

it is saved from a meaningless chaos. Imperfection may be a flaw, yet it is not meaningless. The empirical world comes to be seen as *potentially* forming one rational cosmos in which every deed of human action is explicable as forming a coherent system of meaning. To paraphrase Hegel, the actual becomes the rational and the rational becomes the actual.[18]

The most remarkable point in Weber's account is that creating a teleological metanarrative becomes the essential foundation for generating meaning in the empirical world. Science is seen by Weber as being quite capable of playing a similar function: "Almost all the sciences, from philology to biology, have occasionally claimed to be the sources not only of specialized scientific knowledge but of '*Weltanschauungen*' as well. . . . [T]he inevitable monistic tendency of every type of thought which is not self-critical naturally follows this path."[19]

Indeed, next to religion, science has been the great source of rational teleology. For instance, it has been widely believed that knowledge provides an ascertainable way to a *true* form of everything; thus, "Plato's passionate enthusiasm in the *Republic* is in the end to be explained by the fact that at that time one of the greatest tools of all scientific knowledge was consciously discovered – the *concept*. . . . And from that seemed to follow that if one could only find the correct concept of the beautiful, the good, or even perhaps of courage, of the soul or whatever, one could grasp its true essence."[20] Thus, according to Weber, the ancient Greeks saw no conflict between philosophical practice and the moral education of the citizens; rather, the latter was accepted as the raison d'être of the former. In this respect, the situation changed little even in early modern times, as Weber sees in the claims of da Vinci ("the road to *true* art"), Galileo and Bacon ("the road to *true* nature"), and Descartes ("the road to the *true* god").[21] According to these views, the empirical world may be untrue, abnormal, exceptional, perverse, and *thus* evil, yet it is not a meaningless chaos. In other words, Weber sees in these truth claims a self-conscious linkage of knowledge

[18] G. W. F. Hegel, *Elements of the Philosophy of Right*, ed. A. Wood/trans. H. B. Nisbet (Cambridge : Cambridge University Press, 1991) 20.

[19] Objectivity 167/69.

[20] Science 89–90/15.

[21] Ibid. 93–4/16–17.

and meaning. The secular belief in the grand metanarrative is no less powerful than that which a religion can offer.

In terms of truth claims, the Enlightenment project is no exception.[22] It is certainly true that the most typical French philosophes, men like D'Alembert, D'Holbach, and Helvètius, were aggressively confident in their conviction that they had finally solved the riddle of the nature of good and evil. Their solution, as Hume saw so clearly and said so sharply, rested on a tangle of bad logic and clever puns, but its contemporary force was overriding. To the ancient equation between the good, the right, and the true they added the natural and subtracted the divine. If, they implied, the good was the right, the right was the true, and as scientific inquiry was demonstrating, the right was also the natural (since nature manifestly conformed to reason), the natural must be good. In the form of Natural Law, thus Weber claims, both nature and reason are

regarded as the same, and so are the rules that are derived from them, so that general propositions about regularities of factual occurrences and general norms of conduct are held to coincide. The knowledge gained by human "reason" is regarded as identical with the "nature of things" or, as one would say

---

[22] Robert Pippin argues that two of the defining characteristics of Enlightenment modernity are its radical assertion of historical discontinuity from the premodern world and, moreover, the view that human life after the modern revolutions of the seventeenth and eighteenth centuries is fundamentally better than before (R. Pippin, *Modernism as a Philosophical Problem* [Cambridge: Cambridge University Press, 1991] 4). Weber's understanding of modernity reveals an interesting criticism on both accounts of the epochal self-consciousness based on historical discontinuity and a belief in "progress." Weber rejects these claims through his thesis of rationalization, according to which the modern worldview grew out of the ancient religious doctrines transformed into modern Protestantism – a view later extended and elaborated by Karl Löwith as the "secularization" thesis on the genealogy of modernity. (See K. Löwith, *Meaning in History* [Chicago: University of Chicago Press, 1970].) As is well known, this genealogical view met a challenge from Hans Blumenberg, who argued for the legitimacy of modernity as a fundamentally new historical category and epoch. (See H. Blumenberg, *The Legitimacy of the Modern Age*, trans. R. Wallace [Cambridge, MA: MIT Press, 1991].) Although this Löwith–Blumenberg controversy has many implications for one of the most interesting questions involved in the modernity debate, I do not intend to present here my reading of Weber's rationalization thesis in light of it. The more immediate concern here is Weber's second line of criticism, i.e., demystification of the positivist belief in progress. For those interested in the first line of Weber's criticism of the Enlightenment project, see C. Turner, "Liberalism and the Limits of Science: Weber and Blumenberg," *History of the Human Sciences* 6:4 (1993) 57–79.

nowadays, the "logic of things." The "ought" [*Geltensollende*] is identical with the "is," [*Seienden*] i.e., that which exists in the universal average.[23]

If this was so, then it seemed clear that what was evil was what was unnatural. Use reason to distinguish the natural from the unnatural, they argued, and you will have at once distinguished good from evil.[24] Weber calls this worldview "the great scheme of the natural law and rationalistic *Weltanschauung* of the eighteenth century," which is predicated on an "optimistic faith in theoretical and practical rationalizability of reality," consisting of "a purely 'objective' (i.e., independent of all individual contingencies) monistic knowledge of the totality of reality in a *conceptual* system of metaphysical *validity* and mathematical *form*."[25] In short, the Enlightenment reveals the most secular form of absolute truth claim drawn from the naturalistic reconstruction of a rational teleology in the guise of a scientific "law"; yet in fact it is merely a "naturalistic monism" and "dogma."[26]

The positivist teleology of progress, for instance, of August Comte and Herbert Spencer, was the direct heir to this Enlightenment naturalist metanarrative. History is predestined, runs along a unilinear trajectory toward a grand conclusion, and what conduces to this benign progress of history is deemed true and good; what is not, wrong and evil. Weber contends that according to this kind of positivist evolutionism, "*what was normatively right* was identical . . . with the inevitably emergent.*"[27]

Weber traces the origin of this modern idea of progress to biological science – an idea of organic development in terms of a progressive differentiation. As long as it is used in such a *weak* sense, Weber affirms that the idea of progress can provide social and cultural sciences with useful and value-neutral conceptual measures. From such a perspective, and such a perspective only, we can validate the assertion that, for instance, the modern division of labor signifies a more advanced mode of society than a patriarchal form of domination. Weber goes

[23] Economy and Society 498–9/869.
[24] In agreement is G. Hawthorne, *Enlightenment and Despair* (Cambridge: Cambridge University Press, 1979) 13, 85.
[25] Objectivity 185/85.
[26] Ibid. 186/86.
[27] Ibid. 148/51–2.

on to argue that we can also utilize the concept of progress as long as
it pertains to the development of a *technical* rationality. Weber's prime
examples are found in such areas as engineering and scientific technology, yet he seems willing to accede to a larger claim that any area
under the domination of means–end rationality can be measured on
a progressive scale. What is unacceptable for Weber is the third kind
of claim that the progressive development in the preceding examples
leads to the increase in value and meaning of human life – a justification of progress on a *strong* ground.[28] The third claim presupposes,
falsely in Weber's view, a positive correlation between the increase in
scientific knowledge and the increase of value and meaning, as the Enlightenment truth claims do. For Weber, this claim cannot be validated
in and of itself; rather, it relies on a value-laden belief in an essentially
unascertainable teleology. Thus, he mercilessly exposes its pseudoreligious character: "The concept of 'progress' is required only when the
religious significance of the human condition is destroyed and the need
arises to ascribe to it a 'meaning' which is not only this-worldly, but
also objective."[29] For Weber, this pseudoreligious faith in evolutionary progress signifies "the final twilight of all evaluative standpoints
[*Götterdämmerung aller Wertgesichtspunkte*] in all the sciences."[30]

It is in opposition to what he calls "classical-scholastic epistemology"[31] that Weber positions himself on the question of meaning and
knowledge. As opposed to the preceding belief in the accumulation
of true knowledge as leading to the revelation of meaning, which
Nietzsche ridiculed as being predicated on a hidden "will to truth,"
Weber argues that there exists neither such a direction nor a teleological conclusion in the progress of knowledge. A search for meaning is
utterly incompatible with the nature of the modern scientific enterprise,
according to Weber. It is so because the defining characteristic of modern science is progress, not the Progress with a capital P that amounts to

---

[28] Neutrality 518–26/27–34.
[29] Roscher and Knies 33/229. For a balanced account of Weber's thoughts, it should
also be noted that it was not only positivist and Whig ideas that Weber rejected
as pseudoreligious beliefs; he criticized with no less vigor the Marxian faith in the
inevitable collapse of capitalism, as well as the Hegelian romantic yearning for the
end of history.
[30] Objectivity 186/86.
[31] Ibid. 208/106.

no more than a meaningless change ad infinitum, in which "'purpose' is the conception of a *result* which [immediately] becomes a *cause* of an [next] action."[32] Weber thus saw in Tolstoy the same recognition of the loss of teleology and consequent meaninglessness. For Weber, in other words, modern science is incapable of providing answers to Tolstoy's penetrating questions, "What should we do? How should we live?,"[33] not only because a metanarrative is no longer tenable, but also because it has become utterly impossible in the disenchanted modern world that one single unifying worldview can be universally accepted.

This does not mean, however, that Weber envisions a peaceful co-existence of various value spheres. His argument is *not* that modernity signifies the inability of a universal Christian ethics to hold the world together, and that the result is a modern pluralist culture in which different cultural practices follow their own immanent logic. It is rather that, in the language of current cultural debate, the grand narrative of brotherly love gives way not to a series of local narratives, but to a plurality of alternative grand narratives that attempt to provide answers to the same absolutist questions raised by theology. "[T]he particular dignity of the ethical imperative was obliterated," says Weber, "to the extent that an 'ethical' label was given to all possible cultural ideals."[34] Under the circumstances, the espousal of certain values means "the rejection of certain others," and this point is too easily ignored, Weber cautions, even by those who recognize value fragmentation as the ultimate modern condition.[35]

Weber's favorite example is, of course, the conflict between the logic of politics and absolute ethics: "when they are both completely rationalized, ... politics may come into direct competition with religious ethics at decisive points. ... [O]n the battlefield, the individual can *believe* that he knows he is dying 'for' something. The why and the wherefore of his facing death can, as a rule, be so indubitable to him that the problem of the 'meaning' of death does not even occur to him. ... Only those who perish 'in their callings' are in the same

---

[32] Ibid. 183/83.
[33] Science 93–4/18.
[34] Objectivity 148/52.
[35] Ibid. 150/53.

situation as the soldier who faces death on the battlefield."[36] Weber implies here that, in war, an extension of politics merely by different means, one can put up with existential questions of Tolstoy's kind by accepting the logic of war and politics by which to render a coherent account of one's conduct. In terms of displacing religion, other spheres are no less potent. For instance, the aesthetic sphere also comes in sharp conflict with religion:

[A]rt becomes a cosmos of more and more consciously grasped independent values which exist in their own right. Art takes over the function of this-worldly salvation, no matter how this may be interpreted. It provides a *salvation* from the routines of everyday life, and especially from the increasing pressures of theoretical and practical rationalism. . . . As a matter of fact, the refusal of modern men to assume responsibility for moral judgments tends to transform value judgments [*Werturteile*] into judgments of taste [*Geschmacksurteile*]("in poor taste" [*geschmacklos*] instead of "reprehensible" [*verwerflich*]). . . . This shift from the moral to the aesthetic evaluation of conduct is a common characteristic of intellectualist epochs; it results partly from subjectivist needs and partly from the fear of appearing narrow-minded in a traditionalist and Philistine way.[37]

Each value sphere offers its own measure as good, for each forms a self-contained totality of a meaningful cosmos. In and of itself, each has self-sufficient answers, which are inapplicable to other spheres. That is, these spheres offer radically different answers to the fundamental questions to the point of incompatibility *and* incommensurability. What Weber envisions here is, then, the fragmentation of *and* struggle between value spheres. The result is the loss of a unified notion of goodness, for each sphere claims its own: "And, since Nietzsche, we know that something can be beautiful not only in spite of its lack of goodness, but rather in that very aspect in which it is not good [by the moral standard]."[38]

Weber's polytheistic vision of late modernity is especially salient in the following passage:

[D]ifferent gods struggle with each other and will do for all the time. It is just like in the old world, which was not yet disenchanted with its gods and

---

[36] Rejections 548/335.
[37] Ibid. 555/342.
[38] Science 99/22.

demons, but in another sense. . . . [T]hings are still the same today, but disenchanted and divested of the mythical but inwardly genuine flexibility of
those attitudes. And destiny, certainly not "science," presides over these gods
and their struggles. . . . [T]oday there is the religious nature of "everyday
life." The many gods of old, without their magic and therefore in the form
of impersonal forces, rise up from their graves, strive for power over our
lives and begin once more their eternal struggle among themselves. But what
is so difficult for modern man . . . is to meet the demands of such an *everyday life.*[39]

Weber clearly sees the irony of disenchantment. Disenchantment
with the magical worldview had ushered in that of the monotheistic,
salvation religions. This, in practice, means that ad hoc maxims for
life conduct had been gradually displaced by a unified total system of
meaning and value. In the Puritan ethic of life conduct, Weber claims,
this direction of disenchantment reached its apex in a total teleology
that governs every corner, no matter how trivial, of everyday life. The
irony for Weber originates from the fact that disenchantment was an
ongoing process nonetheless. Disenchantment in its second and late
phase pushed aside monotheistic religion as something irrational, thus
delegitimating it as a value-rendering total teleology in the modern
secular world. Modern science, which was initially welcomed as an
effective surrogate for a religious teleology, became the next victim of
the force of disenchantment. With science delegitimated, various value
spheres, each equipped with its own system of meaning and value, are
struggling to take the position vacated by religion first and then by
science – but all in vain. The results are the epistemological impossibility of any teleological justification of a unifying worldview and the
attendant fragmentation into incommensurable value spheres. Human
life conduct has once again fallen under ad hoc maxims without a co-
ordinating principle. The modern world has become one that seems
to have gone back to the time of Hellenistic polytheism. By expelling
religion – to be more precise, monistic teleology in general – into the
realm of the irrational, the modern world has become again religious.[40]
The modern world is reenchanted as a result of disenchantment. For

[39] Ibid. 99–101/23.
[40] Ibid. 107–10/29.

we "still prefer to will nothingness," to paraphrase Nietzsche, "than not will at all."[41]

Thus disenchanted – or reenchanted, depending on the perspective – the modern world creates a unique *aporia* in terms of individual conduct; it demands that I act according to what are called morality and ethics, and yet it mercilessly demystifies their foundation. The result is a pervasive sense of guilt deeply embedded in modern selfhood. The modern self under such conditions has degenerated, in Weber's view, into a utilitarian hedonist, an aesthetic romantic, a mindless automaton, or simply the "last men." Thus, Weber laments famously, "It might ring true for the 'last men' of this cultural development; 'specialists without spirit, sensualists without heart, these nonentities (*Nichts*) imagine that they have attained a stage of humankind (*Menschentum*) never before reached.'"[42]

The late modern conditions thus articulated pose a serious dilemma to Weber, since, with secure normative and epistemological foundations gone irretrievably, the modern self no longer entertains an unflinching sense of duty, affords to take a principled moral action, and *thus* becomes unfree. At stake, in short, is the very possibility of a responsible agency on which is predicated, according to Weber, our freedom itself. To understand this dilemma of Weber's, we now examine his ethical project proper.

CONVICTION, RESPONSIBILITY, AND DECISION

The most prominent feature of Weber's ethical project is the sharp distinction between the ethic of conviction (*Gesinnungsethik*) and the ethic of responsibility (*Verantwortungsethik*). It has been alleged that here Weber positioned himself against the revolutionary romanticism then sweeping through postwar Germany, on the one hand, and, on the other, Kantian intentionalism. Although in practice these two ideologies of the radical left and liberal Kantianism were oriented in almost opposite directions, Weber, it is argued, saw that they were united since both represented an essentially *apolitical* ethic. By establishing the ideal type of the ethic of conviction, Weber tried to recapitulate the apolitical

[41] Nietzsche (1994) 128.
[42] Protestant Ethic 189/182.

nature of these ethics and to expose clearly its contrast to the ethic of responsibility, which was supposed to form the ethical core of modern political practice. The implication is that at worst Weber was the modern Machiavelli, who attempted to drive any residues of ethical concerns from the political sphere, and that at best Weber was trying to salvage the political sphere from the intrusion of subjectivist fanaticism, thereby refounding political life on a more rational basis. The former depicts Weber as a cold-blooded realpolitiker; the latter, as a classical liberal.

On this score, Wolfgang Schluchter's argument is instructive. His reading underscores the absolute contrast between Weber's two ethics of conviction and responsibility: "there is no complementariness between the two ethics.... In spite of some remarks to the contrary, the two concepts denote in the final analysis two diametrically opposed political ethics."[43] He then goes on to assert that "Weber indeed 'devalues' the ethic of conviction."[44] According to Schluchter, it is in the ethic of responsibility (politics) and value neutrality (science) that Weber sought the source of meaningful life, that is, professionalism free from subjective value concerns. Schluchter's reading amounts to saying that Weber proposed a strict compartmentalization of modern life spheres – he calls it "institutionalized value spheres," drawing from Jürgen Habermas – according to the different values of each sphere; by following the value of the life sphere one belongs to, one can fulfill one's calling and become a "personality."[45] In Schluchter's account, then, value commitment becomes less subjective and more institutionalized. Under these circumstances, the most urgent demand for the modern self is to live up to the *Weltanschauung* of one's chosen sphere of life rather than to choose a value itself. The most important requirement for Weber's ethical project becomes a willful *identification* rather than a *decision*, and the consequence becomes a Lutheran piety rather than a Calvinist agency.

Schluchter is not without grounds in arguing that Weber presumed an absolute dichotomy between the ethic of conviction and the ethic of

---

43 W. Schluchter, "Value Neutrality and the Ethic of Responsibility," in W. Schluchter and G. Roth, *Max Weber's Vision of History* (Berkeley: University of California Press, 1979) 88.

44 Ibid. 87.

45 Ibid. 74–5; also see 92–106.

responsibility. Although not directly quoted by Schluchter, Weber indeed confirms that "[i]t is not possible to unite the ethic of conviction with the ethic of responsibility, nor can one issue an ethical decree determining which end shall sanctify *which* means, if indeed any concession at all is to be made to this principle."[46] Even if we concede this claim of incompatibility, however, it still remains unclear whether Weber "devalued" the former against the latter. For a candid recognition of the logical incompatibility between two ethics does not necessarily, or at least not immediately, entail a moral claim that one of those two ethics was devalued by Weber. What is meant by "devaluation"? What is it that is devalued by Weber? The answer depends on what Weber means by the ethics of responsibility and of conviction – the latter being simply accounted for by Schluchter under the general rubric that Weber was arguing against the revolutionary ideologies of postwar Germany.[47]

In my reading, the ethic of conviction reflects not merely political ideologies in vogue in Weber's time, but also something less ephemeral, and deeply rooted in Weber's thought. By definition, the ethic of conviction for Weber is predicated on an absolute belief in the innate goodness of a certain action that transcends time and space and that, by virtue of its goodness, can even remove the burden of responsibility for its consequences. The ethic of conviction is unique in that it is likely to rely on a foundational system of value and meaning of the world as an Archimedian point by which the meaning of every action can be illuminated. It is no wonder that Weber considers monotheistic religious ethics, such as a certain aspect of Puritan life conduct, to be the most radical expression of this sort of ethics. Thus, Weber reminds us that the ethic of conviction originates from the ethical irrationality of the empirical world and the tension it creates vis-à-vis the rational and meaningful cosmos – from the same psychological anxiety that underlies the rational monotheist religion: "The man who espouses an ethic of conviction cannot bear the ethical irrationality of the world. He is a cosmic-ethical 'rationalist'."[48] According to his

[46] Politics 239–41/362.
[47] It must be noted that, in a recent restatement on the same issue, Schluchter substantially toned down his earlier assertion about the incompatibility between two ethics. See his *Paradoxes of Modernity: Culture and Conflict in the Theory of Max Weber* (Stanford, CA: Stanford University Press, 1996) 48–101.
[48] Politics, 239–41/361.

cosmic-ethical-rational system of meaning, a moral dilemma becomes an evil to be removed without remainder.

In terms of moral psychology, Weber's ethic of conviction prescribes a moral attitude in which an unmitigated consistency and integrity between belief and (in)action becomes the supreme virtue. In one of Weber's favorite anecdotes, the Protestant missionaries in China show an unflinching sense of divine mission that commands them to spread the Gospel. Yet Weber notes that they preach in their own native tongue to the Chinese! According to Weber's interpretation, of utmost importance for the missionaries is the fact that they are engaged in certain actions prescribed and deemed intrinsically good by their belief, and its outcome (here, proselytization of the Chinese heathens) is not in their power but in God's.[49] Their belief is capable of guaranteeing the intrinsic good of certain actions, and the content of their ethical conduct is exhausted by carrying out the action itself. "'Consequences'... are no *concern* of absolutist ethics. *That* is the decisive point."[50] In short, that one's action is required to maintain the unmitigated integrity of the belief that relies on the foundational system of value is indeed what Weber means by the ethic of conviction. A human action becomes the end of an ethical reflection, and the integrity becomes its supreme virtue.

By contrast, Weber maintains that an action based on the ethic of responsibility draws its justification from the consequences it causes: "one must answer for the (foreseeable) *consequences* of one's action."[51] This view dictates that the rectitude of my action be subject to its causal consequences instead of to an absolute ethical maxim. An action predicated on the ethic of responsibility is understood as a part of cause and effect in the empirical world, since, otherwise, it becomes utterly impossible to locate the exact responsibility. That an action is put in causal terms constitutes the most elemental precondition for the ethic of responsibility.

The ethic of responsibility, in practice, demands that one's action be subject to the means–end scheme. As Weber holds causality to be an inverse expression of the means–end narrative, that an action is validated in terms of causality means in effect that it falls under the choice

---

[49] Protestant Ethic 202–3/225–6.
[50] Politics 235–7/359.
[51] Ibid. 235–7/360.

dictated by the means–end considerations.[52] An action becomes signified as an ascertainable means to a certain end, and an ethical question is reduced to a question of technically correct procedure of reason and will. Virtue becomes a rational understanding of the possible causal effect of action and willful rearrangement of the elements of action in such a way as to achieve the desired consequence. In short, Weber prescribes a reorientation from an ethical integrity between intention and action to one between action and consequences.

In Weber's ethic of responsibility, then, we seem to have a clear case of what is called an "ethical consequentialism" based on means–end rationality. In terms of consequentialism alone, that is, Weber's ethical project becomes utterly indistinguishable from utilitarianism. As is well known, nevertheless, Weber flatly rejects any utilitarian ethics.[53] Weber's ethics cannot accept utilitarian ethics on two grounds: first, utilitarian ethics presuppose a foundationalist system of human psychology to which the meaning of human action is reduced in the last instance; second, utilitarian foundationalism is based on a hedonistic account of human psychology, or what he calls, rather disdainfully, "the balance of pleasure [*Lustbilanz*]."[54] Weber's opposition to utilitarianism focuses on its relentless will to resolve moral dilemmas without remainder (a feature it shares with Kantianism) and also on its treatment of the moral self as the agent of utility rather than as the bearer of integrity (a feature that sharply distinguishes utilitarianism from its Kantian alternative).[55] From Weber's perspective, the former becomes another instance of a metaphysical foundationalism that is no longer sustainable in light of the fragmented value spheres of the modern world and the latter is simply a distasteful as well as an unrealistic moral psychology.

The question then becomes: If the ethic of responsibility is clearly antithetical to the ethic of conviction, how does it differ from utilitarianism? This question brings out another aspect of characteristically Weberian questions: If human action is validated as an

[52] Neutrality 526/35.
[53] On Weber's critical attitude to utilitarianism, see Schluchter (1996) 50–3.
[54] Freiburg 558/14.
[55] For a similar criticism of ethical consequentialism, see B. Williams, "A Critique of Utilitarianism," in J. J. C. Smart and B. Williams, *Utilitarianism: For and Against* (Cambridge: Cambridge University Press, 1973).

ascertainable means to achieve a certain consequence, how is the validity of the consequence per se ascertained? In what light can one validate a judgment that a certain consequence is better than another? For what purposes does one need to direct one's activities under a means–end scheme? Utilitarianism solves these questions by reducing human motivations to the pleasure-pain calculus: what increases pleasure and decreases pain is deemed good; what does not is considered bad. Weber's ethic of responsibility, however, does not provide, in and of itself, any clue to the matter.

This is why Weber comes to assert what appears contradictory to his earlier statement: "the ethic of conviction and the ethic of responsibility are not absolute opposites. They are complementary to each other, and only in combination do they produce the true human being who is *capable* of having a 'vocation for politics.'"[56] What Weber says is that validity cannot be ascertained by the ethic of responsibility alone; the only element by which one can validate the goodness of a certain consequence is the cause [*Sache*] of the action – a "passionate commitment to a 'cause', to the god or demon who commands that cause."[57] For Weber, thus, "the problem is precisely this: *how are hot passion and cool judgement to be forced together in a single soul?* . . . Only if one accustoms oneself to distance, in every sense of the word, can one achieve that powerful control over the soul which distinguishes the passionate politician from the mere 'sterile excitement' of the political dilettante. The 'strength' of a political 'personality' means, first and foremost, the possession of these qualities."[58]

Evidently, Weber prescribes a cohabitation within one soul of conviction and responsibility. It is the ethic of *absolute* conviction, and not any conviction, that Weber eventually rejects – "some kind of belief must always be present. Otherwise (and there can be no denying this) even political achievements, which, outwardly, are supremely successful will be cursed with the nullity of all mortal undertakings."[59] On the contrary, one might even say that for Weber the value of conviction becomes more necessary the more one subscribes to the

[56] Politics 250/368.
[57] Ibid. 227–8/353.
[58] Ibid. 227–8/354 (italics added).
[59] Ibid. 230–1/355.

ethic of responsibility, for otherwise the latter can easily degenerate
into a utilitarian ethic. Some contrary statements notwithstanding,
pace Schluchter, conviction and responsibility must form a "dialectical
combination."[60]

The *causa differentia* of genuine conviction in the disenchanted modern world lies, according to Weber, in that it derives its source of justification from nothing external to the individual self, as opposed to
absolute conviction, which relies on a teleological metaphysics. With
the teleological construction of meaning no longer tenable, the latter
demands that the modern individual do something unembraceable. In
the value-fragmented modern spiritual world, the modern individual
constantly encounters the dilemma situation in which "it is really a
question not only of alternatives between values but of an irreconcilable death-struggle, like that between 'God' and the 'Devil.' Between
these, neither relativization nor compromise is possible."[61] It is, in
other words, a world that constantly demands that one make ethical decisions in order to become what Weber calls a "personality," a free and
autonomous moral agent: "ultimately life as a whole, if it is not to be
permitted to run on as an event in nature but is instead to be consciously
guided, is a series of ultimate decisions through which the soul –
as in Plato – chooses its own fate, i.e., the meaning of its activity and
existence."[62] Unfortunately, there is no ascertainable ground for such
decisions, and one should not attempt in vain to discover one. One
should still make ethical decisions, and out of nothing, ex nihilo; it is
first and foremost "a matter of *faith*."[63] The litmus test for a genuine
conviction for Weber is whether one can embrace this modern tragedy

---

[60] This is Lawrence Scaff's term in his *Fleeing the Iron Cage: Culture, Politics, and Modernity
in the Thought of Max Weber* (Berkeley: University of California Press, 1989) 182. It
still remains an open question as to how this cohabitation of heteronomous ethics
can be maintained without causing internal conflicts or how the potential conflict
can be managed. It is no wonder that Weber described the psychological state of a
Puritan *Berufsmensch* as hysteria (China 518/232). In this respect, Charles Larmore's
indication – and I am inclined to agree – that Weber's goal was to preserve and amplify
this potential contradiction to create a constantly agonizing moral agent may provide
one answer. See his *Patterns of Moral Complexity* (Cambridge: Cambridge University
Press, 1987) xiii–xiv, 144–6. Weber's *Berufsmensch* may be a unified personality, yet
it does not have to be a harmonious soul.

[61] Neutrality 507/17.

[62] Ibid. 507–8/18.

[63] Objectivity 152/55.

and rise up to create meaning for one's actions, "to give account of the ultimate meaning of his own actions."[64]

Admittedly, the assumption which I am presenting here derives from the one fundamental fact – that life, as long as it is to be understood in its own terms, knows only the unending struggle between those gods. Put literally, that means the incompatibility of the ultimate *possible* attitudes towards life and therefore the inconclusiveness of the battle between them. It is thus necessary to *decide* between them.[65]

In summary, Weber attempts to find an antifoundational (in the sense that moral dilemma is accepted as an unavoidable reality of the modern world) and at the same time a nonutilitarian (in the sense that the moral self is the agent of integrity rather than of utility) solution to the ethical dilemma the late modern self confronts. It can be said that, if the proposed ethic of responsibility is conceived principally for the former, the emphasis on a passionate conviction is conceived for the latter agenda. Weber's ethical prescription culminates in this symbiosis of subjective ethical decisionism and objective consequentialism. To emphasize, we might even say that to the extent that the consequentialist ethic is recommended, so is the ethical decisionism in order to avoid a utilitarian conclusion.

PRACTICE OF THE SELF I: REALPOLITIK

That Weber's ethical thinking culminates in the syncretism of objective consequentialist and subjective decisionist strands is crucial in understanding the *Berufsmensch* under the late modern conditions of disenchantment. It of course has direct relevance to Weber's definition of a genuine politician; the essentially identical elements are, however, no less crucial for a scientist's calling. Weber's example of a genuine politician with a vocation can be called a realpolitiker who becomes more clearly comprehensible by contrast with vain power politicians and revolutionary syndicalists; likewise, he calls his ideal scientist a specialist in opposition to a "specialist without heart," "subject matter specialist," and academic exhibitionist. The virtues that constitute both types of

[64] Science 104–5/26.
[65] Ibid. 104–5/27.

Berufsmensch are essentially identical – calm intellectual integrity and passionate value commitment. These seemingly incompatible virtues are demanded by Weber of the modern secularized *Berufsmensch*.

First, the genuine realpolitiker can be more easily accounted for by investigating who is not. Many members of the audience to whom Weber delivered "Politics as a Vocation," mostly university students in times of revolution, shared a political belief prevalent in postwar revolutionary Germany – an attitude Weber takes as one of his main targets of criticism in the address.[66] Their beliefs are justified on the grounds of the intrinsic goodness of their actions rather than their political consequences, and these revolutionary sentiments can be said to reflect a latter-day ethic of absolute conviction, which is no longer tenable in Weber's disenchanted world. They try to impose universal ethical standards on the political sphere, which is incompatible with such categories not only because there exists by nature an innate tension between the ethical end and the demonic means of violence that defines the essence of politics, but also because an absolute ethic ceases to govern the value-fragmented modern world, of which politics forms merely one part. Maintaining the double ethical dilemma modern politics confronts, that is, outer (with other value spheres) and inner tension (between means and end), Weber attempts to expose the ignorance and naiveté of these young revolutionaries. It is, in other words, not because they have strong belief and conviction per se, but because they have the untenable kind of conviction in light of the new modern reality that Weber condemns the young revolutionaries. Thus, he urges them to surrender not their conviction, but their ignorance and naiveté with a phrase drawn from Goethe: "The devil is old, so become old enough to produce the human being who is *capable* of having a 'vocation for politics.'"[67] Weber charges that otherwise it leads to "sterile excitement" and mere "romanticism of the intellectually interesting."[68] Even worse, lacking a matter-of-fact grasp of the new modern reality, the revolutionary romantics' belief in the intrinsic goodness of their action easily degenerates into a vain moral self-indulgence.

[66] Weber gave this speech on 18 January 1919. For the circumstances surrounding the addresses and the tense atmosphere of the time, as well as the dating, I rely on Marianne Weber's account in Biography 664 and Schluchter's Nachwort in MWG I/17.
[67] Politics 248–50/367. Originally, Goethe, *Faust*, Part II, Act II, Scene 1, lines 6817–18: "Der Teufel ist alt; so werdet alt, ihn zu verstehen."
[68] Ibid. 227–8/353.

Second, however, Weber makes it clear in the same address that he does not mean to affirm the opposite pole of the political gamut – what he calls the "vain glorification of power." The latter is often invoked when he criticizes the foreign policies of Wilhelmine Germany, especially during the First World War.[69] Even before the war, although a deeply committed nationalist, he frequently pointed out that the German adventurist and confrontational foreign policy was based on mere "vanity" (*Eitelkeit*). The problem of this policy, according to Weber, is that the exercise of political power is purposeless and becomes a "worship of power for its own sake." He attributes the problem to the German political leadership: "The mere 'power politician,' a type whom an energetically promoted cult is seeking to glorify here in Germany as elsewhere, may give the impression of strength, but in fact his actions merely lead into emptiness and absurdity. . . . [This disposition] stems from a most wretched and superficial lack of concern for the *meaning* of human action."[70] Instead of a genuine conviction, a vain power politician is ruled by either an attitude of "adaptation to the chances, real or imaginary, for immediate success in the selection of one's ultimate value-standpoint from among the many possible ultimate value-standpoints (this is the type of realpolitik which our government has followed for the last twenty-seven years with such notable success!)" or a bureaucratic ethic of adaptation "of the means for attaining a given ultimate goal in a particular situation (realpolitik in the narrower sense)."[71]

In other words, what Weber sees in the so-called power politicians much celebrated in Germany is not only the bureaucratic lack of value commitment, but also the situation in which the purposes and values of a certain political action are determined solely in terms of its chance to satisfy their own vain lust for power. Despite its deceptive façade of passion, it reflects a sterile bureaucratic attitude of adaptation and mere vanity in which a genuine concern for and choice of ultimate end are thoroughly removed. The inertia of the German politics Weber deplores comes largely from the leaders' lust "personally to stand in the forefront as clearly as possible" at the expense of a genuine concern for the ideals and meaning of their actions and the bureaucrats' obedience

[69] See, for example, Parliament 248–58/196–209.
[70] Ibid. 228–30/354–5.
[71] Neutrality 515/25.

to the blind satisfaction of the vanity of the leaders. The problem is identified as exactly opposite to that of a revolutionary syndicalist, since this type of personality, whom he calls a power politician, lacks any sense of normative convictions. Weber's criticism cannot be more pointed:

On the whole, people are strongly inclined to adapt themselves to what promises success, not only – as is self-evident – with respect to the means or to the extent that they seek to realize their ideals, but even to the extent of giving up these very ideals. In Germany this mode of behavior is glorified by the name realpolitik. . . . In a sense, successful political action is always the "art of the possible." Nonetheless, the possible is often reached only by striving to attain the impossible that lies beyond it . . . [as opposed to] the only consistent ethic of "'adaptation' to the possible," namely, the bureaucratic morality of Confucianism.[72]

As opposed to the vain glorification of power on the one hand and the revolutionary romanticism lacking a firm grasp of reality on the other, the genuine realpolitik that Weber presents in the controversial Freiburg Inauguration Lecture of 1895 well summarizes his view of an ideal political personality. In the lecture, Weber identifies the crucial problems facing German politics as twofold – one coming from the permeation of a utilitarian, eudaemonistic understanding of politics that puts its highest priority on the well-being of the people, and the other coming from the overall political apathy, nihilism, and ennui prevalent among the industrial classes, a symptom of what he calls "the age of epigones." These two problems are related in that they in effect prevent, each in its own way, the cultivation of a public personality that is able to "place these power interests [of the nation] above all considerations" – an ability that defines what he calls "political maturity."[73] To Weber, for whom the fundamental concern of modern politics is "not the *well-being* human beings enjoy in the future but what kind of people they will *be*," this poses a serious problem.[74] At stake is, moreover, not only the "pettiness" that these attitudes will instill in a political personality, but also the overall social integration of rapidly

[72] Ibid. 513–14/23–4.
[73] Freiburg 565/20–1.
[74] Ibid. 559/15. The political preoccupation with social welfare is satirized by Weber as the "Austrianization of Germany [*die Verösterreicherung Deutschlands*]" that breeds "beerly compliancy." See Democracy 160/88.

industrializing Germany; "The aim of our sociopolitical activity is not to make everybody happy but the *social unification* of the nation, which has been split apart by modern economic development, and to prepare it for the strenuous struggles of the future."[75] And both purposes – that is, maintaining sufficiently public personalities in political leadership and social integration – are betrayed in Germany by the lack of a "political sense of purpose [*Sinn*]."[76] The problem Weber sees is, in short, the public loss of purpose and conviction by which alone one can give a meaningful account of one's political action.

Ironically, power politics on an even grander scale is invoked by Weber as a remedy to this situation caused by the practice of power politics. After lamenting the lack of political maturity in Germany, he turns his attention to the political education of the English working class. He attributes their political maturity to nascent nationalism, which is strengthened by the fact that England is actively involved in world power politics. He seems to believe that England's long involvement in European power politics and its active pursuit of imperial gains abroad have introduced a new dimension of political education at the mass level that enabled the people to realize the harsh reality of politics as "eternal struggle" and put the public interest of the nation over the parochial interests of classes.[77] According to Weber, international politics based on power and the resulting nationalism constitute two of the most important pillars of political maturity of the English people.[78] And these comprise the decisive difference from the German situation.

---

[75] Ibid. 572/27.

[76] Ibid.

[77] Ibid. 560/16.

[78] For Weber's understanding of the English political system, see G. Schmidt, *Deutscher Historismus und der Übergang zur parliamentarischen Demokratie: Untersuchungen zu den politischen Gedanken von Meinecke, Troeltsch, Max Weber* (Lübeck: Matthiesen Verlag, 1964) 269–70, 277, 292. For the implications of Weber's view on England, see R. Factor and S. Turner, "Weber, the Germans, and 'Anglo-Saxon Convention': Liberalism as Technique and Form of Life," in R. Glassman and V. Murvar (eds.), *Max Weber's Political Sociology: A Pessimistic Vision of a Rationalized World* (Westport, CT: Greenwood, 1984). A more historiographical examination of Weber's attitude toward England is contained in G. Roth, "Weber the Would-Be Englishman: Anglophilia and Family History," in H. Lehmann and G. Roth (eds.), *Weber's Protestant Ethic: Origins, Evidence, Contexts* (Cambridge : Cambridge University Press, 1995) and his new book, *Max Webers deutschen-englische Familiengeschichte 1800–1950* (Tübingen: J. C. B. Mohr/Paul Siebeck, 2001).

Once again there [in England] is above all a *political* factor involved [in their political education], namely the *reverberations of a position of world power* which constantly confronts the state with great power-political tasks and exposes the individual to "chronic" political schooling.... The question of whether politics on the grand scale can make us aware once more of the significance of the great political issues of power is also decisive for *our* development.... [I]t would have been better, on the grounds of expense, to leave it [German unification] undone if it was to have been the end rather than the beginning of Germany's involvement in world politics.[79]

Even in his earlier political view as presented in the Freiburg address, Weber disdained the conflation of political and ethical ends as "an unspeakably philistine softening of sensibility."[80] He also maintains, nevertheless, that politics, and to be more precise, its characteristic of power struggle should serve a higher goal. In the Freiburg lecture, he counts among the ultimate ends of politics social integration and, more important, the fostering of a unique heroic personality who can put public interest over parochial private and class interests. Weber sees the problem of modern politics, especially in Germany, as its lack of public consciousness in the political leadership as well as among the general population and regards realpolitik as providing a good political education while expecting it to instill a new sense of purpose and conviction in the modern political sphere. Weber thus concludes his lecture with a guarded hope for a nation of public citizens permeated with youthful conviction.

[Y]outh has the right to stand up for itself and for its ideals. Yet it is not years which make a man old. He is young as long as he is able to feel the *great* passions nature has implanted in us. Thus – allow me to conclude here – it is not the burden of thousands of years of glorious history that causes a great nation to grow old. It will remain young as long as it has the capacity and the courage to keep faith with itself and with the great instincts it has been given, and if its leading strata are able to raise themselves into the hard, clear air in which the sober work of German politics flourishes, an atmosphere which, however, is also filled with the earnest grandeur of national sentiment.[81]

[79] Freiburg 572/26.
[80] Ibid. 573/27.
[81] Ibid. 573–4/28.

Weber's realpolitik is about naked power struggle, devoid of moral contents and based on a cold, calculating mind; yet it is never embraced as an end in itself, but only as a means to achieve certain ultimate values that are not drawn from inside the political sphere. Realpolitik is affirmed only insofar as it fosters a moral personality that Weber deems ideal. This personality that Weber expects to be fostered as a result of an active participation in realpolitik consists of a calm, matter-of-factness and a passionate conviction that claim equal presence in one soul. Weber thus rejects both vain glorification of power and revolutionary romanticism for lacking either of two virtues. It points to a Machiavellian statecraft, yet without Machiavelli's agenda – that is, in Sheldon Wolin's words, to a complete severance of "the old alliance between statecraft and soulcraft."[82] It might be said, to the contrary, that Weber's Machiavellian realpolitik entails a Platonic politics of the soul that aims to "reconnect" statecraft and soulcraft.[83]

PRACTICE OF THE SELF II: IDEAL TYPE

If striving for an ideal and calm, objective matter-of-factness define the politician with a vocation, the essentially same set of virtues is also recommended to the sphere of science [*Wissenschaft*] by Weber. In "Science as a Vocation," after reviewing the modern conditions, both institutional and spiritual, that characterize the academic world, he concludes that the modern scientist cannot but be a specialist. The most important aspect of Weber's advice to those aspiring to take science as a vocation is that they be aware of and embrace "specialization" as an indispensable part of the modern enterprise of science. For him, specialization is the benchmark by which to evaluate whether one has the genuine "inner vocation for science."[84]

This must have been a bold statement on science in Weber's time, when the critique of "cold, lifeless, narrow-minded rationality," an

[82] S. Wolin, *Politics and Vision: Continuity and Innovation in Western Political Thought* (Boston: Little, Brown, 1960) 237.
[83] The word "reconnect" belongs to Harvey Goldman in *Politics, Death, and the Devil: Self and Power in Max Weber and Thomas Mann* (Berkeley: University of California Press, 1992) 163. For more on this reading of Weber and Machiavelli, which is cast in conscious opposition to Jacob Mayer's, see ibid. 161–4.
[84] Science 79–80/8.

exaltation of feeling, sense, and intuition, and a praise for generalists all in the name of personality, on the one hand, and the classic ideal of *Bildung*, on the other, were in great vogue, especially in German academia.[85] The uniquely German discourse of *Bildung* aimed at fostering a well-rounded generalist. Its ideal was to create a harmonious totality out of different, and even conflicting, human faculties, such as reason and sensibilities, that can be achieved in the course of a life-long cultivation of mind.[86] As captured in the popular idiom *Bildung und Besitz* (cultivation and property), a Faustian character remained very much an attractive ideal for the German bourgeoisie in general. On the other hand, although of more recent and different origin, another popular ideal at that time, that the individual is entitled to and obliged to develop the self to its fullest, giving expression to the authentic personality thus formed, also aimed at fostering a generalist. This neo-romantic ideal of self-flourishing was a more direct reaction against what was perceived to be the modern threats in turn-of-the-century Germany to the organic totality of human life. Stefan George and Hugo von Hoffmanstahl were two of the most conspicuous figures frequently associated with this movement.[87] The *Bildungsideal* and fin-de-siècle romanticism shared the critique that modern science created a man of specialized, fragmented, and parochial personality.

[85] For a general survey of the German academy's reaction to modernity at the turn of the century, Fritz Ringer's classic study, *The Decline of the German Mandarins: The German Academic Community, 1890–1933* (Cambridge, MA: Harvard University Press, 1969), is still useful. For a more recent synopsis, see R. vom Bruch, "The Academic Disciplines and Social Thought," in R. Chickering (ed.), *Imperial Germany: A Historiographical Companion* (London: Greenwood, 1996).

[86] For a conceptual survey of this uniquely German tradition of *Bildung* humanism, see R. Vierhaus, "Bildung," in O. Brunner, W. Conze, and R. Koselleck (eds.), *Geschichtliche Grundbegriffe: Historische Lexicon zur politische-sozialen Sprache in Deutschland*, Vol. I (Stuttgart: Ernst Klett Verlag, 1972), 508–51. For more on the German ideal of *Bildung* as it relates to Weber's methodological positions, see Goldman (1992) 25–50.

[87] For this fin-de-siècle romanticism and its yearning for organic totality, see C. Schorske's *Fin-de-siècle Vienna: Politics and Culture* (New York: Vintage, 1961), which is particularly good on Hoffmanstahl and the Secessionist Movement. Also see H. Broch, *Hugo von Hoffmanstahl and His Time: The European Imagination, 1860–1920* (Chicago: University of Chicago Press, 1984). For Weber's fascination with the George circle, see Marianne Weber's account in Biography 463–72/455–64.

Weber flatly rejects such transvaluation of science, calling the propagandists of such a view "mere dilettantes" who, in his view, have either no grasp of the meaning of modern science or no courage to confront the new reality.[88] Given the highly developed division of labor within modern science, such a call for the generalist appears to him either anachronistic or unheroic. Instead, Weber claims that "renunciation of the Faustian universality of man . . . is a condition of valuable work in the modern world."[89]

Weber's endorsement of specialization reveals, however, something more than his resigned acceptance of the evolutionary division of labor in the modern, especially sociocultural sciences (*Geisteswissenschaften*); it also points to what he calls "one-sidedness" (*Einseitigkeit*) in the methodological essays. One-sidedness is critical in this context because he believes that there is no way of grasping sociocultural reality in its totality. Following a neo-Kantian epistemology, Weber holds that social reality is "an infinite multiplicity of successively and coexistently emerging and disappearing events" and that "the absolute infinitude of this multiplicity" cannot be grasped in its totality by the finite human mind.[90] Thus, a scientist does not reproduce or discover a coherent account as it empirically exists, but constructs it, imputing a certain conceptual structure to reality. Weber calls this cognitive activity "attributing cultural significance."[91] So-called social reality as a subject of scientific interest has already undergone the researcher's cognitive process of value-laden signification by which certain fragments of infinite social reality are thematized.[92] This cognitive process is subjective in the sense that it can never be validated on objective grounds. From this perspective, both raw empiricism and sweeping idealism become suspicious, for the former assumes the self-evident existence of a reality that can be discovered and reproduced in a scientist's mind, and the latter assumes the universal validity of a scientist's cognitive process.

From Weber's perspective, in particular, the so-called scientific law in sociocultural science becomes utterly problematic. If by a scientific

---

[88] Science 80–3/10–11.
[89] Protestant Ethic 187/180. Cf. Neutrality 494/5–6.
[90] Objectivity 171/72–3.
[91] Ibid. 161/64.
[92] Ibid. 163–4/65–6.

law we mean that every sociocultural phenomenon is subject to one single, all-inclusive scheme of causal mechanism irrespective of time and space, it is not only impossible but also meaningless. His argument here points more to agnosticism; there may be a law, yet it lies beyond human cognitive capacity, for the human mind cannot grasp social reality in its totality, and without totality a scientific law can never be validated. What we have as the subject matter for scientific interest is only a fragment of social reality that is problematized by the researcher's subjective value concern; we can establish a causal mechanism within or among the fragments, yet that we can do so neither ascertains nor invalidates the existence of the universal valid scientific law. A discussion of scientific law is simply meaningless, for "an *exhaustive* causal investigation of any concrete phenomenon in its full reality is not only practically impossible – it is simply an absurdity."[93] The problem of so-called scientific law in sociocultural science as Weber sees it arises because the proponents of such a view assert something that cannot be proven, and such a view merely reflects the ignorance of the subjective predicament of modern science.

In the sociocultural sciences, the knowledge of the universal or general is never valuable in itself. . . . Firstly, because the knowledge of social laws is not knowledge of social reality but is rather one of the various aids used by our minds for attaining this end; secondly, because knowledge of *cultural* events is inconceivable except on a basis of the *significance* which the concrete constellations of reality have for us in certain *individual* concrete situations.[94]

While rejecting the value of lawlike causal explanation in sociocultural sciences, Weber nevertheless denies that a rational, causal account itself is meaningless. If not human nature, then our culture (of course, the Occidental culture of Weber's time) still demands that the infinite chaos of sociocultural multiplicity be meaningfully and coherently accounted for. That is to say, if the infinite social reality cannot be reproduced in the finite human mind, the reality still needs to be conceptualized, and it cannot but be appropriated with finite concepts. Weber fully acknowledges this epistemological tragedy; although subjective presuppositions should be affirmed, still it remains a truism that "it is

93 Ibid. 178/78.
94 Ibid. 180/80.

entirely *causal* knowledge exactly in the same sense as the knowledge of significant concrete natural events which have a qualitative character."[95] Weber affirms that, for instance, such a sweeping generalization as Benjamin Constant's dichotomy of ancient versus modern liberty is not a meaningless endeavor. The problem for Weber seems less to do with the fact that a finite causal generalization is derived from and imposed on the infinite reality, which is unavoidable, than with the fact that it is done under the self-delusion of a universally valid law. In this respect, what he calls the "evolutionary scheme" in sociocultural sciences raises a similar problem, Marxism being the representative example in Weber's view. The problem is that these schemes too easily forget that they are preceded by subjective signification. So-called scientific law is not free from such subjective elements; in claiming to be so, it is merely self-deceptive.

Weber's perspectivism in methodology thus should not be taken simply as an affirmation of value relativism or, even less, nihilism. Relativism is only a beginning of Weber's problematic in methodology, unlike what he calls "syncretism," one of the possible methodological practices predicated on value relativism. Syncretism, according to Weber, denies the value of objectivity in sociocultural science and attempts to combine various perspectives in research, merely steering a middle course between them. It further claims that, by doing so, it achieves the only possible form of value-neutral objectivity in the modern sociocultural sciences. Not committing themselves to one value position, the proponents of syncretism believe that they can maintain a neutral position by which to avoid value judgments in sociocultural science.[96] Weber emphatically denies that this is identified with what he calls "value freedom" (*Wertfreiheit*). For Weber, such a practice is not only impossible, for there is no knowledge unpreceded by subjective signification, but also *unethical*, for it avoids "the practical duty [of scientists] to stand up for our own ideals."[97] Value relativism should be confronted face to face, yet it need not be affirmed as such.

Contra both positivism in the form of scientific law and value relativism née syncretism, Weber proposes to embrace the very root of

[95] Ibid. 182/82.
[96] Ibid. 154–5/57–8.
[97] Ibid. 155/58.

this epistemological dilemma in sociocultural science – that is, its inescapable "one-sidedness." By one-sidedness, Weber means a self-conscious commitment to a certain perspective in research, no matter how subjective it may be. First, it is *unavoidable*, for otherwise no meaningful knowledge is possible: "only through the presupposition that a finite part alone of the infinite variety of phenomena is significant does the knowledge of an individual phenomenon become logically meaningful."[98] Second, and more important, it is *necessary*, for otherwise the unavoidable value position of the researcher would not be brought out clearly and admitted as such – not only to the readers but also to oneself. He says, "[t]he practical evaluative attitude can be not only harmless to scientific interests but even directly useful, and indeed mandatory."[99] Weber's emphasis on one-sidedness not only affirms the subjective nature of scientific knowledge but also demands that the researcher be self-consciously one-sided. This perspective of Weber's shares with positivism that it imposes finite conceptual constructs on infinite reality; it shares with syncretism that there is no way of scientifically validating a certain value position.

In that it is self-consciously subjective, however, the one-sided perspective differs from a scientific law; in that it makes a commitment to a one-sided perspective of one's own, it differs from value relativism. The methodology of the "ideal type" is the principal methodological carrier that caters to Weber's concern for the unavoidable and necessary one-sidedness in sociocultural science. Thus he defines the ideal type as follows:

An ideal type is formed by the one-sided *accentuation* of *one* or *more* points of view and by the synthesis of a great many diffuse, discrete, more or less present and occasionally absent *concrete individual* phenomena, which are arranged according to those one-sidedly emphasized viewpoints into a unified *analytical* construct [*Gedankenbild*]. In its conceptual purity, this mental construct cannot be found empirically anywhere in reality. It is a utopia.[100]

The ideal type is a purely conceptual construct; it never seeks to claim its validity in terms of a reproduction of social reality or in terms of a correspondence. It is keenly aware of its fictional nature, for it is

[98] Ibid. 177/78.
[99] Ibid. 156/59.
[100] Ibid. 191/90.

predicated on a subjective problematization or cultural signification of the infinite multiplicity of social reality. Its validity can be ascertained only in terms of adequacy. This is not only unavoidable (which is ignored by the proponents of scientific law), but also necessary (which is denied by the proponents of syncretism), for if unavoidable, a researcher's subjective value needs to be clearly exposed so as not to deceive either the readers or the researcher himself or herself. Thus, Weber says that "[o]nly through ideal-typical concept-construction do the viewpoints with which we are concerned in individual cases become explicit."[101] "*Only* as an ideal type," that is, can subjective value – "that unfortunate child of misery of our science" – "be given an unambiguous meaning."[102] The solution Weber proposes in the form of the ideal type is a conceptual construct that enables the researcher to clearly articulate and promulgate one's prejudices.

Now we are better prepared to understand what Weber means by the alleged advocacy of the strict distinction between value judgment and value freedom. For him, there is no completely value-free knowledge; at the same time, he believes that a value judgment should be kept apart from the classroom or scientific research. This seemingly contradictory demand can be made meaningful when we realize that he does not mean to remove value commitments from scientific research. On the contrary, he urges that one foreground one's value position as clearly as possible and admit it as a nonascertainable value assertion without any delusion of scientific objectivity. The ideal-type methodology is meant to serve this purpose, for it is devoid, unlike scientific law, of objective pretensions. It is self-consciously subjective, requiring the subjective ground to be known to the researcher himself or herself as well as to the readers.

The modern scientist with a genuine sense of vocation is, according to Weber, never free from value assertions; to the contrary, he or she is painfully aware of the inundation of unascertainable and incommensurable values in the modern world. What is important for Weber is that the scientist assert a clear value commitment with a full knowledge of its subjective nature. Failing to do so leads to what Weber disdains most – a conflation of value judgment and value freedom in the guise of

[101] Ibid. 212/110.
[102] Ibid. 209–10/107.

scientific objectivity. Objectivity in sociocultural science can be maintained only by affirming and making explicit the subjective foundation of its presuppositions: "The *objective* validity of all empirical knowledge rests exclusively upon the ordering of the given reality according to categories which are *subjective* in a specific sense, namely, in that they present the *presuppositions* of our knowledge and are based on the presupposition of the *value* of those truths which empirical knowledge alone is able to give us."[103] Thus, the specialist Weber proposes is neither a "specialist without heart" nor a "subject-matter specialist" (*Stoffhuber*), but an "interpretative specialist" (*Sinnhuber*),[104] whose virtues consist of passionate conviction, uncompromising intellectual integrity, and, most important of all, a Socratic knowledge of one's own self.

CONCLUSION : MODERNITY, CONSCIENCE, AND DUTY

Rationalization and disenchantment have created, according to Weber, a world with no objectively ascertainable ground for one's conviction. Under the circumstances, Weber saw the modern self as torn between the irresponsible agitation of subjective value and bureaucratic petrification of objective rationality, and thus incapable of taking disciplined moral action. Modern individuals tend to act only in accordance with their aesthetic impulse to express subjective convictions, the motive Weber believed to undergird, for example, the syndicalist anarchism of such figures as Ernst Toller.[105] The majority of those who cannot even act on their subjective convictions lead the life of a "cog in a machine," failing to take any principled action. The two poignant images by which Weber captured the essence of modernity, the Hellenistic polytheism of warring deities and the imminent iron cage of bureaucratic petrification, in fact constitute merely different faces of the same coin that can be called the "inertia" of the modern individual and the disempowerment of agency.

[103] Ibid. 213/110.
[104] Ibid. 214/112.
[105] See D. Dahlmann, "Max Weber's Relation to Anarchism and Anarchist: The Case of Ernst Toller," in W. Mommsen and J. Osterhammel (eds.), *Max Weber and His Contemporaries* (London: Allen & Unwin, 1987).

Culminating in the later works of "Politics and Science as a Vocation," Weber's problematic provides a thread that runs through his comparative sociology of religion, methodological essays, and political writings. Also maintained consistently was his prescription: a Kantian self-empowerment predicated on transcending subjective value and objective rationality. According to Weber, when this balance tilts, modern ethics easily degenerate into either moral self-indulgence or utilitarianism; modern politics, into either vain glorification of power or infantile political romanticism; and modern science, into either unreflective positivism or academic exhibitionism. Although each value sphere suggests different forms of *aporia*, what Weber calls the person of vocation or personality amounts to a single person of innermost conviction who soberly confronts objective reality and methodically organizes everyday life according to a sense of duty. And underlying this type of self-empowerment was a heroic attempt at recoupling the dichotomized subjectivity and objectivity – a restoration of the balance once achieved in the Puritan person of vocation who can position the self on a nonnegotiable and principled basis, agonizingly proclaiming, as Luther once did, "Here I stand, I can do no other."[106]

---

[106] Politics 248–50/367.

5

Liberalism, Nationalism, and Civil Society

> Peace and unanimity are commonly considered as the principal founda-
> tions of public felicity; yet the rivalship of separate communities, and
> the agitation of a free people, are the principles of political life, and the
> school of men. How shall we reconcile these jarring and opposite tenets?
>
> Adam Ferguson[1]

INTRODUCTION: LIBERALISM AND NATIONALISM

To argue that the relationship between liberalism and nationalism
reveals a profound ambivalence seems to be an understatement.
For some, liberalism and nationalism are irreconcilable antagonists.
Michael Oakeshott maintains that nationalism is a product of the
uniquely modern miscegenation between "political rationalism" and
"political romanticism," combining, despite the nationalist pretext of
atavism, the fanatic zeal for a complete breach from an immediate past
and the utopian longing for a refounding once and for all of political
society. Thus understood, nationalism is held responsible for the degeneration of the liberal social foundation. It erodes value pluralism and
the procedural rule of law embedded in "civil associations [*societas*],"
only to replace them with "enterprise associations [*universitas*]" in the
name of administration and management. On account of the mode
of political society it promotes, then, nationalism is no less a foe to

[1] *An Essay on the History of Civil Society*, ed. F. Oz–Salzberger (Cambridge: Cambridge
University Press, 1995) 62–3.

liberalism than socialism and totalitarianism – spiritual cousins of nationalism according to Oakeshott's genealogical account of political modernity.[2]

Without denying the logical tension between the liberal-individualist ideal of civil society and the organic-communitarian vision of national society, others hold that nationalism entails a set of values and beliefs more complicated than Oakeshott exposes and even at times self-contradictory. According to Ernest Gellner, "it speaks of *Gemeinschaft*, and is rooted in a semantically and often phonetically standardized *Gesellschaft*."[3]

This complication reflects the historical elective affinity between civil society and national society. Industrialization demands the transfer of local, parochial loyalties to a wider context in which a certain sociocultural homogeneity will be generated and maintained so as to facilitate communication and mobility. This functional congruence, which Gellner calls the "objective need for homogeneity,"[4] contributed to the historical formation of the liberal–national alliance in nineteenth-century Europe.[5] Miroslav Hroch and Geoff Eley also underscore the codetermination of national and civil societies in the historical development of the European nation-state in which they focus on the national formation of literacy and education, intellectual and popular culture, and media and the press, all of which are rooted in the new universe of (largely bourgeois) voluntary associational life – or in short, the rise of the public sphere à la Jürgen Habermas. Not only in Western Europe during early modern history, but also in large parts of the rest of late-nineteenth-century Europe, the emergence of nation-states was simultaneously that of the public sphere and civil society.[6]

---

[2] M. Oakeshott, "On the Character of a Modern European State," in *On Human Conduct* (Oxford: Oxford University Press, 1975) and "Rationalism in Politics," in *Rationalism in Politics and Other Essays* (Indianapolis: Liberty Press, 1991). For further articulation of nationalism from this conservative perspective, see E. Kedourie, *Nationalism* (Oxford: Blackwell, 1993).
[3] E. Gellner, *Conditions of Liberty: Civil Society and Its Rivals* (New York: Penguin Books, 1994) 107.
[4] E. Gellner, *Nations and Nationalism* (Oxford: Blackwell, 1993) 46.
[5] Gellner (1994) 103–12.
[6] M. Hroch, "From National Movement to the Fully-Formed Nation: The Nation-Building Process in Europe," *New Left Review* 93:198 (1993) 3–20. In agreement is Geoff Eley in his "Nations, Publics and Political Cultures: Placing Habermas in

The implication is that *some* form of nationalism is a foe of liberalism and civil society, and other forms are not.[7] Thus, many an attempt has been made to develop a morphological approach by which to divide nationalism according to emancipatory or integral force, early or late development, Western or Eastern experience, normal or aberrational path, or internal or external orientation. Whether they are understood in terms of associational versus organic nationalism (Hans Kohn) or of territorial versus ethnic nationalism (Anthony Smith), the assumption is that there are good and bad variants of nationalism.[8] One of the recent restatements of this classical approach categorizes nationalism into "ethnic" and "civic" modes.[9] According to this view, ethnic nationalism relies on a collective identity with boundaries drawn firmly according to presumed linguistic and ethnic primordiality, thereby tending to be exclusive and particularistic. Inclusive in principle, by contrast, civic nationalism is predicated on a shared loyalty to potentially universalizable ideals and values that draw a more flexible boundary of identity. The latter is seen to promote liberal values of tolerance and civility toward heterogeneous groups within its national society, whereas the former emphasizes homogeneity and unison of its national population. In short, nationalism does not necessarily antagonize liberal values embedded in civil society, and inversely, the presence of civil society can be an important benchmark by which to distinguish different modes of nationalism.[10]

This differentiated understanding of the liberal–national relationship constitutes our starting point in discussing Max Weber's vision of modern civil society. It is critical for the present project, since the

the Nineteenth Century," in C. Calhoun (ed.), *Habermas and the Public Sphere* (Cambridge, MA: MIT Press, 1993).

[7] See, for example, J. A. Hall, "In Search of Civil Society," in J. A. Hall (ed.), *Civil Society: Theory, History, Comparison* (Cambridge: Polity Press, 1995) 12–14.

[8] H. Kohn, *The Idea of Nationalism* (New York: Macmillan, 1944); J. Plamenatz, "Two Types of Nationalism," in E. Kamenka (ed.), *Nationalism: The Nature and Evolution of an Idea* (New York: St. Martin's, 1976); A. D. Smith, *The Ethnic Origins of Nations* (Oxford: Blackwell, 1986); P. Alter, *Nationalism* (London: Edward Arnold, 1989); and T. Todorov, *On Human Diversity: Nationalism, Racism and Exoticism in French Thought* (Cambridge, MA: Harvard University Press, 1993).

[9] R. Brubaker, *Citizenship and Nationhood in France and Germany* (Cambridge, MA: Harvard University Press, 1992).

[10] C. Bryant, "Civic Nation, Civil Society, Civil Religion," in Hall (1995) 136–57 and Brubaker (1992).

dominant exegetic practice tends to accentuate Weber's authoritarian political values, tracing them to his faith in nationalism, imperialism, and the power state (*Machtstaat*). As exemplified by Wolfgang Mommsen in his classical study, this reading reaffirms the liberal–national dichotomy by maintaining that, crudely put, Weber was a national, thus illiberal thinker.[11]

Without denying the nationalist predicaments in Weber's political thinking or the problematic character of German nationalism, however, one can still suspect Mommsen's simplistic formula, which forecloses different possibilities of nationalism. After all, Weber always maintained a critical distance between Wilhelmine nationalism-imperialism, both its political and social manifestations, and a nationalist standpoint of his own. It is this idiosyncrasy of Weber's nationalism that tends to be unduly overshadowed in Mommsen's attempt to place Weber squarely in the authoritarian tradition of German nationalism.[12] What this one-sided portrait lacks is a differentiated understanding of nationalism when reading Weber's political ideas in the context of Wilhelmine politics.

This chapter investigates Weber's visions of national society and of civil society. These two agendas are inseparably intertwined. On the one hand, discussing civil society in Weber's political thinking needs to be preceded by overcoming the simple liberal–national dichotomy, since otherwise it is difficult to investigate Weber's political thinking as allowing room for a liberal, pluralistic civil society. On the other

---

[11] W. Mommsen, *Max Weber und die deutsche Politik, 1890–1920* (Tübingen: J. C. B. Mohr, 1959), translated by M. Steinberg as *Max Weber and German Politics, 1890–1920* (Chicago: University of Chicago Press, 1984). In Mommsen's recent statement, liberal flirtation with national imperialism "is tantamount to a repudiation of liberal ideals" (W. Mommsen, *Imperial Germany, 1867–1918* [London: Routledge, 1995] 73). Cf. "an idea of nation . . . nurtured increasing enthusiasm for power and thereby became less and less capable of vindicating the view that the exercise of power involved the use of tools of 'diabolical' origins" (Mommsen [1984] 64).

[12] In fact, Mommsen appears ambivalent, and even at times self-contradictory, when he assesses Weber's nationalism in relationship to the Wilhelmine nationalist discourse. Especially in the account of Weber's theoretical understanding of nations (which I will also analyze shortly), Mommsen acknowledges the profoundly different nature of Weber's attitude, which, nevertheless, simply leads to the conclusion that "Weber shared the tragic overvaluation of the principles of power and their ideal fulfillment in the concept of the nation that was characteristic of the imperialist epoch – an over-valuation that was to lead the old Europe to catastrophe" (Mommsen [1984] 67).

hand, the presence of a liberal vision of civil society in Weber's political thinking can mitigate the allegation of authoritarian nationalism without denying the nationalist dimension of his ideas. In short, by investigating and reconstructing Weber's vision of pluralistic civil society, I intend to relativize the one-sidedly authoritarian reading and, instead, to illustrate a unique symbiosis of liberal and national ideals in Weber's political ideas.

First, I will examine Weber's account of the category of nation in order to stress his nonethnic and nonlinguistic understanding, which foreshadowed the present social constructionist theories of nation. The point of this exercise is to show that Weber's nationalism is utterly devoid of the ethnic nationalist obsession with primordiality that pervaded German nationalism, and that, by implication, it does not necessarily recommend a homogeneous national population. Second, I will bring this implication forth more clearly as I investigate Weber's commentaries on Wilhelmine associational life, in which the critique of bourgeois refeudalization and of socialist party leadership figures prominently. Here I will underscore Weber's repeated emphasis on social self-organization constructed along class lines and galvanized by public-nationalist concerns. Third, I will turn my attention to Weber's postwar writings, which reveal a principled opposition to bureaucratic corporatism and an alternative vision of the political, economic, and social mechanism of checks and balances among various voluntary organizations. In conclusion, I will discuss Weber's symbiosis of liberalism and nationalism in light of his own larger political project as well as the contemporary discussions of liberal nationalism.

NATIONAL IDENTITIES, NATION-STATES, AND THE POLITICAL

The idea of the sovereign nation-state had enjoyed enormous cultural and political prestige in turn-of-the-century Europe, and Germany was certainly no exception. The dominant scholarship had reconstructed modern European history as a teleological consolidation of nation-states that in Germany culminated in the unification under Prussian hegemony. The exclusion of Austria from the German nation building was justified historically on the grounds of its multinational foundation, which indicated for Heinrich von Treitschke its lack of historical mission and backwardness in comparison to Prussia.[13] In political economy, the Prussian state as a Hegelian carrier of historical mission was generally affirmed when, for example, Adolf Wagner emphasized its role as the benign protector and guardian of the German market. In a similar, albeit more progressive, vein, patronizing social policies by the state were advocated by the *Kathedersozialisten*, with whom Weber had close association via the *Verein für Sozialpolitik* (hereafter *Verein*).[14] In all this, the state epitomized the public reason and universal morality that stood over and arbitrated the conflicts immanent in the private interest–driven civil society. According to Leopold von Ranke, the father of modern historiography, nation-states are "spiritual substances...thoughts of God."[15]

Moral aura had accrued to the state, distinguishing it from other social institutions, and it was the bureaucracy that was to execute this moral mandate given to the state. Thus, Gustav Schmoller, the doyen of *Kathedersozialismus* and one of Weber's mentors, studied the administrative history of Prussia and portrayed its rational and efficient bureaucracy as progressively achieving a moral mission by clearly establishing itself over civil society. Essentially, bureaucracy was conceived of as an independent political force, endowed with the qualities of wisdom and disinterestedness, and hence supremely well suited to direct the affairs of society. Among the older generation of the *Verein*, the magnificent achievements of the German bureaucracy formed a constant refrain to their zeal for social reform, and their anxiety over political democratization was predicated on their trust in the state bureaucracy, which, they feared, would be replaced by the interest politics of party and class. Through a historical-teleological reconstruction, in short, Schmoller and others translated the rationality and efficiency

[13] See, for example, H. Treitschke, *Politics*, ed. H. Kohn (New York: Harcourt, Brace & World, 1963) 203–4, in which he compares Prussia and Austria, respectively, to (progressive) Athens and (backward) Sparta.
[14] For the political position of the older generation of the *Verein* members as well as that of Wagner and Schmoller, see D. Lindenlaub, *Richtungskämpfe im Verein für Sozialpolitik: Wissenschaft und Sozialpolitik im Kaiserreich vornehmlich vom Beginn des "neuen Kurses" bis zum Ausbruch des ersten Weltkrieges (1870–1914)*, Vol. I (Wiesbaden: Franz Steiner Verlag, 1967) 141–95.
[15] L. von Ranke, *The Theory and Practice of History* (Indianapolis: Bobbs-Merrill, 1973) 119.

of Prussian bureaucracy into the moral authority of the German state.[16]

Against this background, Weber's whole oeuvre on bureaucracy can be read as a subtle criticism of the prestige of bureaucracy and, by extension, of the Prusso-German state. That is to say, Weber's emphasis on the *technical* achievement and *instrumental* value of bureaucratic administration was meant to propel an immanent subversion of its "uncritical moral glorification [*kritiklosen Verherrlichung*]" in Germany.[17] Weber's critical attitude toward German bureaucracy was particularly apparent in an Oedipal debate with the older generation of the *Verein* that managed to break out at its 1909 convention.[18] In this debate, Weber's point was that although bureaucracy embodied the perfection of formal rationality – itself a judgment that could have been prejudiced by the German tradition of its glorification – it had no more or less than an *instrumental* value. As its rationality was merely formal and technical, bureaucracy for Weber was also less disinterested than it was believed to be. It had a tendency to form a closed status group with its own power and material interests while leveling the whole of civil society.[19] Weber thus claimed later that this fundamentally partisan interest "and nothing else is what is meant here by the 'nonpartisan' character of rule by officials."[20] Especially in Germany, he further accused, the state bureaucracy tended to "promote this guild-like closure of officialdom [*zunftartige Abschließung der Beamtenschaft*]," as one

---

[16] In agreement on the *Verein*'s prejudice and subsequent limit is David Beetham in his *Max Weber and the Theory of Modern Politics* (London: Allen & Unwin, 1974) 63–4. Note that there are dissenting opinions among Weber scholars. Martin Albrow, for one, opines that Weber's ideal type of bureaucracy in essence continues the German idiomatic practice of setting (good) *Beamtentum* against (bad) *Büreaukratie*. See M. Albrow, *Bureaucracy* (New York: Praeger, 1970) 40. It should also be noted, however, that Weber does not follow this idiomatic distinction strictly in his critique of bureaucracy.

[17] Biography 421/417.

[18] See Marianne Weber's vivid depiction of this debate, in which Alfred Weber also actively participated, in Biography 420–3/415–18. Also see D. Krüger, "Max Weber and the Younger Generation in the *Verein für Sozialpolitik*," and E. Demm, "Max and Alfred Weber in the *Verein für Sozialpolitik*," in W. Mommsen and J. Osterhammel (eds.), *Max Weber and His Contemporaries* (London: Allen & Unwin, 1987).

[19] See, for example, Economy and Society 569/985.

[20] Parliament 500–2/190.

could see in the Prussian officer corps, which was hailed as one of the
moral backbones of the Prusso-German state.[21] In short, he trivialized
the meaning of bureaucracy – by implication, the state – as a moral
agent and a disinterested party by stripping it of its sacred halo; on the
contrary, the state for Weber was an instrument that could be made to
serve any moral purpose.[22]

> The state itself has no *intrinsic* value in that it is a purely technical instrument
> for the realization of other values from which alone it derives its value, and
> that it can retain this value only as long as it does not seek to transcend this
> merely auxiliary status [*Handlungerberuf*].[23]

Weber's purely formal, instrumental, and antiessentialist account
of the state seems to be in accord with his understanding of the nation. With regard to nation, I first emphasize that Weber categorically rejected any causal explanation in terms of national character or
identity. A good example of this is contained in *The Protestant Ethic
and the Spirit of Capitalism*, which depends in part on a sharp distinction between Anglo-American Puritanism and German Lutheranism.
It has been argued that the subtext of Weber's Protestant ethic thesis reflects the German discursive context, which, albeit disguised
in theological terms, attempted to articulate the German *Sonderweg*
by contrasting it with the Anglophone experience of modernization.
In this sense, Weber's contrast between Puritanism and Lutheranism
can in fact be seen as building on this German discourse of national
juxtaposition.[24]

All the more interesting, however, is the fact that despite this strong
undercurrent, Weber refused to trace this differentiation through any

---

[21] Economy and Society 553/960.
[22] Jeffrey Praeger's misguided criticism that, compared especially to Durkheim,
Weber failed to grasp the normative dimension in the modern state ironically affirms Weber's politically motivated intention behind the ideal typical construction of
bureaucracy. See J. Praeger, "Moral Integration and Political Inclusion: A Comparison
of Durkheim's and Weber's Theories," *Social Forces* 59:4 (1981) 918–50.
[23] Neutrality 540/47.
[24] See F. W. Graf, "The German Theological Sources and Protestant Church Politics,"
in H. Lehmann and G. Roth (eds.), *Weber's Protestant Ethic: Origins, Evidence, Contexts* (Cambridge: Cambridge University Press, 1995). For the political subtext of the
German theological discourses, see G. Rupp, *Culture-Protestantism: German Liberal
Theology at the Turn of the Century*, American Academy of Religion: *Studies in Religion*,
Vol. 15 (Missoula, MT: Scholars Press, 1977).

mythical genealogy back to Tacitus's *Germania* and idealized Germanic tribal life in explaining national variation, including the different formation of Reformation dogmas.[25] On the contrary, it was the difference in religious dogmas, rather than an immortal national identity, that brought about the different national characters in Germany and England. According to Weber, "the appeal to national character [*Volkscharakter*] is generally a mere confession of ignorance, and in this case it is entirely untenable."[26]

Weber's attitude built on his more theoretical rejection of nation as a linguistic community. Until Ferdinand de Saussure's synchronic and structuralist linguistics emerged, nineteenth-century philology, mainly historical-comparative, was preoccupied with identifying the historical link between language and ethnic-racial community formation.[27] The key to this paradigm was that nations had primordial and essentialist bases in the formation of common language that reflected and determined the collective character of a nation. On a more general level, these philological studies were predicated on a sharp distinction between Indo-European and Semitic languages that corresponded to the contemporary historians' occupation with the Germanist genealogy of national-ethnic-racial differentiation. That which belied this assertion reflected, as Edward Said has famously argued, the search for an objective essentialist foundation of Western European identity that was constructed by imagining the equally absolute and essentialist, yet contrasting, foundation of an Oriental alterity.[28] Language was understood to provide an objective basis for the formation of different national identities.

---

[25] For the nationalist manipulation of history in Germany, see G. Mosse, "Ancient Germany Rediscovered," in his *The Crisis of German Ideology: Intellectual Origin of the Third Reich* (New York: Schocken Books, 1981) 67–87 and G. Iggers, "The Origins of German Historicism," in *The German Conception of History: The National Tradition of Historical Thought from Herder to the Present* (Hanover, NH: Wesleyan University Press, 1968). For England, see J. W. Burrow, *A Liberal Descent: Victorian Historians and the English Past* (Cambridge: Cambridge University Press, 1983). For France, see M. Thom, "Tribes within Nations : The Ancient Germans and the History of Modern France," in H. Bhabha (ed.), *Nation and Narrative* (London: Routledge, 1994).

[26] Protestant Ethic 74–5/88–9.

[27] See J. Culler, *Ferdinand de Saussure* (Ithaca, NY: Cornell University Press, 1986) 65–77.

[28] See E. Said, "Islam, Philology and French Culture: Renan and Massignon," in *The World, the Text and the Critic* (London: Faber, 1984).

Weber's philological account of the idea of "calling" (*Beruf*) consistently rejected such a paradigm.[29] For instance, Weber's argument can be read as defying any discernible association of ethnic-linguistic group in Indo-European languages with the idea of calling. It was rather Luther's innovative translation of the Hebrew Bible that first brought this word and idea into vernacular use.[30] Two observations can be made here. First, Weber ascribed decisive importance to an individual's innovation in historical change – a tendency commonly found in his sociology of religion. More important in our context, Weber here traced the etymological origin of "calling" to a Hebrew word, which defied the common dichotomy between Indo-European and Semitic linguistic-cum-ethnic identities. Minimizing the importance of linguistic primordiality in the formation of national identity, Weber boldly claimed: "Today, in the age of language conflict, a community based on a common language [*Sprachgemeinschaft*] is preeminently considered the normal basis of national identity [*nationalen Gemeinsamkeit*] . . . [yet] a common language is also insufficient in sustaining a so-called sense of national identity [*Nationalgefühl*]."[31]

Even less sufficient for sustaining national identity was the concept of ethnic-racial community. Again, Weber's position can be highlighted once juxtaposed to the discursive context of his time. As is well known, there was an intense interest in what can broadly be called "physical anthropology" and in such pseudosciences as eugenics, racial hygiene, and anthropometrical criminology. In part influenced by the prestige of biological science in the nineteenth century (Darwinism, for example), this popular interest was spearheaded mostly by biologists and physicians who turned their attention to social policies.[32] This background accounts for Weber's heated debate with Alfred Ploetz, one such physician turned social scientist in Germany, which took place in

---

[29] In agreement is H. Liebersohn, "Weber's Historical Concept of National Identity," in Lehmann and Roth (1995) 124–5.

[30] Protestant Ethic 97–100/207–10.

[31] Economy and Society 242/395 and 528/922. For the insufficiency of common language as a ground for *any* community formation [*Vergemeinschaftung*], see ibid. 22–3/ 42–3.

[32] For a recent and most comprehensive survey of racist-cum-nationalist ideology in Germany, see P. J. Weinding, *Health, Race and German Politics: Between National Unification and Nazis* (Cambridge: Cambridge University Press, 1989) 11–60. For Ploetz, see ibid. 119–47.

1910 during the first meeting of the German Sociological Association at Frankfurt.

The surviving record of this encounter shows that the debate took place in the course of Ploetz's presentation on the ethnic-racial determinism of sociocultural phenomena (titled *Die Begriffe Rasse und Gesellschaft*), interrupted frequently by Weber's characteristically volcanic objections. Weber, for instance, raised a furious objection as soon as Ploetz suggested that the demise of ancient Greek civilization should be attributed to its ethnic degeneration, by which he attempted to account for the modern (inferior) state of the Greek people and culture, and again when Ploetz attributed American racial problems to the inferiority of the "Negro."[33] According to Weber, however, what was commonly addressed as the "Negro problem" (*Negerfrage*) in this meeting was "*socially* determined by the previously sketched tendency toward the monopolization of social power and honor, a tendency which in this case happens to be linked to race."[34]

The passionate objection to Ploetz seems to have a deeper theoretical root in Weber. Despite Weber's ongoing interest in the possibility of physical anthropology, which he insisted be incorporated as an independent section into the German Sociological Association,[35] an equally abiding attitude of Weber's seems to indicate his determined rejection of the approach that eventually lent support to ethnic-primordial nationalism. Weber thus ends his 1920 introduction to the *Gesammelte Aufsätze zur Religionssoziologie* by expressing strong suspicions about the potential of physical anthropology, which might also have been triggered in part by Werner Sombart's quasi-racial and potentially anti-Semitic genealogy of modern capitalism – one that clearly rivaled Weber's own genealogy in his contemporary Germany.[36]

I see up to the present no way of exactly or even approximately measuring either the extent or, above all, the form of its influence [of heredity] on the

---

[33] Sozialpolitik 456–62: Also see *Verhandlungen des ersten deutschen Soziologentages* (Frankfurt a. M: Sauer & Auvermann, 1969) 157–64.

[34] Economy and Society 235/386.

[35] *Verhandlungen* (1969) 215. For more on Weber and the race issue within the German Sociological Association, see H. Liebersohn, *Fate and Utopia in German Sociology, 1870–1923* (Cambridge, MA: MIT Press, 1988) 116–18.

[36] On Sombart and Weber, see J. Osterhammel, "Personal Conflict and Ideological Options in Sombart and Weber" in Mommsen and Osterhammel (1987).

development investigated *here* [in *Religionssoziologie*] ... an appeal to heredity would therefore involve premature renunciation of the possibility of knowledge attainable *now*, and would shift the problem to factors at present still unknown.[37]

Consistently held throughout his career – from as early as 1904 through 1920, the year of his death – Weber's antagonism to the account of nation in terms of either linguistic or ethnic-racial primordiality was given its most theoretically explicit, albeit truncated, elaboration in *Economy and Society*. Weber's argument here culminates in one single point: nation is fundamentally a *political* concept. "Time and again, we find that the concept of 'nation' directs us to its relationship to political power."[38] By using the word "power," he meant to underline two characteristics embedded in the concept of nation. One is that, contrary to contemporary scholarly belief, the formation of political communities and actions precedes that of national identity, and not vice versa; the other is that ethnic-national identity is an "artificial product [*Kunstprodukt*] of the political community [*politischen Gemeinschaft*]"[39] constructed for political purposes and usually devoid of any objective ground.

We shall call "ethnic groups" those human groups that foster a *subjective* belief in their common descent ... it does not matter whether or not an objective blood relationship exists. Ethnic identity [*Gemeinsamkeit*] differs from the kinship group precisely by being an *imagined* identity [*geglaubte Gemeinsamkeit*], not a community with concrete social action, like the latter. In our sense, ethnic identity does not in itself constitute a group; it only facilitates group formation of any kind, particularly in the political sphere. On the other hand, it is primarily the political community, no matter how artificial a construction [*künstlichen Gliederungen*], that cultivates the belief in common ethnicity.[40]

Without delving further into Weber's sweeping historical and intercivilizational comparisons of the categories of ethnic-linguistic nations, suffice it to say for the moment that Weber's argument does not

---

[37] Protestant Ethic (Vorbemerkung) 24–5/30–1. Also see his proposal for the *Verein* study of contemporary working-class life, in which he cautions his colleagues against the "conventional, altogether unclear concept of the folk character." See Sozialpolitik 28.

[38] Economy and Society 244/397–8.

[39] Ibid. 241/393; also see 529–30/925–6.

[40] Ibid. 237/389 (italics mine).

accord well with scholarship contemporary with his that was predicated on what is now called the "objectivist-essentialist" account of nation. Albeit in a rudimentary form, Weber's concept of nation foreshadowed the current understanding of nationalism that is succinctly thematized as *The Imagined Communities*. Rejecting the linguistic and ethnic ground of nationalism, Weber's understanding instead strongly points to a subjectivist-constructivist idea of nation.

NATIONALISM, CITIZENSHIP, AND PERSONALITY

The fact that Weber's nationalism lacks an essentialist ground for legitimation invites suspicion of the claim that his "ultimate" values were fixated on the power of the German nation-state. Even in the Freiburg address (1895), which reveals the strongest version of Weber's nationalist commitments, no such claim surfaces unambiguously despite passionate polemics. To see this point, we need to revisit this well-known speech.

Weber appears in the address to have in mind two distinct yet overlapping audiences: social scientists and the bourgeois class in general. He first addressed his fellow scholars; at issue was the value-neutral pretension of the study of political economy. Using his earlier investigation of the East Elbian problem as an example, Weber pointed out that, in terms of the Darwinian law of adaptation and survival, the Polish displacement of German agrarian laborers in East Prussia was perfectly justifiable; the Poles simply proved to be a stronger "race" when it came to the competition for survival. From the perspective of allegedly value-neutral political economics, which Weber identified with social Darwinism, political intervention into this economic problem on behalf of German *Kultur* could not be legitimated scientifically. Nor could it properly account for the motivation behind the emigration of the German population, since the reason was far from being dictated by the naturalistic law of survival. It was rather rooted in the "half-conscious urge towards far off places [wherein] lies hidden an element of primitive idealism... the magic of *freedom*."[41] The grave error of contemporary political economics consisted in its ignorance

---

[41] Freiburg 522/8.

of the fact that social sciences were unavoidably value laden.[42] Notoriously, Weber went on to assert that the social sciences should actively serve the reason of the nation-state.[43]

This testimony to Weber's ardent nationalism was nonetheless quickly followed by the justification of his value position, which was elaborated as an answer to a self-imposed question: Is the "nationalist value judgment" a mere prejudice?[44] It was, according to Weber, not a prejudice to be set aside in the name of scientific objectivity – not because it relied on some sort of subjective existentialist decision, as Raymond Aron implied,[45] but because it served the ultimate ethical question of human characterology.

> The question which stirs us as we think beyond the grave of our own generation is not the *well-being* human beings will enjoy in the future but what kind of people they will *be*, and it is this same question which truly underlies all work in political economy. We do not want to breed well being in people, but rather those characteristics which we think of as constituting the human greatness and nobility of our nature.... A science [*Wissenschaft*] concerned with *human beings* – and that is what political economy is – enquires above all else, into the *quality of the human beings* reared under those economic and social conditions of existence.[46]

Shortly following this stern moralizing is the notorious dictum that "the science of political economy is a *political* science."[47] We might as well substitute "moral science" for "political science" in the dictum.

This unique conflation of the categories of the national, the political, and the moral persisted in the second theme of the address, which was directed to the bourgeois class in general: political maturity (*Reifung*) and education (*Schulung*). Diagnosing the Wilhelmine political situation as a stalemate between declining agricultural Junkerdom and rising industrial classes, whether bourgeois or proletariat, Weber urged his fellow bourgeois class to rise to the responsibility of leading

[42] Neutrality 536–9/44–6.
[43] Freiburg 558/13; also see 560–1/16–17.
[44] Ibid. 558/13–14.
[45] R. Aron, "Max Weber and Power-Politics," in O. Stammer (ed.), *Max Weber and Sociology Today* (Oxford: Oxford University Press, 1971).
[46] Freiburg 559/15.
[47] Ibid. 561/16.

the nation politically, identifying political education as the most urgent task for this national leadership. While the founding generation's political achievement was duly acknowledged, Weber chose to highlight its failure to institutionalize the proper political education of the masses. The consequence of this poor political education that concerned Weber most was the bourgeois class's failure to "grasp... the nation's enduring economic and political *power* interests and their ability... to place these interests above all other considerations."[48]

This diagnosis does not mean, however, that Weber endorsed the German practice of power politics. In fact, the pursuit of power for its own sake troubled Weber greatly, and he believed it to be deeply rooted in the Wilhelmine political culture of "vanity" (*Eitelkeit*).[49] The German fascination with power reflected merely the political immaturity and vanity of the bourgeois and Junker classes, which, instead of espousing national-public spiritedness and somber realism, embraced a misguided glorification of vain power politics, as reflected in the popular longing for a new Bismarck and mass support for overseas expansions.[50] Weber holds, to the contrary, that no economic gain from an authoritarian practice of politics and imperialism "can substitute for such [political] education."[51] Despite the polemical elevation of power politics in the Freiburg address, thus, it was never glorified as the *ultimate* aim of nationalist galvanization. On the contrary, when elevated to an ultimate value in itself, it merely indicated to Weber a lack of genuine conviction and sense of purpose. For ultimate values cannot be drawn from within either politics or science; "rather they are *the old, general types of human ideals.*"[52]

From the perspective of *The Protestant Ethic*, which was not published until 1904, the meaning of these 1895 references to the old human ideals is evident.[53] As I argued in Chapter 4, Weber's delineation

---

[48] Ibid. 565/20.
[49] On the concept of "vanity" in Weber, see R. Titunik, "Status, Vanity and Equal Dignity in Max Weber's Political Thought," *Economy and Society* 24:1 (1995) 101–21.
[50] Freiburg 566–70/22–5.
[51] Ibid. 570/25.
[52] Ibid. 563/19.
[53] Even within the address, the immediate point of reference of the "old humanist ideals" is the earlier passage in which he discussed the motivation for the German emigration from the East Prussia and attributed it to the "magic of *freedom.*" This should have

in the address of the idealized character who combines a somber realism of power politics and a passionate conviction in nationalist causes clearly foreshadows the ideal type of the Puritan man of vocation (*Berufsmensch*), who represents a principled aversion to vanity, undisciplined passion, and bureaucratic-hierocratic conformism. This type of agency surfaces in Weber's work under various names – personality, charismatic individual, or politician and scientist with vocation. Critical for the formation of these types of self, which Weber regarded as the anthropological foundation for the exercise of modern individual freedom, autonomy, and agency, was to sustain the methodical, disciplined, and purposive action of individuals, and such a pattern of action was seen to be galvanized in the context of collective purpose that permeated the everyday life of the tightly organized, disciplinary community Weber called sectlike society (*Sektengesellschaft*) – and thus Weber's somewhat infelicitous neologism, "sect man" (*Sektenmensch*). This sociological formula for the uniquely modern empowerment of individual agency seems to repeat itself in Weber's polemical elevation of nationalism. As the collective purpose of a sectarian life reinforced, ironically, the autonomous and voluntary characteristics of its members, Weber seems to have conceived of the nationalist sentiments as an alternative way of imbuing secularized modern society with a sense of collective purpose that would contribute to the formation of autonomous personalities.

It is this dimension of ethical characterology that is unduly repressed in the authoritarian account of Weber's nationalist conviction. In Weber's political writings, although accorded the status of the single most urgent necessity in German politics, nationalist-imperialist involvement in international power politics appears at times to be merely of *instrumental* value to Weber. Just as Weber's Puritan *Berufsmensch* approached political participation with a sense of duty under certain circumstances, while steadfastly refusing to sanctify political activities as possessing intrinsic values, power politics and the attendant nationalist galvanization were critical for Weber, since it was through active participation in power politics that genuine public personalities,

been clear to the audience, since Weber had also said in the earlier passage that these "libertarian ideals of our early youth have faded, and . . . have now gone into historical decline" (ibid. 552/8).

especially on a mass level, were formed. By "protecting [their] own rights and sharing in the responsibility for the fate of the nation," modern individuals would be gradually transformed into public citizenry.[54]

In fact, the conscious link between nationalist patriotism, public citizenship, and individual agency is a familiar theme in the tradition of liberal political theory. In the historic lecture "What Is a Nation?" (1882), for example, Ernest Renan, Weber's near contemporary, declared that a nation "is summarized . . . by a tangible fact, namely, consent, the clearly expressed desire to continue a common life. A nation's existence is . . . a daily plebiscite."[55] In order to maintain his attachment to liberal values, and thus to the primacy of individual will and freedom, without renouncing loyalty to his country, Renan took the route of affirming that one belongs to a nation by the exercise of one's free will alone. Nationalism, or patriotism, gains legitimacy by resorting to the individual decision based on free and autonomous will; conversely, individual self-determination, a universal value in itself, is supported by remaining loyal to the particularistic national society to which one belongs. According to Tzvetan Todorov, from this point on, one can be a patriotic nationalist and a humanitarian cosmopolite at the same time in good conscience – thereby transcending the Rousseauite dichotomy of "man and citizen."[56]

The second half of Renan's equation is more clearly captured by Alexis de Tocqueville. The danger of democracy, as Tocqueville insists tirelessly, lies in the fact that each individual may be exclusively preoccupied with his or her own interests and that citizens may no longer aspire to any public ideal. The danger lies in "the taste for material well-being and softness of heart . . . , the gradual softening of mores, the abasement of the mind, the mediocrity of tastes."[57] Coupled with the danger of conformism inherent in modern mass democracy, at stake for Tocqueville was the individual capacity to make an autonomous decision, and one remedy, under the circumstances, was to revitalize

---

[54] Biography 143/135.

[55] E. Renan, "What Is a Nation?" in G. Elley and R. Suny (eds.), *Becoming National: A Reader* (Oxford: Oxford University Press, 1996) 53.

[56] Todorov (1993) 222.

[57] Alexis de Tocqueville, *Selected Letters on Politics and Society*, trans. J. Toupin and R. Boesche/ed. R. Boesche (Berkeley: University of California Press, 1985) 150–1.

national pride. "It is necessary that those who march at the head of
such a nation [a democratic nation] should always keep a proud attitude, if they do not wish to allow the level of national mores to fall
very low."[58] Of course, the other, and more celebrated, antidote to this
malady of political modernity was, for Tocqueville, the proliferation
of intermediary associations between the state and individuals.

It is not a mere coincidence that John Stuart Mill, the addressee
of Tocqueville's letter quoted here, echoed this combination of public-
spirited patriotism and the proliferation of voluntary associational life,
especially when he tried to propose the latter in terms of the former.
For Mill defended a pluralistically organized civil society on the ground
that it would take people

out of the narrow circle of personal and family selfishness, and [accustom] them
to the comprehension of joint interests, the management of joint concerns –
[habituate] them to act from public or semipublic motives, and guide their
conduct by aims which unite instead of isolating them from one another.[59]

Insofar as we identify Mill's and Tocqueville's main theme as the
question of mass democracy and political education, for which both
associational empowerment and nationalist galvanization are suggested in equal measure as prescriptions, Weber's nationalism seems
to resonate with an unambiguously Tocquevillean and even Millian
agenda.[60] For Weber also recognized that, in order for autonomous personalities and robust citizenship to be maintained in a modern mass
democracy, a heightened sense of nationalist patriotism needs to be
complemented by the proliferation of intermediary associations that
can constantly and institutionally engage the masses in the public affairs of their own self-government. Thus, Weber held in his commentary
on the Russian Revolution of 1905: "It can clearly only be solved by the
organs of self-government, and for this very reason it seems vitally important for liberalism to understand that its vocation still lies with the

[58] Ibid. 151.
[59] J. S. Mill, *On Liberty and Other Writings*, ed. S. Collini (Cambridge: Cambridge University Press, 1989) 109–10.
[60] For more on Tocqueville and Weber, see S. Kalberg, "Tocqueville and Weber on the
Sociological Origin of Citizenship: The Political Culture of American Democracy,"
Citizenship Studies 1:2 (1997) 199–222. For Weber and Mill, see A. Ryan, "Weber
and Mill on History, Freedom and Reason" in Mommsen and Ostehammel (1987).

struggle against both bureaucratic and Jacobin *centralism* and working to spread the old, fundamental individualist notion of 'inalienable
human rights' among the masses."[61] To this second pillar of Weber's
agenda for political education we now turn.

POLITICS OF THE CLASSES: REFEUDALIZATION AND
EMBOURGEOISEMENT

Weber's concern with political education, public citizenship, and self-
government appears especially salient in his ambitious agenda for
collective research at the new German Sociological Society. Put forward in a speech given at the first convention of the society in 1910,
this agenda contained two independent, yet related, projects – one
concerning journalism (*Zeitungswesen*) and the other voluntary associational life (*Vereinswesen*). His call for an extensive investigation into
what is now called the "public sphere" in German civil society, however, fell on deaf ears, and the proposed research did not materialize
despite Weber's enthusiastic leadership. When the research proposals
were finally dropped in 1912, he withdrew from the activities associated
with the society, which he had played a critical role in founding.[62] The
nature of Weber's problem appears, however, sufficiently clear in the
speech.[63]

According to Weber, these projects were meant to address a broadly
conceived question of the late modern self. The sociology of journalism has to deal with inquiries into the "nature of the modern public
sphere [*Öffentlichkeit*]," its role in the modern "balance of power," or
the implications of monopolization and capitalization of the press –
inquiries that eventually culminate in the questions "What does it

[61] Russia 268–9/108.
[62] See Biography 425–30/420–5.
[63] For more on the biographical and intellectual context surrounding this speech, see
Sung Ho Kim, "Max Weber and Civil Society," *Max Weber Studies* 2:2 (2002) 186–
98, which frames my translation of the second half of the speech [*Vereinsewesen*]
with an introduction and annotation (M. Weber, "Voluntary Associational Life
[*Vereinswesen*]," ibid.). The first half on the sociology of the press has been translated by K. Tribe as "Preliminary Report on a Proposed Survey for a Sociology of
the Press" and introduced by W. Hennis as "The Media as a Cultural Problem:
Max Weber's Sociology of the Press," *History of the Human Sciences* 11:2 (1998)
107–20.

[modern journalism] contribute to the *making of modern man?* ... How are the objective, *public cultural values [überindividuellen Kulturgüter]* influenced, what shifts occur, what is destroyed and newly created with regard to the beliefs and hopes of the masses, of the '*Lebensgefühlen*' – as they say today – what part of the potential viewpoint is destroyed forever and newly created?"[64] In short, Weber's proposed research on journalism is mainly concerned with the way in which the modern self is constituted in a public sphere.

The same thematic rubric continues to inform the proposed investigation of the voluntary associational life. Weber began with his observation on the contemporary dynamism in German civil society and called the modern self "associational man" (*Vereinsmensch*).[65] He proceeded to draw an analogy with American associational life to underscore the decisive influence different modes of association exerted on the formation of various personalities. And he concluded the opening remarks of this speech with the statement that, in contrast to "institution" (*Anstalt*), "the archetype [*Urtypus*] of all voluntary associational life [in America]...is the sect in the specific sense of the word."[66] This ideal type of Anglo-American associational life seems to pose for Weber a fine counterexample to that in Germany, since he formulated the two main questions for the research in the following way. First, "democracy in America is no heap of sand"; then "how does it stand to us?...Where? With what consequences? Where not? Why not?" The second question was "How does a certain associational membership influence the inner workings [*innen*] of the individual members or the personality [*Persönlichkeit*] as such?", a question he once again linked back to the Anglo-American counterexamples, such as the "Greek Letter Society" in American colleges.[67] After expounding at length on the various aspects of the relationship between the associational mode and personality formation, Weber related this question of association and individual back to the "making of the individuals and then the making of objective, public cultural values [*Kulturgüter*]" in contemporary Germany.[68]

[64] Sozialpolitik 441.
[65] Ibid. 442.
[66] Ibid. 442–3.
[67] Ibid. 443.
[68] Ibid. 447.

Even in this research proposal, however, Weber's attitude toward the nascent associational dynamism and the attendant bourgeois public sphere in Germany – which "range from bowling clubs to political parties" – was far from value-neutral. Despite their seeming vigor, for instance, the various aesthetic sects and even Freud's disciples in his contemporary Germany were lumped together and given varying degrees of critical attention, as Weber suspected that they all contributed to the formation of personalities likely to resign from this world and withdraw into a purely private sphere of mystic contemplation (as in the George circle) or quietism in the name of mental hygiene and emotional sublimation (as in Freudian sects).[69] To give another example, the popular culture of neighborhood choral societies (*Gesangvereinskunst*) deserved close investigation, since a member of such a club

will become a person who, to put it succinctly, will easily become a "good citizen" in the passive sense of the word. No wonder that monarchs have such a great predilection for entertainments of that kind. "Where people sing, you may safely settle." Great, strong passions and great actions are lacking there.[70]

Weber's criticism seems to be predicated on the recognition that all of these organizations fail to cultivate the idealized citizen he calls a "personality," who is capable of readily taking principled and even defiant moral actions with a passionate conviction and sober sense of responsibility. What German civil society lacks, then, is not so much the numerical proliferation of institutions of socialization as the direction that this kind of civic education takes. Thus, Weber laments, "the quantitative distribution of the voluntary associational life does not always go hand in hand with qualitative significance" in Germany.[71]

Weber's suspicion that German civil society bred mostly passive and conformist personalities continued in his later political writings. First, the German associations tended to emphasize "*schoolboy subordination*" in the governing of internal matters. In contrast to "English

---

[69] Ibid. 446.
[70] Ibid. 445. Also see Weber's letter to Karl Bücher dated 1 February 1909, in which he compares the "singing talent" of the black population in the southern United States to that of German choral societies, highlighting "concurrent" political quietism. MWG II/6, 49.
[71] Ibid. 442.

clubs ... [in which] *all gentlemen are equal,"* they emphasized *"training for the discipline of office"* and "ritualized conventions." Second, Weber was critical of these internal cultures, because this "nonsense" was disguised as personality training, which in fact was strictly followed by the members "in order to ingratiate themselves in higher places." Lacking, in Weber's view, was the genuine cultivation of free and autonomous personalities capable of taking principled moral action – a crucial defect that eventually led to vain "boasting about the wealth of one's *parents"* and zeal to be incorporated into the "society" (*Gesellschaft*). Weber's interest in German civil society was, in short, motivated by his suspicion that it produced men of passive conformism.[72]

This kind of status consciousness, and its consequent conformism, was particularly problematic in Germany, Weber believed, because, unlike other European nations, Germany had no honorable tradition of aristocracy for the Wilhelmine bourgeoisie to emulate. It is this perspective that made Weber particularly harsh toward the strand of public discourse that was eventually rendered as the so-called "German Idea of 1914."[73] Weber categorically dismissed this earlier and positive articulation of the German *Sonderweg* as "dilettantism [*Literatenprodukt*]."[74] In 1917, for instance, Weber isolated this popular myth as his main target for criticism, along with corporatist proposals, against which he advocated the democratization of the Prussian three-class suffrage and the broad parliamentarization of Germany. In this text, Weber's rhetorical strategy was to pit the alleged aristocratic value against itself.

[72] Democracy 381–6/115–17. Again, Weber's contrast between "American" and "German" associational cultures has a precedence in Tocqueville when "French" associations are criticized for producing a passive and servile attitude in opposition to "American" counterparts. See his *Democracy in America* (New York: Harper & Row, 1988) 198.

[73] An outcome of an intense search for the meaning of the First World War, this idea reflected an intellectual attempt to articulate the peculiarity of German spiritual *Kultur* allegedly cramped between the Oriental despotism of Russia and the material *Zivilisation* of the West. Institutionally, integral to this idea was the rejection of, among other things, the political institutions of the West rooted in parliamentary liberal democracy as well as a free market economy. Instead, the Idea of 1914 celebrated what it perceived to be the uniquely Germanic institutions of the Prussian monarchy, the bureaucratic state, and benignly paternalistic aristocracy. Counterposed to the so-called French Idea of 1789, the Idea of 1914 gained immediate popularity upon the outbreak of war, and was supported by such eminent intellectuals as Plenge, Rathenau, Troeltsch, Sombart, and even Weber's own brother, Alfred.

[74] Neutrality 540/47.

For Weber, true aristocracy should be able to address universal and national concerns free from partisan social and economic interests.[75] The Prussian Junkerdom, by contrast, strictly followed its narrow class interests as agricultural entrepreneurs, especially in East Prussia, and its feudal gestures and aristocratic pretensions were mere devices to camouflage its *"physiognomy of the parvenu [Parvenüphsyognomie]."* Weber continued: "The plebeian traits of the way we conduct ourselves in the world ... derive at least in part ... from suggesting to sections of society who quite simply lack the qualification to do so that they should play the part of aristocrats."[76] Despite popular belief, Weber thus boldly asserted that *"it* [true aristocracy] *simply does not exist"* in Germany[77] and that the Junkers were in fact plebeians who merely "stylize [themselves] as an 'aristocracy'."[78]

Similar complaints continued in Weber's pointed comments on German student fraternities. In an address delivered to the university teachers' convention in the autumn of 1911, for example, Weber deplored the popular striving to adopt feudal lifestyles, such as "worthiness to fight a duel" [*Satisfaktionsfähigkeit*]. He found this attitude even among the bourgeois students of newly founded business schools, which were supposedly modern in comparison to more traditional universities.[79] What drove Weber to be so harsh – he even later declared explosively in front of uniformed university students that "anyone who belongs to a uniformed corporation [in German universities] ... is a son of a bitch [*Hundsfott*]"[80] – was his belief that such status consciousness and misguided upward mobility (*Standeshebung*) "cannot be democratized; rather, it formally constitutes a caste convention which, materially speaking, is not aristocratic but *plebeian* in nature."[81]

In sum, Weber's critical comments on Wilhelmine bourgeois associational life and his repeated emphasis on the necessity for a genuinely public sphere and a pluralistic civil society reveal the same thematic concern that motivated his polemicized call for nationalist

[75] Democracy 373–6/108.
[76] Ibid. 381–3/115.
[77] Ibid. 376–7/109.
[78] Ibid. 380–1/114.
[79] Biography 431–3/426–8.
[80] Ibid. 644/632.
[81] Ibid. 599/588.

galvanization – a theme that ultimately goes back to the ethical characterology in modern mass democracy. It is premature to conclude,
however, that Weber's concern with the formation of public citizenship
among the bourgeoisie was class-biased or class-limited. For Weber's
so-called refeudalization thesis[82] not only concerned the bourgeois zeal
to emulate and identify with feudal caste values; it was also directed at
the German bourgeois preoccupation with distinguishing their social
status from that of the working classes. Even in the Freiburg address,
he explicitly acknowledged the importance of the bourgeois partnership with the working class in governing an industrial nation.[83] To
the extent that he emphasized in the address the necessity of political
education and maturation of the bourgeois class, Weber thus paid comparable attention to the political consciousness of the working class.
Weber's prescription amounted to a nationalist agitation for the political education of both classes; no less critical in this endeavor than his
concern for bourgeois empowerment was the issue of self-organization
of the working class.

Turning his attention to the working class, Weber also criticized
their lack of political maturity, sharply contrasting it with the English
example. He believed that England's long involvement in European
power politics and active pursuit of imperial gains abroad had enabled
the English working class to put the interest of the nation over the
parochial class interests. This public spiritedness was reinforced by
collective participation not only in economic struggles but also in nationalist deliberations, engaging them "in a chronic political education
[*Schulung*]" – "whereas for us [Germans] it is only received when our
borders are threatened, i.e., in acute cases."[84]

Weber attributed this lack of public consciousness among the
German working class to the Social Democratic Party (SPD) leadership.

[82] For a later development of this theme as a critique of Wilhelmine political culture,
see R. Dahrendorf, *Society and Democracy in Germany* (Garden City, NY: Doubleday,
1967) 46ff. In a different sense, Habermas also uses the concept to describe the rise of
interest groups and the subsequent demise of the public sphere in the modern welfare
state. See "Public Sphere" in *Jürgen Habermas on Society and Politics: A Reader*, ed.
S. Seidman (Boston: Beacon, 1989) 236.
[83] For more on this theme, see M. Weber, "Über Deutschland als Industriestaat," in
Verhandlungen des achten Evangelische–sozialen Kongresses (Göttingen: Vandenhoeck
& Ruprecht, 1897).
[84] Freiburg 571/26.

Weber's criticism seems twofold. At the SPD conventions in 1906 and 1907, on the one hand, he was alarmed to hear the empty phraseology of revolutionary fervor among the party leaders, although they had long followed a decidedly revisionist course. Not only was it the sort of intellectual hypocrisy he most disdained, this revolutionary phraseology was seen by Weber as contributing to the quietism of the German working class. The problem was that, uncritically embracing the Marxist historical determinism that postulated inevitable stages of historical evolution, the empty emphasis on revolution instilled an infertile utopian illusion that in effect steered the working class away from any sort of activism. This was not entirely an honest tactical mistake on the part of SPD leadership, Weber believed, since the emphasis on "inexorable development" led toward preservation of the party apparatus "for its own sake."[85]

On the other hand, the fact that the SPD established itself as a mainstream political party, with a vested interest in its organizational perpetuation, prompted Weber to chide its members at their annual convention of 1906 for lack of revolutionary commitment.[86] The law of organizational oligarchy, later given a definitive statement by Robert Michels, from whom Weber acquired much of his knowledge of socialism, can be found in embryonic form in Weber's criticism here.[87] Far from being the medium of democratic participation and mass revolution that the party was originally meant to be, the SPD leadership had increasingly become a petit bourgeois class with its own status interests.[88] The embourgeoisement of the leadership, which ran parallel to the party's bureaucratization, Weber found particularly problematic, since it was accustoming its "followers to a submissiveness in the face of dogmas and party authorities." At stake are once again

[85] M. Weber, "Verhältnis der Kartelle zum Staaten," in *Schriften des Vereins für Sozialpolitik*, Vol. 116: Verhandlungen der Generalversammlung in Mannheim, 28 September 1905 (Leipzig: Dunker & Humboldt, 1906) 389–90.

[86] Letter to Robert Michels (8 October 1906) cited in L. Scaff, "Max Weber and Robert Michels," *American Journal of Sociology* 86:6 (1981) 1271.

[87] On Michels and Weber, also see D. Beetham, "From Socialism to Fascism: The Relation between Theory and Practice in the Works of Michels," *Political Studies* 25:1 (1977) 3–24, and W. Mommsen, "Max Weber and Robert Michels: An Asymmetrical Partnership," *European Journal of Sociology* 22:1 (1981) 100–16.

[88] M. Weber, "Der Sozialismus" (1918), in MWG (SA) I/15, 623–4.

the formulation of public citizenship and liberal character formation among the working-class masses.

There is not the faintest likelihood that economic "socialization" could encourage the growth of inwardly "free" personalities or "altruistic" ideals. Do we find the slightest seeds of anything of the kind among those who, in their opinion, are borne along by "material development" to inevitable victory? The Social Democrats, who excel in "correctness," drill the masses to perform a sort of spiritual goose step. They preach a this-worldly paradise to them, instead of an otherworldly paradise – which in Puritanism could *also* claim some notable achievements in the service of this-worldly "liberty" – thereby turning the Social Democratic Party into a sort of smallpox vaccination which is to the advantage of those interested in the preservation of the status quo.[89]

This observation, however, should not be taken as reflecting Weber's abandonment of hope for working-class organization. Weber instead urged the German bourgeoisie to embrace an alternative organizational source for working-class empowerment: trade unionism. Criticizing Bismarck's legacy, Weber proclaimed:

[I]n everyday life,...the sense of *honour and comradeship* [*Ehre und Kameradschaft*] produces the only decisive moral forces for the education of the masses, and that these forces must therefore be given free rein.... [T]*his and this alone* [unionism] is what "social democracy" means in an age which will inevitably remain capitalist for a long time to come.[90]

For Weber believed that "within the SPD," only the trade unions had "taken the education of the masses in hand."[91] He recognized that the task of the political education of the working class was not easy. Neither the patronizing intervention of the state bureaucracy nor the well-meaning guidance offered by the left-liberal leadership could displace political maturation, which could be nurtured only by active participation in and deliberation on national public considerations in an autonomously organized associational life of the working class's own. For these reasons, he strongly affirmed "the equal participation of the workers in the collective determination of working conditions"

[89] Russia 272/109–10.
[90] Parliament 447–9/143.
[91] Sozialpolitik 398.

and "the strengthening of their organizations, which spearhead this effort." He went on to claim "the comradeship and class dignity that develops in this way [have] a positive cultural value" since "we want to live in a land of citizens, not of subjects."[92] Weber viewed the public participation of the working class to be at once an urgent necessity and their right.

The modern working class wants more than forbearance, compassionate understanding, and charity; they demand the recognition of their right to reflect about the same things, and in the same way, as the so-called educated people.... Their intellect has emancipated itself from bondage to tradition, and we should not only "understand" this and view it with indulgence, but *take it into account* and recognize it as something justified.[93]

It is from this perspective that Weber chided as naive "dilettantes" the founding members of the *National-sozialer Verein* (1896–1903), a left–bourgeois coalition that probably came closest to the practical realization of Weber's political ideals.[94] Although he regarded Friedrich Naumann, its leader, as "a single ray of hope,"[95] Weber was harshly critical of the *Verein*'s platform of 1896, which embraced optimistic coalitionism by which to lure the working class away from the SPD and incorporate it into the *Verein*. Instead, he urged that the platform pay more attention to German power politics and surrender the working-class elements in order to make the *Verein* represent a pan-bourgeois political voice. Less indicative of the "Nietzschean-elitist" character of Weber's political thinking, as Mommsen alleged,[96] this criticism was directed rather at the unrealistic paternalism of the reform-minded bourgeoisie. It was the same motivation that underpinned his address to the *Verein für Sozialpolitik* in 1905. He accused

---

[92] Memorandum of 15 November 1912, quoted in Mommsen (1984) 120.

[93] Biography 141/133.

[94] For this important bourgeois political organization, see W. R. Ward, *Theology, Sociology, and Politics: The German Protestant Social Consciousness, 1890–1933* (Berne: P. Lang, 1979). For Friedrich Naumann's politics, see B. Heckart, *From Basserman to Bebel: The Grand Block's Quest for Reform in the Kaiserreich, 1900–1914* (New Haven, CT: Yale University Press, 1974). On the relationship between Weber and Naumann, see P. Theiner, "Friedrich Naumann and Max Weber: Aspects of a Political Partnership," in Mommsen and Osterhammel (1987).

[95] Weber's letter to Lujo Brentano (6 February 1907) quoted in Biography 405/400.

[96] See, for example, Mommsen (1984) 101, 128–9.

the bourgeoisie, even those of left-liberal leanings and those benignly
disposed to the working class, of entertaining "authoritarian sentiments."⁹⁷ He proceeded to express his belief that the workers are entitled to defend their interests, and then to condemn both the mild
authoritarianism of the bourgeoisie and legal restrictions on trade
unions. He concluded with the bold assertion that unions had a value
in themselves (*Eigenwert*) and challenged "every proposal that threatened the union's essence [*Wesen*]."⁹⁸ As the Junker paternalism hin-
dered the political education of the bourgeois class, the bourgeois
leadership would only hamper the political maturation of the working class. The working class had to be organized independently and
autonomously.

In sum, spanning as they do his entire career, these comments
strongly indicate Weber's desire to maintain a vibrant associational
life galvanized by national public deliberations and constructed along
class lines – a robust civil society, in other words, that can be empowered by, and in turn strengthen, the national body politic. Nevertheless,
much to his dismay, Weber discovered in Wilhelmine society the erosion of the public sphere and the rise of castelike exclusivities. The
consequent "refeudalization" of civil society was to be countered by
the galvanization of associational life. This nationalist galvanization
was no less critical for the working class, which, Weber believed, deserved a partnership in the governing of modern industrial society. Yet,
in this regard, Weber believed that the working class should form its
own class-based associational life independent of bourgeois leadership.
Experience with autonomous public deliberation was an important exercise in the formation of national citizens, not only for the bourgeoisie
but also for the working class.

POLITICS OF CHECKS AND BALANCES: CORPORATISM
AND PARLIAMENTARISM

Corporatism had a long history in German political thought. It could
be attributed with little difficulty to the classical Idealists such as Hegel
and Müller. On a different spectrum, the German Catholic thinkers also

⁹⁷ Sozialpolitik 396.
⁹⁸ Ibid. 399.

had long celebrated the traditional social groups against the centralizing state backed, for different reasons, by the Prussian Junkers and the anticlerical National Liberals. The common denominator among these diverse ideas was a critical attitude toward the allegedly atomistic individualism that was held responsible for the social discontents brought about by rapid modernization and the parliamentary representation that these thinkers perceived to rely on mechanistic majority rule. Instead, they broadly converged on a blueprint of a political society in which public decisions are made via "organic," harmonious deliberation among various religious, vocational, and status groups that were to be officially incorporated as subjects of formal rights.[99]

By the time of the war's end, these divergent ideas had received two definitive stamps. One was the so-called Idea of 1914, and the other was the German war economy. Integral to the Idea of 1914 was the rejection, along with parliamentary democracy, of the materialistic market economy (the so-called anarchy of production), the attendant class struggle, and the proposed adoption of a "communal economy" (*Gemeinswirtschaft*). The wartime economic regime orchestrated by Walter Rathenau in a sense put this traditional agenda into practice. As a leader of the domestic logistics efforts during the war, Rathenau constructed a planned economy that was managed by organized consultation among government bureaucrats and big industrialists, sprinkled with paternalistic gestures of appeasement toward the working class. At the end of the war, Rathenau, along with Wichard von Moellendorf, an undersecretary of the Economic Ministry, emerged as a forceful voice for the reconstruction of the German economy and society along the lines of wartime experiments with a planned economy and functional-vocational representation. The postwar German bourgeoisie proved to be exceptionally vulnerable to the corporatist gospel of sustained economic productivity free of market competition

---

[99] For the Catholic tradition as well as German corporatist ideas in general, Ralph Bowen's classical account is still helpful. See R. Bowen, *German Theories of the Corporative State: With Special Reference to the Period 1870–1919* (New York: Russell & Russell, 1949). Another classical survey, and probably more authoritative, by virtue of its author's direct participation in these debates, will be found in K. Landauer, *Corporate State Ideologies: Historical Roots and Philosophical Origins* (Berkeley: University of California Press, 1982).

and class struggles. Although this proposal, at least in the original form Rathenau and Moellendorff outlined, was eventually defeated in 1919, when it was dropped at the cabinet meeting and then in the National Assembly, it remained an influential idea during the immediate postwar era and was partially reflected in the new Weimar constitution in the form of a National Economic Council (*Reichswirtschaftsrat*).[100]

It is against this background that Weber's extended criticism of corporatism makes better sense.[101] In his first sustained discussion of postwar German reconstruction, in November 1917, which was published in Naumann's periodical *Hilfe*, Weber set up corporatism as one of three or so main targets against which he attempted to advocate the pressing need for universal suffrage and attendant parliamentarization in Prussia. Corporatism seemed to Weber a natural target of criticism, especially given its functional representation scheme that would potentially sidestep universal suffrage and parliamentary empowerment.

Weber's critique of corporatism became more directly engaged as he examined the corporatist proposals as an extension of the wartime economy. First and foremost, the corporatist suggestion that peacetime capitalism be modeled after the wartime economy was simply unacceptable to Weber, who earlier had taken care to celebrate the novelty of modern capitalism by contrasting its entrepreneurship with mercantilism that was political in essence. Given his genealogical understanding of modern economy, such an economic reconstruction meant to Weber the "Golgotha of *all* economic ethics."[102]

Weber also opposed in unambiguous terms the corporatist scheme of functional representation. He cited difficulties associated with the instability of vocational categories in a rapidly changing industrial

[100] For Rathenau's own corporatist manifesto, see his *The New Society*, trans. A. Windham (New York: Harcourt, Brace, 1921). For a brief yet theoretically informed historical survey of the debates surrounding corporatism in postwar Germany, see C. Maier, "Society as Factory," in his *In Search of Stability: Explorations in Historical Political Economy* (Cambridge: Cambridge University Press, 1987) 39ff. Maier is especially good on contextualizing this postwar discourse in the wider comparative perspective of Western Europe and America. For more detailed accounts, see his earlier *Recasting Bourgeois Europe: Stabilization in France, Germany, and Italy in the Decade after World War I* (Princeton, NJ: Princeton University Press, 1975), especially the "Introduction" and "Part I: The Containment of the Left."
[101] On the relationship between Weber and Rathenau, see E. Schulin, "Max Weber and Walter Rathenau," in Mommsen and Osterhammel (1987).
[102] *Democracy* 356–8/ 89–91.

society; under the circumstances, functional representation would run the risk of imposing a rigid regime on the fluid social reality. The unrealistic politicization of the economy and society would, moreover, deepen the instability of these categories, since political interests would cut across the occupational divisions, creating more fractures across these purely economic and social categories.[103] The fact that political decisions do not necessarily correspond to economic interests was something of a truism to Weber, who had earlier concluded his East Elbian studies by sharply juxtaposing the agrarian classes' economic interests with the political interests of the industrial classes and the nation. And after all, the institutional representation of organized interests was, Weber grudgingly added, already reflected in the Bismarckian constitution, albeit partially, in the form of the Upper Chamber (*Erste Kammern*).

Shifting gears to a more explicitly political mode, Weber then derided what he called the "corporatist politics of compromise" by juxtaposing it to the contrasting principle of exacting decisionism in a parliamentary representative system.

Naturally, compromise also prevails in parliamentary politics. . . . *But*, it must be stressed, there is *always* the ultimate ratio of the *voting slip* in the background. . . . There is no getting away from the fact that the real and approximate *counting* of votes is an integral and essential element both of modern electoral contests and the conduct of business in parliament.[104]

This assertion by Weber brings out an interesting point of contrast with Carl Schmitt's critique that parliamentary democracy is based on the principle of compromise. For it was precisely for this reason that Schmitt criticized liberal parliamentarism as anathema to the essence of "the political" that, in his view, culminates in an existentialist distinction between friend and enemy.[105] This contrast is all the more interesting since Weber in fact isolated the same reason for the necessary empowerment of parliamentary representation as that listed by Schmitt for his rejection of liberal parliamentarism – that is, the mutual penetration of the state and society.

[103] Ibid. 358–61/ 94–5.
[104] Ibid. 367–9/102.
[105] See C. Schmitt, *The Concept of the Political* (Chicago: University of Chicago Press, 1996) and *The Crisis of Parliamentary Democracy* (Cambridge, MA: MIT Press, 1988).

The Weberian momentum is apparent in Schmitt's understanding of the "neutralization" (*Neutralisierung*) of the modern political sphere.[106] Understood essentially as an outcome of teleological rationalization and secularization, the neutralized political sphere posed a problem to Schmitt since it reflected the undifferentiated domination of formal rationality in the state, market, and civil society alike. Under the circumstances, Schmitt posited his main question as how to preserve the "substantive value," or existentialist core, of the political sphere. In order to counter the encroachment of formal rationality, Schmitt saw that some kind of "politicization" was necessary, and Weber's call for nationalist agitation can also be understood as coming from a similar concern.[107] Here, however, the similarity seems to end. The difference between the kinds of politicization Weber and Schmitt put forward appears most stark in the different agencies proposed for such a task.

For Schmitt, the mutual penetration of the state and society, one unavoidable outcome of neutralization, had led to the rise of what he called the "total state." Liberal parliamentarism, with its principle of "representation" as opposed to "identity" between leader and the ruled, provided an illuminating example of this interpenetration, since its function had degenerated to compromise and articulation among competing societal interests. The total state, however, also opened up a dialectical possibility of self-redemption – that is to say, the flip side of the societalization of the state is the politicization of society.[108] Schmitt thus urged that the total state not only be accepted empirically, but also affirmed on a normative ground. One critical precondition for the affirmation was the institutionalization of the absolute "sovereign," a plebiscitary leader who would guard the value core of the political sphere by deciding authoritatively on the "exception."[109] Given the amalgamated structure of the total state, furthermore, the sovereign's

---

[106] For the concept of neutralization, see C. Schmitt, "The Age of Neutralizations and Depoliticizations," trans. M. Konze and J. P. McCormick, *Telos* 96 (1993) 119–42.

[107] For more, see G. L. Ulmen, "The Sociology of the State: Carl Schmitt and Max Weber," *State, Culture and Society* 1:1 (1985) 3–57 and J. McCormick, "Antinomies of Technical Thought: Attempting to Transcend Weber's Categories of Modernity," in his *Carl Schmitt's Critique of Liberalism: Against Politics as Technology* (Cambridge: Cambridge University Press, 1997).

[108] *The Concept of the Political* 22.

[109] C. Schmitt, *Political Theology* (Cambridge, MA: MIT Press, 1988) 5.

decisions would not only guard the value of the political sphere, but also counter the technical-economic rationality prevalent in civil society. Eventually, the total state in this positive formulation was given more enthusiastic legitimization as Schmitt developed an eclectic theory of democracy as a principle of "homogeneity elevated into an identity" between leader and the ruled.[110]

In stark contrast to Schmitt's argument for a democratic homogeneity, Weber's criticism of corporatism amounts to the question of how to maintain *heterogeneity*. Unlike Schmitt, who regarded compromise as a product of gradual neutralization, that is, as a uniquely modern phenomenon, Weber found its typical expression in the semifeudal principles of the *Ständestaat*.[111] In a note attached to his theoretical discussion of *Ständestaat*, Weber warned that "[t]oday the theory of 'representation by occupational groups' is very much in vogue. The advocates of this proposal for the most part fail to see that even under these conditions *compromises* rather than majority decisions would be the only feasible means."[112] By contrast, the modern ideal of a democratic state was predicated on competition and conflict, leading ultimately to an exacting political decision cast by ballots. This kind of "democracy of numbers [*Zifferndemokratie*]"[113] could be most effectively preserved in parliamentary representation, as opposed to the functional representative scheme proposed by corporatism.

One critical precondition for the effective empowerment of the parliamentary system was for Weber a preservation of the voluntary character of societal organizations. It was because he consciously implicated the political rendering of exacting decisions, competition of numbers, and voluntary associations: "the essence of all politics . . . is *conflict, the recruitment of allies and a voluntary following*."[114] In other words, this contrast between compromise and decisionism stemmed from the different natures of the organizations that underpin the status or interest groups and voluntary political parties: "The ballot as a basis of final decision is characteristic of settling and expressing the compromise of

[110] The Crisis 14. Also see C. Schmitt, *Verfassungslehre* (Berlin: Dunker & Humboldt, 1928/1983) 234.

[111] Democracy 366–9/100–1.

[112] Economy and Society 162/276.

[113] Democracy 369–70/103.

[114] Parliament 481–3/173.

parties. It is not, however, characteristic of the occupational interest groups."[115]

Regarded as the "central phenomenon of all social organization,"[116] therefore, the political parties for Weber were voluntary associations par excellence; they were "essentially voluntarily created organizations directed at free *recruitment.*"[117] Voluntary associations are in essence based on the principles of free recruitment and free following, on which was also predicated the capacity of political parties "to determine policy through the *numbers* of their supporters." The similar voluntary principle also underpinned the modern capitalist economy, especially in its principle of (formally) free recruitment of labor. Both political and economic principles of voluntarism were in grave danger in the "attempt to compel them to unite on the model of an official department of state," which would put an end to their "inner life," that is, their voluntary basis.[118] The displacement of voluntary associations by bureaucratic agencies under state corporatism would eradicate the competition among political parties, which would contribute to the absence of political decisions. In this package of political decisionism, majoritarian rule, and voluntary associations lay Weber's principled opposition to corporatism, and the same reason underlay his rejection of the socialist utopia, as we saw in the previous section. Contra Schmitt, in short, Weber asserted a stake in heterogeneity.

In terms of political institutions, it was along this line that Weber proposed an elaborate scheme of institutionalized checks and balances for the postwar reconstruction. In fact, Weber's suggestion for the Weimar constitution consisted in a series of balances of power among various institutions in civil society and the state. For one, he wanted to strengthen presidential power and authority so that it could counterbalance the administrative bureaucracy and the fully empowered legislature.[119] In order to achieve the same balance, permanent and specialized

---

[115] Economy and Society 175/298.
[116] Ibid. 539/939.
[117] Parliament 454–5/149.
[118] Democracy 364–6/99.
[119] Reichspräsident 304–8. Mommsen argues that Weber's strong advocation of the plebiscitary presidency signifies a critical turn in an authoritarian direction in his political ideas. This reading is not entirely supported by the reasons for the advocation

subcommittees in parliament were to be empowered so as to compen-
sate for the bureaucratic command over technical expertise and administrative secrecy.[120] The plebiscitary president could in turn be checked
between elections only by the parliament, since it was to be equipped
with impeachment power.[121] Weber also advocated a federalist solution
to the uniquely German problem of regional particularism and Prussian
domination in the belief that relatively autonomous regional powers
could provide an effective antidote to the central state institutions.[122]

This series of counterbalancing mechanisms among the constitutional institutions was in the final analysis predicated on the robust
pluralism of civil society. For only a robust civil society can sustain
the elements of dynamism and even struggle both inside and outside
associational life. Thus, Weber was always interested in the manner in
which leadership is formed through competition inside voluntary associations, and what competition between associations, especially political parties, does to the individual members. Political parties, especially
ideological parties (*Weltanschauungsparteien*), were important to Weber
since they present a selection process for leaders under whose direction political parties in turn become a medium for group dynamism
in modern society.[123] In other words, the political leaders could be

he enumerated in an article published in March 1919. In this short article, "Reichspräsident," it is apparent that Weber's plebiscitary presidency is conceived more in
terms of an institutional balance of power vis-à-vis the Reichstag, the Bundesrat,
Prussia, and regional particularism than simply of a charismatic leadership.

[120] Parliament 487–9/178.

[121] Ibid. 471–4/165–6, 539–41/222.

[122] Weber also suggested a similar federal solution to the ethnic problem facing the
Russian Revolution of 1905 (Russia 54–63). Weber's attitude toward federalism
is, however, far from consistent. In the draft meeting for the Weimar constitution,
Weber clearly advocated a more federal approach in opposition to Hugo Preuss's
unitary solution to the Prussian problem. Although he later moved closer to Preuss's
position, it needs to be borne in mind that Weber's primary concern in conceding to
a more unitary solution was the destruction of the Prussian hegemony that served as
a conservative bastion in the Kaiserreich. For Weber on federalism, see Parliament
551–96/233–71. For various theoretical positions associated with the constitutional
question of German federalism and Prussian particularism, see R. Emerson, *State
and Sovereignty in Modern Germany* (New Haven, CT: Yale University Press, 1928)
92ff. For an analysis of Weber's position in the constitutional draft committee, especially regarding federalism, see G. Schulz, *Zwischen Demokratie und Diktatur, Vol. I:
Verfassungspolitik und Reichsreform in der Weimarer Republik* (Berlin: Walter de
Gruyter, 1987) 114–42.

[123] Sozialpolitik 447.

identified and gain training only from the bottom up – through intense struggle and competition within and among political parties rooted in the active associational life of the lay citizenry. In the form of the "battlefield of modern elections" among political parties, the political leaders would have to survive an intense process of checks and balances within civil society before they could be entrusted with controlling bureaucracy – the most urgent task, according to Weber, in sustaining a vibrant political society under modern circumstances. In contrast to state corporatism, which would homogenize civil society by subjugating it to the single monolith of bureaucratic structure, the parliamentary system Weber advocated would embed itself in and actively promote pluralism and competition within civil society. A vibrant civil society itself was expected by Weber to provide a sociocultural precondition to resisting state power.

Weber entertained no illusions, however. The novelty of his theory of bureaucracy depends little on suspicion of the societal petrification caused by the bureaucratized state – itself a judgment little different from a banal liberal vilification of the state. It resides rather in his recognition that also transformed by bureaucratization are the social and market organizations. Thus, the same phenomenon that could potentially empower political parties, that is, the modern electoral battle, also contributed to their bureaucratization.[124] Under this increasing convergence between the organizational modes of the state and civil society, Weber's liberal credentials seem all the more solid. For, while fully understanding the pervasive power of modern bureaucracy, Weber nonetheless endorsed a vigorous civil society to the extent that associational pluralism can arrest the social petrification brought about by a bureaucratic Leviathan.

Of course, the fate and character of economic life will be determined increasingly and irrevocably by this iron cage if the *opposition* between state bureaucracy and the bureaucracy of private capitalism is replaced by a system of bringing firms under "communal control" by a *unitary* bureaucracy to which the workers will be subordinated and which would no longer be counterbalanced by anything outside itself.[125]

---

[124] Parliament 449–52/146.
[125] Democracy 356–7/90.

In short, Weber's vision of postwar reformed Germany was filled with a guarded hope for competition and struggle among various voluntarily organized associations, economic interest groups, and political parties – all culminating in a national, democratically constituted parliament that would counterbalance administrative democracy (and, it should also be noted, the plebiscitary presidency) while giving decisive direction to the whole nation.

CONCLUSION: "THE SCHOOL OF MEN"

In his political writings, Weber consistently directed his harshest criticism of late modernity to the normalization of the tension and conflict that once sustained the dynamism of the earlier modernity. As a part of this larger project, he envisioned a pluralistically organized society, or what we would now call a civil society, in which competition and even struggle among various political and social voluntary associations are to be embedded. A voluntary associational life is to instill a habit of purposive action in its individual members. This requires a specific mode of associational life, which is at once pluralized, small-scale, egalitarian, selective, deliberative, and public – in short, a secularized version of Puritan sects. In his contemporary Germany, Weber believed that a nationalistic galvanization would facilitate the breaking of the social bondage imposed on Wilhelmine civil society by incorporating the industrial classes into the public sphere of participatory deliberation. Weber's political proposal postulates nationalism as a critical ally of a liberal reform agenda – a classical formula that once resonated in the Paulskirche during the Revolution of 1848. Standing on this unique juncture of philosophical anthropology, liberal institutional reform, and nationalist valorization are Weber's politics of civil society, which form an integral part of his larger critique of late modernity. And it is in this light that the following lament, which concludes one of Weber's swan songs, makes much sense:

[T]he fate of our age, with its characteristic rationalization, intellectualization, and above all disenchantment of the world, is that the ultimate, most sublime values have withdrawn from public life, either into the transcendental realm of mystical life or into the brotherhood of immediate personal relationships between individuals. It is no accident that our greatest art is intimate rather than monumental, nor is it fortuitous that today only in the smallest group, between individuals, something pulsates in pianissimo which corresponds to the prophetic pneuma which formerly swept through great communities like fire and welded them together.[126]

Evidently, and only few will disagree, to dichotomize liberalism and nationalism in theory and practice is a simplistic conceptual framework. In fact, liberalism during its earlier incarnation tended to advance along with nationalist causes as it did in many postcolonial nations of the twentieth century, especially when liberal principles are understood in terms of self-determination for both individuals and groups. Weber's liberal nationalism reminds us of this theoretical and historical elective affinity. Another lesson from Weber's liberal nationalism is that, contra recent well-known efforts to resuscitate liberal nationalism, national groups are first and foremost *political* in nature – not cultural groups and certainly not ethnic or linguistic ones.[127] This highly politicized understanding of national groups tends to highlight the individual member's self-determination when it comes to group affiliation and identity with more facility than a cultural understanding of liberal nationalism can. I believe that this theoretical link between individual self-determination, galvanization of political actions in civil society, and patriotism-cum-nationalism is worth a close look, especially at a time when nationalism is liberalized and sanitized through "depoliticization."

By contrast, Weber's *political* vision of civil society was to be organized by diverse voluntary associations constructed along class lines, which could provide a balance of power in opposition to the rapidly bureaucratizing state. Rather than an ultimate goal, nationalism was instrumental to this ideal, insofar as it contributed to maintaining the public spiritedness of the voluntary associations, thus preventing them from degenerating into sheer interest or status groups. In this political synthesis of liberal civil society and national patriotism, then, we find a concern that was dear to both Tocqueville and Mill. Seen in this light, Weber's formula for liberal nationalism may be vulnerable to a charge of anachronism – as its affinity with the *Vormärz* liberalism

---

[126] Science 22–3/30.
[127] On liberal nationalism, see Y. Tamir, *Liberal Nationalism* (Princeton, NJ: Princeton University Press, 1993) and R. McKim and J. McMahan (eds.), *The Morality of Nationalism* (Oxford: Oxford University Press, 1997).

widely shared among the German generation of 1848 seems evident.[128] Weber's dependence on nationalism may have been misguided in turn-of-the-century Europe, where nationalism no longer retained its traditional call for collective self-determination and basic political and civil rights of the individual citizens as its corollary, and instead gravitated steadily toward collective homogeneity and racial ideologies. For a political thinker, anachronism can be a charge as grave as any other. It remains undeniable, however, that Weber's liberal nationalism cannot be placed squarely in the authoritarian tradition of Wilhelmine nationalism. For, in the end, nation and civil society formed an integrated ideal in Weber's liberal nationalism, all for the purpose of empowering our agency and cultivating a self-governing individual-cum-citizen.

---

[128] Guenther Roth argues that Weber's fundamental value orientation was embedded in his cosmopolitan bourgeois family background, which is characterized by market globalism in economic outlook and "cosmopolitan nationalism" in political loyalty. Evidently, both sets of ideas were reflective of the bygone bourgeois era and were profoundly outdated by the turn of the century, when trade protectionism and ethnic nationalism were on the rise. See Guenther Roth's recent *Max Webers deutschen-englische Familiengeschichte 1800–1950* (Tübingen: J. C. B. Mohr/Paul Siebeck, 2001).

6

Max Weber's Politics of Civil Society

In our allegedly postmodern world, we see the ever-growing recognition of Max Weber as one of the first political and social thinkers whose main question centered on what is now called modernity. Weber's recent reputation seems to rest on two potent images by which he captured our (post)modern predicaments – the imminent iron cage of bureaucratic petrification and the Hellenistic polytheism of warring deities. This seemingly contradictory imagery of modernity in fact reflects different faces of the same coin. Whether the problem of modernity is accounted for in terms of a permeation of objective, instrumental rationality or of a purposeless agitation of subjective values, Weber viewed these two images as constituting a single problem insofar as they contributed to the inertia of modern individuals, who fail to take principled moral action. According to Weber, in other words, a modern individual tends to act only in accordance with his or her aesthetic impulse to express arbitrary convictions; the majority of those who cannot even act on their convictions lead the life of a "cog in a machine." This problem of modern individuals and the disempowerment of their agency have provided the central theme that runs through my reinterpretation of Weber's vast opus.

Once things were different, Weber claimed. An unflinching sense of conviction that relied on nothing but one's innermost personality once issued in a highly methodical and disciplined conduct of everyday life – or, simply, life as a duty. This type of self drew its strength solely from within in the sense that one's principle of action was determined by one's own psychological need to gain self-affirmation. Also, the way in which this deeply introspective subjectivity was materialized, that is, in self-mastery, involved a radically objective stance toward oneself and the outside world. Subjective value and objective rationality once formed an "unbroken unity." Weber called the agent of this unity the "person of vocation" (*Berufsmensch*) in his religious writings, "personality" (*Persönlichkeit*) in the methodological essays, and "charismatic individual" in *Economy and Society*.

Once different, too, was the mode of society constituted by and in turn constitutive of this type of agent. Weber's social imagination revealed its keenest sense of irony when he traced the root of the cohesive integration, intense socialization, and severe communal discipline of the sectlike society (*Sektengesellschaft*) in America to the isolated and introspective subjectivity of the Puritan *Berufsmensch*. The irony was that the anxiety-ridden, egotistical, depersonal, and even antisocial virtues of the *Berufsmensch* could be sustained only in the disciplinary environment of small-scale associational life. Membership in exclusive social associations is open, and it is such membership, or "achieved quality," that guarantees the ethical qualities of the individuals with whom one interacts. "The old 'sect spirit' holds sway with relentless effect in the intrinsic nature of such associations," Weber wrote, for the sect was the first mass organization to combine individual agency and social discipline in this way. It seems clear that what Weber was trying to outline here was an archetypal form of social organization that can empower free agency by sustaining group dynamism in a mass democratic society.

Within Weber's schema, nevertheless, this relatively coherent vision of the modern project generates a tension with his historicist understanding of modernity. Weber's problem with modern*ity* originates precisely from the fact that it required a historically unique constellation of cultural values, and yet modern*ization* has effectively undermined the normative basis for transcendental individualism and its attendant principle of disciplinary civil society, which together had given the original impetus to modernity. The modern project has fallen victim to its own success. With the evaporation of the transcendental dimension, the legitimacy of modern individualism has come to rely mostly on a utilitarian ethical justification, that of civil society, on a no less utilitarian logic of production and consumption. In Weber's view, this degeneration ushers in an extreme value pluralism and fragmentation in self-constitution, on the one hand, and a thorough bureaucratic petrification of society, on the other. Under the circumstances, Weber's question is: What remnants of earlier modernity can be salvaged and in what way? In short, the tension between modernity and modernization in Weber's social imagination prompts him to confront the Nietzschean reality with an essentially Kantian agenda.

It is important to recognize this coherent vision of modern self and pluralistic civil society and their subsequent degeneration, which Weber tried to capture with the theory of rationalization. Its importance is especially salient in understanding Weber's political ideas, since the two parts of this vision constituted a single image by which to assess the political, social, and cultural predicaments of his "late modern" age, propelling his sustained critique of them. It is true that Weber's political ideas were deeply embedded in the particular context of his time and place, yet Weber's critical distance from major discursive positions in Wilhelmine politics, both right and left, cannot be properly accounted for in isolation from his visions of modernity and modernization, which were conceived in universal terms. Thus, for example, Weber's ambivalence to realpolitik, as it was revered and glorified in his contemporary Germany, reflects his principled rejection of a practice of self that bred capricious vanity and unbridled opportunism among the bureaucracy; he was no less critical of the revolutionary syndicalism of the left, since he believed that it led merely to an expressionist and irresponsible agitation of subjective convictions. Weber's defiant nonpartisanship was predicated on his belief that these political practices of the right and left all reflected the "dissolution" of the inner unity of subjectivity and objectivity and their uncontrolled rampage. This dissolution also accounts for Weber's simultaneous critiques of state bureaucracy and the local associational life of Wilhelmine Germany. Weber's critical attitude to bureaucracy and suspicion of its moral glorification hardly needs further comment; more interesting is Weber's recognition, contra our contemporary Durkheimian-cum-Tocquevillean salutation to civil society, that the mere presence of "bowling clubs" does not suffice for the formation of liberal democratic citizenship. On the contrary, Weber saw that the mode of associational life prevalent in his contemporary

Germany actively contributed to the spread of passive citizenship that made the whole nation susceptible to authoritarian political rule. Not all civil society is normatively desirable; moreover, some forms of associational life are active accomplices in facilitating "passive democratization" by the bureaucracy. Hence Weber's simultaneous critique of civil society and bureaucracy as they existed in Germany.

As the Protestant ethic thesis stabilizes Weber's critical gaze, it also contributes to delineating Weber's prescription for the late modern world. In the face of the individual inertia and social petrifaction unleashed by value pluralism, Weber understood politics and science, albeit constituting incommensurable "spheres of values," as converging on a practice of self that issues in an empowerment strategy for the late modern agency. Herein lies the significance and peculiarity of Weber's ethical project. Despite his acute understanding of the conflict between ethical intentionalism and consequentialism, Weber still insisted that they be forcefully combined. In fact, resolving this analytical inconsistency in terms of certain ethical edicts does not seem to interest Weber much. For his ethical project is not about formal analysis of moral maxims, nor is it about substantive virtues that are reflective of some kind of ontic telos. It is too formal to be an Aristotelean virtue theory, and it is too concerned with a moral character to be a Kantian deontology. His aim is, rather, to cultivate a character that can bring together these conflicting virtues of conviction and responsibility in order to create what he called a "total personality" in which passion and reason are properly ordered by sheer force of individual volition. In this light, the virtue of Weber's *Berufsmensch* resides not simply in a subjective intensity of value commitment or in a detached intellectual integrity, but in their willful combination in a unified soul. This virtue Weber described as "maturity" in his last speeches on politics and science and as "charisma" in *The Protestant Ethic* and other religious writings.[1]

Thus understood, Weber's ethical project of charisma and maturity makes itself vulnerable to two kinds of critiques: antiliberal nihilism and antidemocratic elitism. On the one hand, Leo Strauss charges that Weber's ethic of responsibility is inconsistent and cannot be made

---

[1] For a useful discussion of Weber's concept of ethical personality and the virtue of maturity, see D. Owen, *Maturity and Modernity: Nietzsche, Weber, and Foucault and the Ambivalence of Reason* (London: Routledge, 1994).

compatible with that of conviction in the end. Given his nihilistic rejection of objectivity, Weber's ethical project culminates in an uncritical celebration of subjective value conviction as the only source of normativity, and the ethic of responsibility is at best only a disingenuous façade for Weber's dangerous moral decisionism. The bottomless irrationality that underpins the virtue of charisma is, according to Strauss, the main problem especially in Weber's leadership ideal. On the other hand, for Wolfgang Mommsen, Weber's leadership ideal itself is no less a problem than its irrational quality. For Weber's basic premise that the hierarchical relationship between the ruler and the ruled is an ineradicable essence of politics already harbors a dangerous authoritarianism. His emphasis on the irrational and accidental virtue of charisma as the leadership quality simply reinforces this wall between the ruler and the ruled, making the institutionalized participation of ordinary citizens all but inconceivable. From this perspective, Mommsen alleges, Weber's ideal of the charismatic politician is incapable of serving as a principled argument against the kind of authoritarian dictatorship that emerged with tragic consequences after his death – a *reductio ad Hitlerum* conclusion that Strauss also shares.

Strauss's critique, although persuasive in many respects, tends to exaggerate the problematic nature of Weber's ethical project. First, Strauss's charge of inconsistency between conviction and responsibility would hardly be new to Weber; Weber himself emphasized the "abysmal contrast" that separates the two. Rather, Weber thought it all the more important to insist that this *logical* inconsistency did not entail the *moral* claim that conviction and responsibility be separated. What Strauss tends to ignore is the fact that this inconsistency rarely undermines Weber's ethical project; on the contrary, such a tension only reinforces the urgency with which Weber emphasized the need to cultivate this willful personality he describes as mature and charismatic. Second, Strauss is overstating his case when it comes to Weber's alleged moral nihilism. His perspectivism does not assert that a rational, objective deliberation is impossible in and of itself; on the contrary, the charismatic personality is obliged to engage in a rational debate about various moral issues. This recognition follows from the fact that Weber's ethic of responsibility demands a constant self-examination, intellectual integrity, and an objective assessment of the issue, which cannot but compel us to engage in public intellectual deliberation. Weber's perspectivism merely maintains that a rational discussion between reasonable people does not necessarily yield a universal agreement on objective truth, and it is futile to predicate our public engagement on such an unwarranted optimism. Rational people, in other words, can have a *rational disagreement* about almost anything and everything when it comes to moral deliberations. This kind of Millian disagreement, however, does not immediately license irrationalism, relativism, nihilism, or even moral corruption, as Strauss seems to believe. Third, Strauss's critique makes better sense when it comes to Weber's admonishment that rational disagreement should not result in quietism, docility, and inaction in the public sphere. In order to avoid public inertia, we urgently need to take action with an unflinching sense of conviction, and, according to Weber, the virtue of charisma and maturity is necessary to empower our agency. Following Strauss, then, one may still ask on what rational ground one can have a conviction robust enough to act upon when rational disagreement is the norm, and this can be a legitimate critique. It is still an overstatement, nonetheless, to paint this principled action as something completely unfounded and irrational. After all, Weber found the most moving illustration of his ethical position in what Luther had to say at the Diet of Worms – "Here I stand; I can do no other." Note that Weber is as moved by the second clause as by the first – that is, "I can do no other" – and, if I may add, at the end of a long, arduous day.

In fact, I am also inclined to believe that Weber's ethical project falters in the end, although not for the reasons that Leo Strauss has suggested. It crumbles rather under its own weight, since it harbors a self-defeating project. The ultimate goal of Weber's ethical characterology is to (re)empower our agency under the iron cage circumstances, but in all likelihood it will culminate in its further disempowerment. For it demands something nearly impossible without clear persuasion but by resorting to an invocation of our mysterious will. It not only demands that we remain constantly alert to the abysmal contrast between conflicting ethical maxims, but also demands that we combine them, and combine them in a systematic way so as to create a total personality – all this by sheer force of will. In all likelihood, these demands will create a constantly agonizing moral agent who is highly unlikely to take immediate action at the end of a long, arduous day. In short, Weber's Nietzschean call for heroism is likely to end up in a Socratic agnosticism.[2] If Weber still demanded that these agonizing moral agents throw themselves into action, I think we would have to bring Strauss back in and be persuaded by his charge of dangerous nihilism. I suspect, though, that Weber would still be pleased to see these agonies, for although they discourage instant action, these constantly agonizing moral agents would not be content to live as cogs in a machine. At least, that is, they would not become the self-content "last men" for whom happiness was invented.

Even if charisma cannot be identified unambiguously with a diabolical irrationalism, however, Weber's ethical project is still vulnerable to the charge that it demands too much of us, the last men. It requires a constant self-examination and introspection, clear intellectual honesty and integrity, steadfast courage to act on our conviction, and an unflinching sense of responsibility for the outcome. It requires enormous willpower to withstand the tension between conflicting demands while striving to craft and maintain integrity between them. It demands, one might say, the virtue of a tragic hero, which is too rigorous an ethic for ordinary souls. Charisma is an antidemocratic, elitist virtue. Or is it necessarily so?

It is true that Weber's charisma makes rigorous ethical demands, and it assumes that, in theory, not all of us are capable of rising up to these calls. Charisma is hardly a democratic virtue. It needs to be borne in mind, however, that Weber carefully emphasized the sociocultural foundation for the rise of charismatic leadership and mature personality in general. It is, in fact, less a historical accident than Weber's formal definition of charisma might suggest. Weber saw localized, yet public, associational life as a breeding ground for the formation of charismatic individuals through competition and struggle. Contra Carl Schmitt's concept of the "sovereign," which is predicated on the substantial homogeneity of political society, then, charismatic leadership in Weber's political project requires a heterogeneous and pluralistic organization of civil society. Second, these charismatic qualities are not attributed exclusively to the leaders, and certainly not solely to a caesaristic dictator. When leaders are identified and trained at the level

---

[2] For a useful discussion of Weber's political thought and its complex relationship to Socratic agnosticism, see D. Villa, *Socratic Citizenship* (Princeton, NJ: Princeton University Press, 2001) 186–245.

of, say, neighborhood choral societies and bowling clubs, the alleged elitism comes across as more pluralistic in its conceptualization, far from its usual identification with demagogic dictatorship and unthinking mass following. As Weber held that a sectlike society functions as an effective medium for the horizontal diffusion of charismatic qualities among laypeople, his notion of charisma can retain a strongly democratic tone insofar as he also suggested social pluralism as an effective means of political mass education. Investigating Weber's vision of pluralist civil society, then, reveals the other side of his emphasis on charismatic leadership – namely, that it could function as an ideal for public citizenship rather than for an authoritarian elitism.

As Aron, Habermas, Marcuse, Mommsen, Strauss, and numerous others have contended, we can indeed find a common thematic thread that runs from Weber's earlier nationalism and methodological perspectivism through his postwar emphasis on charismatic leadership. Contrary to the antiliberal and antidemocratic reading of Weber, however, this common theme reveals Weber's preoccupation with ethical characterology and public citizenship in a modern mass democracy. It is in Weber's hitherto ignored vision of civil society that such a thematic thread surfaces unmistakably. And this thematic thread most clearly illustrates Weber's steadfast refusal to separate statecraft and soulcraft in modern times.

PURPOSE, CONTESTATION, AND THE POLITICAL

In order to deepen our understanding of the way in which Weber recoupled statecraft and soulcraft via his politics of civil society, I will take a slight detour now, comparing it with a contemporary theory of civil society – in particular, that of Michael Oakeshott. Oakeshott is chosen because he effectively highlights two main subtexts that have informed my interrogation of Weber so far – one problem pertaining to "liberal neutrality" and the other to "uncivil or bad civil society." That is to say, Oakeshott's ideal type of "civil association" contains an unflinching belief in the liberal principle of procedural neutrality and the formal rule of law. But his own formulation also discloses his recognition that liberal neutrality cannot be sustained without a substantive sociocultural context, as well as certain individual characters and virtues that can uphold and appreciate it. In its concern with the substantive foundation of a formal rule of law, it might be said that Oakeshott's project amounts to a communitarian defense of the liberal principle of neutrality.[3] This strategy, nevertheless, obviously entails a tension, since Oakeshott's belief in liberal neutrality prohibits him from explicitly endorsing the formative influence of civil society. This tension ushers in, as I will argue, a suppressed account of the formative aspects of civil associations that recommends an education in liberal virtues without overtly saying so. Once understood this way, Oakeshott's ideal types of civil association and "cives" reveal an interesting point of contrast, which illuminates how Weber's politics of civil society transcends both liberal and communitarian projects.

In opposition to an "enterprise association" (*universitas*), according to Oakeshott, a "civil association" (*societas*) is a universal organization in that it is capable of embracing heterogeneous types of self and smaller associations. Its universal character relies on Oakeshott's assertion that civil law does not interfere with the substantive purposes of individual actions. It is not only formal and procedural, but also neutral. Oakeshott likens civil law to a road map that supplies "how to" yet does not provide any "where to" knowledge. A road map or a system of roads is neutral with regard to the individual traveler's direction and destination. In this sense, the state in its civil mode can tolerate within its domain heterogeneous types of selves and associations. The only precondition is met when they assent to the procedural and formal prescriptions of civil law and moral practices (Oakeshott tends to identify the two). Once the characteristics of a civil association are transposed onto the state, the state becomes seen as a "*societas cum universitas*" that governs "*sine irae et studio*" – or, simply put, purposelessly.[4] Herein lies, according to Oakeshott, the critical difference between a civil association and a bureaucratic enterprise association.

Utterly devoid of any substantive purpose, however, an ideal typical bureaucracy also rules *sine irae et studio*, Weber says, which "is the specific nature of bureaucracy, and it is appraised as its special virtue."[5] For

---

[3] For Oakeshott in light of the liberal–communitarian debate, see P. Franco, *The Political Philosophy of Michael Oakeshott* (New Haven, CT: Yale University Press, 1990) 230–6.

[4] M. Oakeshott, *On Human Conduct* (Oxford: Oxford University Press, 1976) 201, 144.

[5] Economy and Society 563/215–16.

Weber, bureaucracy is incapable of articulating a substantive purpose, instead relying on a formal rule of procedure. Charles Larmore is right in his "praise of bureaucracy" when he criticizes Oakeshott for failing to understand bureaucracy as the institutional expression of liberal neutrality.[6] The irony is that Oakeshott's ideal type of civil association, which is conceived of as a critique of the petrifying effect of the modern welfare bureaucracy, is defined by features that Larmore – and Weber would certainly follow – sees as the essence of a bureaucratic rule: purposelessness and neutrality.

Weber shows a characteristic ambivalence toward bureaucratic rule especially with regard to its relationship to democracy. On the one hand, he understands that a precise formulation of a formal rule that can be applied universally and neutrally improves the predictability of governing, curtails the arbitrary exercise of political power, and thereby contributes to the empowerment of individual rights. On the other hand, he recognizes that formal neutrality is a highly elusive ideal and that, even if achieved, its purposelessness has a detrimental effect on genuine democracy. Weber, in short, can be no less critical of bureaucratic associations than Oakeshott, yet for altogether opposite reasons.

In part a subtle criticism of Hegel's glorification of bureaucracy as the sole representative of universal interest, Weber's point is that bureaucracy has a tendency to form a status group of its own, in fact striving to establish itself as the only ruling caste over other classes, and its seemingly neutral rule is motivated by a partial class interest thinly disguised as a universal interest.[7] Besides the empirical criticism, however, Weber also maintains that the universal, formal, purposeless neutrality of bureaucracy, even if achieved, will contribute directly to the leveling of the whole political society, ushering in a merely passive democratization.[8] The critical problem Weber sees is that, "in contrast to the democratic self-government of small homogeneous units,"[9] passive democratization will turn the governed into, at

---

[6] C. Larmore, *Patterns of Moral Complexity* (Cambridge: Cambridge University Press, 1987) 40–1.

[7] Biography 420–3/415–18; Parliament 500–2/190.

[8] Economy and Society 569/985–6.

[9] Ibid. 567/983.

best, passive beneficiaries and subjects of bureaucratic rule. This has a detrimental impact on the substantive contents of individual characters and identities; thus, he says, "the bureaucratization of all domination very strongly furthers the development of . . . the personality type of the technical expert [*Fachmenschentum*]."[10] Weber holds that, insofar as responsiveness and accountability to public opinion are concerned, bureaucracy can be made democratic, thus satisfying the procedural requirements for democracy. The problem is that, as a result of bureaucratic rule, public opinion itself has degenerated into merely "communal action [*Gemeinschaftshandeln*] born of irrational sentiments."[11] Contrary self-claims notwithstanding, the purposelessness of passive democracy and bureaucratic rule has been transformed into a purpose itself that justifies the imposition of a specific kind of identity for its citizens at the expense of other identities. A genuine democracy, as opposed to a procedural and passive democracy, becomes a question of the nature of public citizenship and ethical characters for Weber.

Oakeshott's formulation of liberal neutrality can be a good example of Weber's second critique, for it tends to conflict with the new identity of cives imposed on the allegedly heterogeneous selves who constitute a civil association. On the one hand, Oakeshott describes this new identity as a "persona" – a sort of public mask one wears as an associate.[12] By implication, it can be adopted by different types of selves regardless of their substantive dispositions and faculties. On the other hand, cives is only a different name for those whom Oakeshott called in various contexts simply "individual" or "religious man" – that is, a "free agent"[13] who realizes that, by submitting to the procedural prescriptions of moral traditions, customs, and practices only, one can gain the freedom of choosing a substantive purpose.[14] This type of self presupposes a particular set of substantive values that sharply distinguishes it from other types, most notably what he variously called "individual manqué," "anti-individual," or "mass man," that are in

[10] Ibid. 576/998.
[11] Ibid. 566/980.
[12] Oakeshott (1976) 196–7.
[13] Ibid. 112.
[14] M. Oakeshott, "Religion and the World," in his *Religion, Politics, and the Moral Life*, ed. T. Fuller (New Haven, CT: Yale University Press, 1993) 28–30, 33.

need of transformative education. It takes some sort of homogeneity with "a man like me,"[15] according to Oakeshott, for a civil association to be able to sustain itself. Oakeshott's ideal type of civil association is, then, inclusive and exclusive, heterogeneous and homogeneous, or, in his own words, universal and compulsory, all at once.[16]

One way to make sense of Oakeshott's assertion that a civil association is inclusive and exclusive at once seems to be that it provides an educational ground for free agents. Although freedom is intrinsic to human conduct, according to Oakeshott, its exercise is an art, not nature, something to be educated and learned.[17] However, he does not identify this kind of moral education simply as an indoctrination of moral rules and maxims. Learning "technical knowledge" does not exhaust the contents of moral education; it is rather an elusive remainder of the technical learning that prompts individuals to reflect, choose, and act morally and autonomously. It is only in the context of associational life, through "continuous corrective analyses and criticisms" in everyday life,[18] that individuals receive moral education that cannot be exhausted by learning rules. One cannot learn to be a free agent unless one is part of an appropriate moral and customary fabric of an intimate associational life. Civil association is inclusive in that it can embrace heterogeneity; yet it is exclusive in that it purports to generate homogeneity as cives. The universal identity of cives is predicated on the compulsory moral education of heterogeneous selves. Despite the claim of neutrality, as Weber would have insisted, it is not clear that Oakeshott's civil association is not concerned with what can be called a "Platonic politics of the soul"; it simply aims at, one might say, a laissez-faire politics of the soul.

In Oakeshott's formulation of liberal neutrality and its intrinsic tension, in fact, what he chose not to give explicit consideration to is more instructive – that is, what happens to those who refuse to subscribe to this homogeneous identity qua cives? The type of self who fails to live by this "unsought freedom" Oakeshott calls "the poor," who are

---

[15] Oakeshott (1976) 129.
[16] Ibid. 148–51.
[17] M. Oakeshott, *Rationalism in Politics and Other Essays* (Indianapolis: Liberty Press, 1991) 466.
[18] Ibid. 474.

blamed for the emergence of the collectivist "enterprise association" in modern political society.[19] In more urgent need of education and self-transformation into cives are, however, those whom Oakeshott calls the "moral eclectic." The moral eclectic is a moral perfectionist who refuses to accept the customary ethics and claims a knowledge of non-contingent truth; moreover, he or she is a political activist who attempts to change this world according to his or her truth. The moral eclectic is a Platonic seer who has gone out of the cave and seen the light, only to come back to enlighten the cavemen.[20] In making a claim for an unmitigated contact with an otherworldly source of meaning, the moral eclectic exhibits "charisma," a personal quality that poses the most potent threat to what Weber calls "routine" or what Oakeshott calls "moral practice." This is why, in Oakeshott's cave, the charismatic figure is respected, revered, yet in the end ostracized. The moral eclectic's charisma needs to be confined to a purely private sphere; a Freudian sublimation is welcome, yet once spread out into the public sphere, charisma would be treated like an epidemic to be quelled.[21] Charisma has to be subdued and converted into customs – in short, "routinized."[22] In sum, for Oakeshott, the danger to civil association, and by extension to individual freedom, lies in the liberation of charisma from its routine confines.

To Oakeshott, hence, Luther's famous declaration at Worms – "Here I stand; I can do no other" – foreshadows the subsequent tragedies of modern history. For this episode marks the advent of the assertive subjective will that is held responsible for the erosion of the moral fabric of civil society in which individual freedom is embedded. The moral attitude represented by Luther, according to Oakeshott, led only to "fanaticism" and "follies."[23] For Weber as well, Luther's declaration signals a historical watershed, yet for a categorically opposite reason – it movingly illustrates the essence of modern individual freedom.[24]

The contrast could not be clearer. Both projects are predicated on a principled criticism of modern bureaucratic rule, seeking an alternative

[19] Oakeshott (1976) 236, 303.
[20] Ibid. 27–31.
[21] Oakeshott (1991) 472.
[22] Ibid. 485.
[23] Oakeshott (1976) 238.
[24] Politics 248–50/367.

foundation of modern liberal politics in a pluralistically organized civil society. Contra Oakeshott's civil associations, however, the goal of Weber's politics of civil society is precisely to cultivate a moral eclectic, or a charismatic agent, who can take a defiant moral action. This charismatic agent is constantly empowered and disciplined in an associational life in which the sense of collective purpose is sharply enumerated and voluntarily shared among the members. Thus, Weber characterizes sectlike society as culminating in the social mechanism Oakeshott denounces as *"domestica disciplina."*[25] In terms of its emphasis on purpose and discipline, in short, Weber's sectlike society is an "enterprise association" in Oakeshott's terms.[26]

Furthermore, in contrast to Oakeshott's postulation of civil society as a site in which tacit customs and moral practices are preserved and educated, Weber posits a mutually reinforcing relationship between the purposeful and disciplinary nature of sectlike civil society and open contestation, competition, struggle, and even conflict – in short, the political. In opposition to bureaucratic formal neutrality, Weber tried to combine the political, conflict, and voluntary associations. Political contestation depends on the mobilization of voluntary associations; in turn, voluntary associational activities become more robust when the associates take part in political contestations, for this strengthens the locus of identity, sense of common purpose, and individual discipline. Herein lies Weber's other affinity with Carl Schmitt's theory of the political, yet the difference is once again apparent. For Weber's emphasis on the exclusive nature of associational life and the consequent discipline, purpose, and contestation ushers in a robust pluralism and heterogeneity within a civil society, whereas Schmitt's preoccupation with the friend–enemy distinction is meant to generate a social homogeneity in the name of democracy. At this juncture of ethical characterology, activist citizenship, political contestation, and voluntary associational life stands Weber's unique politics of civil society.

In sum, Weber's politics of civil society is to preserve and amplify the element of the political, a goal that enables him to negatively substantiate what he regards as a bad civil society. From this perspective, both the

---

[25] Oakeshott (1976) 284.
[26] In agreement is C. Turner, *Modernity and Politics in the Work of Max Weber* (London: Routledge, 1992) 151–3.

liberal principle of formal and procedural neutrality and associational life conceived one-sidedly in terms of customs and traditions can be active accomplices in the expansion and penetration of bureaucracy into everyday life, contributing to the formation of a passive, complacent, conformist, and even docile citizenry. What is necessary, in Weber's view, is instead a highly alert citizenry that is ready to take principled and defiant public action, and such character traits can be bred only in a small-scale associational life that emphasizes purpose and discipline through various means of membership selection and sanctions. In contrast to the liberal-juridical and communitarian-social models of civil society, one might say, Weber proposed a political model by which he strove to imbue the late modern iron cage once again with vibrancy, enterprise, movement, and dynamism.[27]

BOWLING ALONE

It is an irony of history that, precisely at the moment when the triumph of civil society is loudly proclaimed in many parts of the world, civil society in America, one of its traditional seedbeds, is allegedly in decline. Implicit in this allegation is the more profound and troubling question of whether a liberal democratic regime can sustain itself on its own terms. Identifying the orthodox liberal demarcation of statecraft and soulcraft as the source of the problem, an increasing number of theorists are turning to civil society as a site in which certain kinds of moral personality and civic virtues conducive to liberal democracy are cultivated. Weber's larger reflections on modernity can also be understood as driven by the similarly agonizing question of its sustainability, especially after it has successfully undermined its own normative foundation in the course of rationalization and secularization. Prominent in this troubling tension between modernity and modernization for Weber was the problem of the disempowerment of the modern agency.

In this light, both the neo-Tocquevillean and Weberian projects can be said to share the recognition that liberal democracy cannot be

---

[27] For a contemporary articulation of the political model of civil society, as opposed to the liberal-juridical and communitarian-social models, see C. Mouffe, *The Return of the Political* (London: Verso, 1993) 60–73, although I disagree with her interpretations of Oakeshott and Schmitt in this connection.

sustained in a robust form without a unique sociocultural environment that can cultivate certain kinds of individual virtues. Seen this way, both projects criticize the orthodox doctrine of liberal neutrality that requires citizens to leave behind their private identities before entering the public sphere of rational debate and collective deliberation, strictly prohibiting politics from intervening in the moral and civic education of its citizens. It is on this broadly communitarian and/or civic republican criticism of liberal neutrality that the Weberian and neo-Tocquevillean politics of civil society converge. This similarity, however, cannot be entertained long, and it is in the different degrees of sensitivity to the contents of civil society and individual characters that they diverge. Especially compared to those whom Peter Berkowitz calls the "right-Tocquevilleans," Weber appears more alert to the possibility of bad civil society.[28] To this naive emphasis on the simple presence of spontaneous voluntarism Amy Gutman responds with a question, and Weber would certainly follow: "Should we be horrified about the decrease in associational activity in America, if it has in fact taken place? We cannot assume that the more secondary associations that exist, the better off liberal democracy will be. More of civic importance probably depends on the nature of associations in America than on their numbers."[29] Not all forms of civil society are conducive to the vitality of liberal democratic polity; some might in fact be detrimental to it.

Even when the "nature of associations" is enumerated, those characteristics appear radically different from Weber's project. For Weber, on the one hand, the most critical issue in revitalizing a civil society is to preserve and magnify the elements of contestation under late modern circumstances. Modern individuals need to engage in various associational activities so that they can challenge and compete with each other in a concrete, everyday context in which they will be constantly required to define, redefine, and choose their ultimate values and to take disciplined moral actions based on their choices. For Weber's politics of civil society, in short, the critical issue is to "deepen" the innermost core of the modern self. To "broaden" the self, on the other hand, or

---

[28] P. Berkowitz, *Virtues and the Making of Modern Liberalism* (Princeton, NJ: Princeton University Press, 1999) 187.

[29] A. Gutman (ed.), *Freedom of Association* (Princeton, NJ: Princeton University Press, 1998) 31.

to develop "the I into the We" seems to define some projects especially of right-Tocquevillean persuasion.[30] In this view, a desirable form of associational life is frequently imagined in terms of communal congeniality and group solidarity: the civic virtues, in terms of sociability, civility, cooperation, and trust. In the face of the alleged anomie and disorderliness, then, the issue becomes the recovery of this kind of solidarity through a pluralistic associational life, which as an unintended consequence is expected to engender a more engaged public citizenry and a robust liberal democracy. The difference, in short, lies in the primary function that is assigned to modern civil society – that is, between the cultivation of defiant individual autonomy in Weber's civil society and the recovery of individual sociability and the enhancement of social solidarity in the right-Tocquevillean civil society. Weber's politics of civil society in the end cannot accept a simple celebration of associational life for its own sake.

Sheldon Wolin recently warned that "in the age of vast concentrations of corporate and governmental power, the desperate problem of democracy is not to develop better ways of cooperation, but to develop a fairer system of contestation over time, especially hard times."[31] Weber would wholeheartedly agree, and would add that the question is not only about the "system," but more critically about the proliferation of autonomous and disciplined agents who readily rise up to join "contestations." It is the pluralistically organized civil society Weber called sectlike society that is expected to cultivate these moral dispositions and civic virtues. If our "revivified" civil society, however, can breed only communal congeniality and fuzzy neighborliness, Weber might even say – let people "bowl alone." For, in the absence of better alternatives, ironically, defiantly resisting purposeless group pressure can sometimes be a more visible hallmark of sect man.

---

[30] R. Putnam, "Bowling Alone: America's Declining Social Capital," *Journal of Democracy* 6:1 (1995) 67.

[31] S. Wolin, "The Liberal/Democratic Divide: On Rawls's Political Liberalism," *Political Theory* 24:1 (1996) 115.

References

Max Weber's Works

Italicized titles of Weber's works indicate the abbreviated titles I used in the footnotes and the original year of publication. Page numbers in the footnotes are to the German texts followed by the English editions – for example, Protestant Ethic 116/118–19. Even when the *Studienausgabe* (SA) of *Max Weber Gesamtausgabe* (MWG) was used, I still referred to the original page numbers in the MWG edition that are noted on the margin of the SA.

Freiburg (1895)

"Der Nationalstaat und die Volkswirtschaftspolitik" in MWG I/4-2, 535–74: "The Nation State and Economic Policy (Freiburg Inaugural Lecture)" in *Weber: Political Writings*, ed. and trans. P. Lassman and R. Speirs (Cambridge: Cambridge University Press, 1994) 1–28.

Roscher and Knies (1903–6)

"Roscher und Knies und die logischen Probleme der historischen Nationalökonomie" in *Gesammelte Aufsätze zur Wissenschaftslehre* (GAWL), ed. J. Winckelmann (Tübingen: J. C. B. Mohr/Paul Siebeck, 1985) 1–145: *Roscher and Knies: The Logical Problems of Historical Economics* (New York: Free Press, 1975).

Objectivity (1904)

"Die 'Objektivität' sozialwissenschaftlicher und sozialpolitischer Erkenntnis" in GAWL, 146–214: "Objectivity in Social Science and Social Policy" in *The Methodology of the Social Sciences*, ed./trans. E. A. Shils and H. A. Finch (New York: Free Press, 1949) 50–112.

Nordamerika (1906)

"'Kirchen' und 'Sekten' in Nordamerika: Eine kirchen- und sozialpolitische Skizze," *Die christliche Welt* 20 (1906) 558–62/577–83: "'Churches' and 'Sects' in North America: An Ecclesiastical Sociopolitical Sketch," trans. C. Loader/intro. C. Loader and J. Alexander, *Sociological Theory* 3:1 (1985) 1–13.

Russia (1906)

"Zur Lage der bürgerlichen Demokratie in Rußland" in MWG I/10, 71–280: "Bourgeois Democracy in Russia" in *Max Weber: The Russian Revolutions*, ed./trans. G. C. Wells and P. Baehr (Ithaca, NY: Cornell University Press, 1995) 41–147.

Zeitungswesen (1909)

Nachlaß Tönnies, Schleswig – Holsteinische Landesbibliothek, Kiel: "Preliminary Report on a Proposed Survey for a Sociology of the Press," trans. K. Tribe, *History of the Human Sciences* 11:2 (1998) 111–20.

Schlußwort (1910)

"Antikritisches Schlußwort zum Geist des Kapitalismus" in *Max Weber: Die protestantische Ethik II – Kritiken und Antikritiken*, ed. J. Winckelmann (Gerd Mohn: Gütersloher Verlagshaus, 1978) 283–345.

Vereinswesen (1910)

"Rede auf dem ersten Deutschen Soziologentage in Frankfurt" in Sozialpolitik, 41–9: "Voluntary Associational Life (*Vereinswesen*)," ed./trans. Sung Ho Kim, *Max Weber Studies* 2:2 (2002) 199–209.

World Religions (1913)

"Die Wirtschaftsethik der Weltreligionen: Einleitung" in *Gesammelte Aufsätze zur Religionssoziologie* (GARS), three volumes (Tübingen: J. C. B. Mohr/Paul

Siebeck, 1920–1), vol. 1, 237–75: "The Social Psychology of the World
Religions" in *From Max Weber*, 267–301.

China (1915–16)

"Konfuzianismus und Taoismus" in GARS, vol. 1, 276–536: *The Religion of
China: Confucianism and Taoism*, trans. H. H. Gerth and intro. C. K. Yang
(New York: Free Press, 1968).

Rejections (1915–16)

"Zwischenbetrachtung: Theorie der Stufen und Richtungen religiöser Weltan-
blehnung" in GARS, vol. 1, 536–73: "Religious Rejections of the World and
Their Directions" in *From Max Weber*, 326–59.

Democracy (1917)

"Wahlrecht und Demokratie in Deutschland" in MWG (SA) I/15, 344–96:
"Suffrage and Democracy in Germany" in *Max Weber: Political Writings*,
80–129.

Neutrality (1917)

"Der Sinn der Wertfreiheit der soziologischen und ökonomischen Wis-
senschaften" in GAWL, 489–540: "The Meaning of 'Ethical Neutrality' in
Sociology and Economics" in *Methodology*, 1–49.

Parliament (1918)

"Parlament und Regierung im neugeordneten Deutschland" in MWG (SA)
I/15, 421–596: "Parliament and Government in Germany Under a New Political Order" in *Max Weber: Political Writings*, 130–271.

Science (1917–19)

"Wissenschaft als Beruf" in MWG (SA) I/17, 49–112: "Science as a Vocation,"
trans. M. John in *Max Weber's "Science as a Vocation,"* ed. P. Lassman and I.
Velody (London: Allen & Unwin, 1989) 3–31.

Politics (1919)

"Politik als Beruf" in MWG (SA) I/17, 113–252: "The Profession and Vocation
of Politics" in *Max Weber: Political Writings*, 309–69.

Protestant Ethic (1904–5/1920)

"Vorbemerkung" and "Die protestantische Ethik und der Geist des Kapitalismus" in *Max Weber: Die protestantische Ethik I: Eine Aufsatzsammlung*,
ed. J. von Winckelmann (Gütersloh: Gütersloher Verlagshaus, 2000) 9–277:
The Protestant Ethic and the Spirit of Capitalism, trans. T. Parsons/intro. A.
Giddens (London: Routledge, 1992).

Protestant Sects (1920)

"Die protestantischen Sekten und der Geist des Kapitalismus" in GARS, vol.
1, 207–36: "The Protestant Sects and the Spirit of Capitalism" in *From Max
Weber: Essays in Sociology*, ed./trans./intro. H. H. Gerth and C. Wright Mills
(Oxford: Oxford University Press, 1946) 302–22.

Economy and Society (1921–2)

Wirtschaft und Gesellschaft: Grundriss der verstehenden Soziologie, ed. J. Winckelmann (Tübingen: J. C. B. Mohr/Paul Siebeck, 1972): *Economy and Society*,
two volumes, ed. G. Roth and C. Wittich (Berkeley: University of California
Press, 1978).

Sozialpolitik (1924)

Gesammelte Aufsätze zur Soziologie und Sozialpolitik, ed. Marianne Weber
(Tübingen: J. C. B. Mohr/Paul Siebeck, 1924).

Biography (1926)

Max Weber: Ein Lebensbild (Tübingen: J. C. B. Mohr/Paul Siebeck, 1926): Marianne Weber, *Max Weber: A Biography*, trans. H. Zohn/intro. G. Roth (New
Brunswick, NJ: Transaction, 1988).

MWG (1981–)

Max Weber Gesamtausgabe, ed. H. Baier, M. R. Repsius, W. J. Mommsen, W.
Schluchter, and J. von Winckelmann (Tübingen: J. C. B. Mohr/Paul Siebeck,
1981–).

Other Works

Albrow, Martin. *Bureaucracy* (New York: Praeger, 1970).
Alexander, Jeffrey. *Theoretical Logic in Sociology, Vol. III – The Classical Attempt
at Theoretical Synthesis: Max Weber* (Berkeley: University of California
Press, 1983).

Structure and Meaning: Rethinking Classical Sociology (New York: Columbia University Press, 1989).

Allison, Henry. *Kant's Theory of Freedom* (Cambridge: Cambridge University Press, 1991).

Alter, Peter. *Nationalism* (London: Edward Arnold, 1989).

Arblaster, Anthony. *The Rise and Fall of Western Liberalism* (Cambridge: Cambridge University Press, 1984).

Arnold, Matthew. *Culture and Anarchy and Other Writings*, ed. S. Collini (Cambridge: Cambridge University Press, 1993).

Aron, Raymond. *Main Currents of Sociological Thought, Volume II: Durkheim, Pareto, Weber* (Baltimore: Penguin Books, 1970).

"Max Weber and Power-Politics," in O. Stammer (ed.), *Max Weber and Sociology Today* (Oxford: Oxford University Press, 1971).

Baehr, Peter. "An 'Ancient Sense of Politics'?: Weber, Caesarism, and the Republican Tradition," *European Journal of Sociology* 60:2 (1999) 333–50.

"The 'Iron Cage' and the 'Shell as Hard as Steel': Parsons, Weber, and the *stahlhardes Gehäuse* Metaphor in *The Protestant Ethic and the Spirit of Capitalism*," *History and Theory* 40:2 (2001) 153–69.

Baehr, Peter and Wells, Gordon (eds./trans.). *The Protestant Ethic and the "Spirit" of Capitalism and Other Writings* (New York: Penguin, 2002).

Barber, Benjamin. "The Discourse of Civility" in Elkin and Soltan (1992).

Baumgarten, Eduard (ed.). *Max Weber: Werk und Person* (Tübingen: J. C. B. Mohr/Paul Siebeck, 1964).

Beetham, David. *Max Weber and the Theory of Modern Politics* (London: Allen & Unwin, 1974).

"From Socialism to Fascism: The Relation between Theory and Practice in the Works of Michels," *Political Studies* 25:1 (1977) 3–24.

"Max Weber and the Liberal Political Tradition," *European Journal of Sociology* 30 (1989) 313–23.

Bellamy, Richard (ed.). *Victorian Liberalism: Nineteenth Century Political Thought and Practice* (London: Routledge, 1990).

Bendix, Reinhard. *Max Weber: An Intellectual Portrait* (New York: Doubleday, 1960).

Berger, Stephen. "The Sects and the Breakthrough into the Modern World: On the Centrality of the Sects in Weber's Protestant Ethic Thesis," *Sociological Quarterly* 12 (Autumn 1971), 486–99.

Berkowitz, Peter. *Virtues and the Making of Modern Liberalism* (Princeton, NJ: Princeton University Press, 1999).

Berman, Marshal. *All That Is Solid Melts into Air: The Experience of Modernity* (New York: Penguin, 1982).

Berman, Sheri. "Civil Society and the Collapse of the Weimar Republic," *World Politics* 49:3 (1997) 401–29.

Blum, Fred. "Max Weber: The Man of Politics and the Man Dedicated to Objectivity and Rationality," *Ethics* 70:1 (1959) 1–20.

Blumenberg, Hans. *The Legitimacy of the Modern Age*, trans. R. Wallace (Cambridge, MA: MIT Press, 1991).

Bowen, Richard. *German Theories of the Corporative State: With Special Reference to the Period 1870–1919* (New York: Russell & Russell, 1949).

Breiner, Peter. *Max Weber and Democratic Politics* (Ithaca, NY: Cornell University Press, 1997).

Broch, Herman. *Hugo von Hoffmanstahl and His Time: The European Imagination, 1860–1920* (Chicago: University of Chicago Press, 1984).

Brubaker, Roger. *The Limits of Rationality: An Essay on the Social and Moral Thought of Max Weber* (London: Allen & Unwin, 1984).

 Citizenship and Nationhood in France and Germany (Cambridge, MA: Harvard University Press, 1992).

Bruch, Rüdiger vom. "The Academic Disciplines and Social Thought," in R. Chickering (ed.), *Imperial Germany: A Historiographical Companion* (London: Greenwood, 1996).

Brunner, Otto, Conze, Werner, and Koselleck, Reinhart (eds.), *Geschichtliche Grundbegriffe: Historische Lexicon zur politische – sozialen Sprache in Deutschland* (Stuttgart: Ernst Klett Verlag, 1972).

Bryant, Christopher. "Civic Nation, Civil Society, Civil Religion," in J. A. Hall (ed.), *Civil Society: Theory, History, Comparison* (Cambridge: Polity Press, 1995).

Bryant, Christopher. "Social Self-Organization, Civility, and Sociology: A Comment on Kumar's 'Civil Society'," *British Journal of Sociology* 44:3 (1993) 397–401.

Burrow, John Wyon. *A Liberal Descent: Victorian Historians and the English Past* (Cambridge: Cambridge University Press, 1983).

Cahnman, Werner. *Weber and Tönnies: Comparative Sociology in Historical Perspective* (New Brunswick, NJ: Transaction, 1995).

Chalcraft, David. "Bringing the Text Back In," in L. J. Ray and M. Reed (eds.), *Organizing Modernity: New Weberian Perspective on Works, Organization, and Society* (London: Routledge, 1994).

Chambers, Simone and Kopstein, Jeffrey. "Bad Civil Society," *Political Theory* 29:6 (2001) 837–65.

Chapman, Mark D. "Polytheism and Personality: Aspects of the Intellectual Relationship between Weber and Troeltsch," *History of the Human Sciences* 6:2 (1993) 1–33.

Cohen, Jean and Arato, Andrew. *Civil Society and Political Theory* (Cambridge, MA: MIT Press, 1992).

Constant, Benjamin. *Political Writings*, ed./trans. B. Fontana (Cambridge: Cambridge University Press, 1988).

Coser, Lewis. *Masters of Sociological Thought* (New York: Harcourt Brace Jovanovich, 1971).

Culler, Jonathan. *Ferdinand de Saussure* (Ithaca, NY: Cornell University Press, 1986).

Dagger, Richard. *Civic Virtues: Rights, Citizenship, and Republican Liberalism* (Oxford: Oxford University Press, 1997).

Dahlmann, Dittmar. "Max Weber's Relation to Anarchism and Anarchist: The Case of Ernst Toller," in Mommsen and Osterhammel (1987).

Dahrendorf, Ralph. *Society and Democracy in Germany* (Garden City, NY: Doubleday, 1967).

Demm, Eberhard. "Max and Alfred Weber in the *Verein für Sozialpolitik*," in Mommsen and Osterhammel (1987).

Dibble, Vernon K. "Social Science and Political Commitments in the Young Max Weber," *European Journal of Sociology* 9:1 (1968) 92–110.

Diggins, John Patrick. *The Promise of Pragmatism: Modernism and the Crisis of Knowledge and Authority* (Chicago: University of Chicago Press, 1994).

Max Weber: The Politics and Spirit of Tragedy (New York: Basic Books, 1996).

Donne, John. *Selected Poems* (New York: St. Martin's, 1993).

Dostoevsky, Feodor. *Crime and Punishment* (New York: Literary Guild of America, 1953).

Dumont, Louis. *Homo Hierarchicus: The Caste System and Its Implications* (Chicago: University of Chicago Press, 1970).

"A Modified View of Our Origins: The Christian Beginnings of Modern Individualism," *Religion* 12:1 (1982) 1–27.

Eden, Robert. *Political Leadership and Nihilism: A Study of Weber and Nietzsche* (Philadelphia: Temple University Press, 1983).

Eisen, Arnold. "Called to Order: The Role of the Puritan *Berufsmensch* in Weberian Sociology," *Sociology* 13:2 (1979) 203–18.

Eisenstadt, Shmuel. "Transcendental Visions, Otherworldliness and Its Transformation: Some More Comments on L. Dumont," *Religion* 13:1 (1983) 1–17.

"Comparative Liminaity, Liminality and the Dynamics of Civilizations," *Religion* 15:3 (1985) 315–38.

Eksteins, Modris. *Rites of Spring: The Great War and the Birth of the Modern Age* (London: Bantam, 1989).

Eley, Geoff. "Liberalism, Europe and the Bourgeoisie, 1860–1914," in D. Blackbourne and R. Evans (eds.), *The German Bourgeoisie: Essays on the Social History of the German Middle Class from the Late Eighteenth to the Early Twentieth Century* (London: Routlege, 1991).

"Nations, Publics and Political Cultures: Placing Habermas in the Nineteenth Century," in C. Calhoun (ed.), *Habermas and the Public Sphere* (Cambridge, MA: MIT Press, 1993).

Eley, Geoff and Blackbourn, David. *The Peculiarities of German History* (Oxford: Oxford University Press, 1984).

Elkin, Stephen and Soltan, Karol (eds.). *Citizen Competence and Democratic Institutions* (Philadelphia: Penn State University Press, 1999).

Elshtain, Jean Bethke. *Democracy on Trial* (New York: Basic Books, 1995).

Emerson, Rupert. *State and Sovereignty in Modern Germany* (New Haven, CT: Yale University Press, 1928).

Evans, Richard. *Rethinking German History: Nineteenth-Century Germany and the Origins of the Third Reich* (London: Allen & Unwin, 1987).

Factor, Regis and Turner, Stephen. "Weber, the Germans, and 'Anglo-Saxon Convention': Liberalism as Technique and Form of Life," in R. Glassman and V. Murvar (eds.), *Max Weber's Political Sociology: A Pessimistic Vision of a Rationalized World* (Westport, CT: Greenwood, 1984).

Ferguson, Adam. *An Essay on the History of Civil Society*, ed. F. Oz-Salzberger (Cambridge: Cambridge University Press, 1995).

Fleischman, Eugène. "De Weber à la Nietzsche," *European Journal of Sociology* 5 (1964) 190–238.

Franco, Paul. *The Political Philosophy of Michael Oakeshott* (New Haven, CT: Yale University Press, 1990).

Freund, Julien. *The Sociology of Max Weber* (New York: Vintage, 1969).

Frommer, J. and Frommer, S. "Max Webers Krankheit: Recherchen zur Krankheits – und Behandlungsgeschichte um die Jahrhundertwende," *Fortschritte der Neurologie, Psychiatrie*, 66:5 (1998) 193–200.

Galston, William. *Liberal Purposes: Goods, Virtues, and Diversity in the Liberal State* (Cambridge: Cambridge University Press, 1991).

"Political Economy and the Politics of Virtue: U.S. Public Philosophy at Century's End," in A. L. Allen and M. C. Regan, Jr. (eds.), *Debating Democracy's Discontents: Essays on American Politics, Law, and Public Philosophy* (Oxford: Oxford University Press, 1998).

Gellner, Ernest. *Legitimation of Belief* (Cambridge: Cambridge University Press, 1974).

Nations and Nationalism (Oxford: Blackwell, 1993).

Conditions of Liberty: Civil Society and Its Revivals (London: Penguin Books, 1994).

Giddens, Anthony. *Capitalism and Modern Social Theory: An Analysis of the Writing of Marx, Durkheim and Max Weber* (Cambridge: Cambridge University Press, 1971).

Gierke, Otto von. *Das deutsche Gennosenschaftsrecht*, Vols. I–III (1868–81); trans. (parts). F. W. Maitland as *Political Theories of the Middle Age* (Cambridge: Cambridge University Press, 1901); ed. A. Black/trans. (parts). M. Fischer as *Community in Historical Perspective* (Cambridge: Cambridge University Press, 1990).

Goldman, Harvey. "Weber's Ascetic Practices of the Self," in Lehmann and Roth (1987).

Max Weber and Thomas Mann: Calling and the Shaping of the Self (Berkeley: University of California Press, 1988).

"The Problem of the Person in Weberian Social Theory," in M. Milgate and C. B. Welch (eds.), *Critical Issues in Social Thought* (London: Academic Press, 1989).

Politics, Death, and the Devil: Self and Power in Max Weber and Thomas Mann (Berkeley: University of California Press, 1992).

Graf, Friedrich Wilhelm. "The German Theological Sources and Protestant Church Politics," in Lehmann and Roth (1987).

Gray, John. *Liberalism* (Minneapolis: University of Minnesota Press, 1986).

Green, Bryan S. R. *Literary Methods and Sociological Theory: Case Studies of Simmel and Weber* (Chicago: University of Chicago Press, 1988).

Gutman, Amy (ed.). *Freedom of Association* (Princeton, NJ: Princeton University Press, 1998).

Habermas, Jürgen. *Toward a Rational Society*, trans. J. Shapiro (London: Heinemann, 1971).

"Discussion on Value Freedom and Objectivity" in Stammer (1971).

The Theory of Communicative Action, Vol. 1: Reason and the Rationalization of Society, trans. T. McCarthy (Boston: Beacon, 1984).

Jürgen Habermas on Society and Politics: A Reader, ed. S. Seidman (Boston: Beacon, 1989).

Hall, John A. *Civil Society: Theory, History, Comparison* (Cambridge: Polity Press, 1995).

Hawthorne, Geoffrey. *Enlightenment and Despair* (Cambridge: Cambridge University Press, 1979).

Heckart, Beverly. *From Basserman to Bebel: The Grand Block's Quest for Reform in the Kaiserreich, 1900–1914* (New Haven, CT: Yale University Press, 1974).

Hegel, Georg Wilhelm Friedrich. *Elements of the Philosophy of Right*, ed. A. Wood/trans. H. B. Nisbet (Cambridge: Cambridge University Press, 1991).

Helle, Horst J. "Max Weber über Otto Gross: Ein Brief an Else Jaffe vom September 1907," *Zietschrift für Politik* 41:2 (1994) 214–23.

Hennis, Wilhelm. "Max Webers Thema: "Die Persönlichkeit und die Lebensordnungen," *Zeitschrift für Politik* 31:1 (1984) 11–52; trans. K. Tribe as "Personality and Life Orders: Max Weber's Theme" in Whimster and Lash (1987).

Max Webers Fragestellung: Studien Zur Biographie des Werkes (Tübingen: J. C. B. Mohr, 1987); trans. K. Tribe as *Max Weber: Essays in Reconstruction* (London: Allen & Unwin, 1988).

Max Webers Wissehschaft vom Menschen (Tübingen: J. C. B. Mohr/Paul Siebeck, 1996).

"The Media as a Cultural Problem: Max Weber's Sociology of the Press," *History of the Human Sciences* 11:2 (1998) 107–10.

Henrich, Dieter. *Die Einheit der Wissenschaftslehre Max Webers* (Tübingen: J. C. B. Mohr/Paul Siebeck, 1952).

Herf, Jeffrey. *Reactionary Modernism: Technology, Culture, and Politics in Weimar and the Third Reich* (Cambridge: Cambridge University Press, 1984).

Hirst, Paul. "The State, Civil Society, and the Collapse of Soviet Communism," *Economy and Society* 20:2 (1991) 217–42.

Hobbes, Thomas. *Leviathan*, ed. R. Tuck (Cambridge: Cambridge University Press, 1991).

Hobsbawm, Eric. *The Age of Extremes: A History of the World, 1914–1991* (New York: Vintage Books, 1996).

Holmes, Stephen. *The Anatomy of Antiliberalism* (Chicago: University of Chicago Press, 1993).

Honigsheim, Paul. *On Max Weber* (New York: Free Press, 1968).

Horowitz, Asher and Malley, Terry (eds.). *The Barbarism of Reason: Max Weber and the Twilight of Enlightenment* (Toronto: University of Toronto Press, 1994).

Hroch, Miroslav. "From National Movement to the Fully-Formed Nation: The Nation-Building Process in Europe," *New Left Review* 93:198 (1993) 3–20.

Iggers, Georg. *The German Conception of History: The National Tradition of Historical Thought from Herder to the Present* (Hanover, NH: Wesleyan University Press, 1968).

Jameson, Frederic. "The Vanishing Mediator: The Narrative Structure in Max Weber," *New German Critique* 1:1 (1972) 52–89.

Jaspers, Karl. *Max Weber: Eine Gedenkrede* (Tübingen: J. C. B. Mohr/Paul Siebeck, 1926).

On Max Weber (New York: Paragon House, 1989).

Jellinek, Georg. *The Declarations of the Rights of Man and of Citizens: A Contribution to Modern Constitutional History*, trans. M. Farrand (Westport, CT: Hyperion Press, 1901).

John, Michael. *Politics and the Law in Late Nineteenth-Century Germany* (Oxford: Oxford University Press, 1989).

Kahan, Alan. *Aristocratic Liberalism: The Social and Political Thought of Jacob Buckhardt, John Stuart Mill, and Alexis de Tocqueville* (Chicago: University of Chicago Press, 1992).

Kalberg, Stephen. "The Search for Thematic Orientations in a Fragmented Oeuvre: The Discussion of Max Weber in Recent German Sociological Literature," *Sociology* 13:1 (1979) 127–39.

"The Origin and Explanation of *Kulturpessimismus*: The Relationship between Public and Private Spheres in Early Twentieth Century Germany," *Sociological Theory* 5 (1987) 150–65.

"Tocqueville and Weber on the Sociological Origin of Citizenship: The Political Culture of American Democracy," *Citizenship Studies* 1:2 (1997) 199–222.

Kant, Immanuel. *Foundations of the Metaphysics of Morals*, trans. L. W. Beck (Indianapolis: Bobbs-Merrill, 1969).

Keane, John. *Civil Society: Old Images, New Visions* (Stanford, CA: Stanford University Press, 1998).

Kedourie, Elie. *Nationalism* (Oxford: Blackwell, 1993).

Khilnani, Sunil. "The Development of Civil Society," in S. Kaviraj and S. Khilnani (eds.), *Civil Society: History and Possibilities* (Cambridge: Cambridge University Press, 2001).

Kim, Sung Ho. "Max Weber and Civil Society," *Max Weber Studies* 2:2 (2002) 186–98.

Köhler, Hennig (ed.), *Deutschland und der Westen* (Berlin: Colloquium Verlag, 1984)

Kohn, Hans. *The Idea of Nationalism* (New York: Macmillan, 1944).

Kristeva, Julia. "Word, Dialogue, and Novel," in T. Moi (ed.), *The Kristeva Reader* (New York: Columbia University Press, 1986).

Krüger, Dieter. "Max Weber and the Younger Generation in the *Verein für Sozialpolitik*," in Mommsen and Osterhammel (1987).

Kumar, Krishan. "Civil Society: An Inquiry into the Usefulness of a Historical Term," *British Journal of Sociology* 44:3 (1993) 375–95.

LaCapra, Dominick. *Rethinking Intellectual History: Text, Contexts, and Language* (Ithaca, NY: Cornell University Press, 1983).

Landauer, Karl. *Corporate State Ideologies: Historical Roots and Philosophical Origins* (Berkeley: University of California Press, 1982).

Landschudt, Siegfried. *Kritik der Soziologie und Schriften zur Politik* (Berlin: Hermann Luchterhand Verlag, 1969).

Larmore, Charles. *Patterns of Moral Complexity* (Cambridge: Cambridge University Press, 1987).

The Morals of Modernity (Cambridge: Cambridge University Press, 1996).

Lassman, Peter and Velody, Irving (eds.), *Max Weber's "Science as a Vocation"* (London: Allen & Unwin, 1989).

Lehmann, Helmut and Roth, Guenther (eds.), *Weber's Protestant Ethic: Origins, Evidence, Contexts* (Cambridge: Cambridge University Press, 1987).

Levine, David. *Flight from Ambiguity: Essays in Social and Cultural Theory* (Chicago: University of Chicago Press, 1985).

Liebersohn, Harry. *Fate and Utopia in German Sociology, 1870–1923* (Cambridge, MA: MIT Press, 1988).

Lindenlaub, Dieter. *Richtungskämpfe im Verein für Sozialpolitik: Wissenschaft und Sozialpolitik im Kaiserreich vornehmlich vom Beginn des "neuen Kurses" bis zum Ausbruch des ersten Weltkrieges (1870–1914)*, Bd. I (Wiesbaden: Franz Steiner Verlag, 1967).

Löwith, Karl. *Max Weber und Karl Marx* (Stuttgart: Verlag W. Kohlhammer, 1960).

"Die Entzauberung der Welt durch Wissenschaft: Zu Max Webers 100. Geburtstag," *Merkur* 18 (1964) 501–19.

Vorträger und Abhandlungen: Zur Kritik der christlichen Überlieferung (Stuttgart: Verlag W. Kohlhammer, 1966).

Meaning in History (Chicago: University of Chicago Press, 1970).

Lukács, Georg. "Max Weber and German Sociology," *Economy and Society* 1:4 (1972) 386–98.

Macedo, Stephen. *Liberal Virtues: Citizenship, Virtue, and Community in Liberal Constitutionalism* (Oxford: Oxford University Press, 1990).

"Community, Diversity, and Civic Education: Toward a Liberal Political Science of Group Life" in E. F. Paul, F. Miller, and J. Paul (eds.), *Communitarian Challenge to Liberalism* (Cambridge: Cambridge University Press, 1996).

MacKinnon, Malcolm. H. "Part I: Calvinism and the Infallible Assurance of Grace" and "Part II: Weber's Exploration of Calvinism," *British Journal of Sociology* 39:2 (1988) 143–210.

Maier, Charles. *Recasting Bourgeois Europe: Stabilization in France, Germany, and Italy in the Decade after World War I* (Princeton, NJ: Princeton University Press, 1975).

In Search of Stability: Explorations in Historical Political Economy (Cambridge: Cambridge University Press, 1987).

Marcuse, Herbert. "Industrialization and Capitalism," in Stammer (1971).

Marx, Karl. *Critique of Hegel's Philosophy of Right*, ed./trans. J. J. O'Malley (Cambridge: Cambridge University Press, 1970).

Mayer, Jacob P. *Max Weber and German Politics: A Study in Political Sociology* (London: Faber & Faber, 1944).

McCormick, John. *Carl Schmitt's Critique of Liberalism: Against Politics as Technology* (Cambridge: Cambridge University Press, 1997).

McKim, Robert and McMahan, Jeff (eds.). *The Morality of Nationalism* (Oxford: Oxford University Press, 1997).

Meinecke, Friedrich. "Max Weber" (1927) in R. König and J. Winckelmann (eds.), *Max Weber zum Gedächtnis* (Köln: Westdeutschen Verlag, 1964).

Merquior, José Guilhjerme. *Rousseau and Weber: Two Studies in the Theory of Legitimacy* (London: Routledge, 1980).

Mill, John Stuart. *On Liberty and Other Writings*, ed. S. Collini (Cambridge: Cambridge University Press, 1989).

Mills, C. Wright and Gerth, Hans H. *From Max Weber: Essays in Sociology* (Oxford: Oxford University Press, 1946).

Mitzman, Arthur. *The Iron Cage: An Historical Interpretation of Max Weber* (New York: Knopf, 1969).

Mommsen, Wolfgang. "Die Vereinigten Staaten von Amerika im politischen Denken Max Webers," *Historische Zeitschrift* 213 (1971) 72–96.

Age of Bureaucracy (Oxford: Blackwell, 1974)

Max Weber: Gesellschaft, Politik, und Geschichte (Frankfurt a. M.: Suhrkamp, 1974).

"Max Weber and Robert Michels: An Asymmetrical Partnership," *European Journal of Sociology* 22:1 (1981) 100–16.

Max Weber und die deutsche Politik, 1890–1920 (Tübingen: J. C. B. Mohr, 1959); trans. M. Steinberg as *Max Weber and German Politics, 1890–1920* (Chicago: University of Chicago Press, 1984).

The Political and Social Theory of Max Weber (Chicago: University of Chicago Press, 1989).

"The Return to the Western Tradition: German Historiography since 1945," Occasional Paper #4 (Washington, DC: German Historical Institute, 1991).

Imperial Germany, 1867–1918 (London: Routledge, 1995).

Mommsen, Wolfgang and Osterhammel, Jürgen (eds). *Max Weber and His Contemporaries* (London: Allen & Unwin, 1987).

Mosse, George. *The Crisis of German Ideology: Intellectual Origin of the Third Reich* (New York: Schocken Books, 1981).

Mouffe, Chantal. *The Return of the Political* (London: Verso, 1993).

Nehamas, Alexander. *Nietzsche: Life as Literature* (Cambridge, MA: Harvard University Press, 1985).

Nelson, Benjamin. "Max Weber's 'Author's Introduction' (1920): A Master Clue to his Main Aims," *Sociological Inquiry* 44:4 (1974) 269–78.

"Max Weber, Ernst Troeltsch, Georg Jellinek as Comparative Historical Sociologists," *Sociological Analysis* 36:3 (1975) 229–40.

Neuenhaus, Petra. *Max Weber und Michel Foucault: Über Macht und Herrschaft in der Moderne* (Pfaffenweiler: Centaurus-Verlagsgesellschaft, 1993).

Nietzsche, Friedrich. *The Gay Science,* trans. W. Kaufmann (New York: Random House, 1974).

On the Genealogy of Morality, ed. K. Ansell-Pearson/trans. C. Diethe (Cambridge: Cambridge University Press, 1994).

Oakes, Guy. *Weber and Rickert: Concept Formation in the Cultural Sciences* (Cambridge, MA: MIT Press, 1988).

Oakeshott, Michael. *On Human Conduct* (Oxford: Oxford University Press, 1976).

Rationalism in Politics and Other Essays (Indianapolis: Liberty Press, 1991).

Religion, Politics, and the Moral Life, ed. T. Fuller (New Haven, CT: Yale University Press, 1993).

O'Connor, Daniel. "Good and Evil Disposition," *Kant-Studien* 76:3 (1985) 288–302.

Osterhammel, Jürgen. "Personal Conflict and Ideological Options in Sombart and Weber," in Mommsen and Osterhammel (1987).

Owen, David. "Autonomy and 'Inner Distance': A Trace of Nietzsche in Weber," *History of the Human Sciences* 4:1 (1991) 79–91.

Maturity and Modernity: Nietzsche, Weber, and Foucault and the Ambivalence of Reason (London: Routledge, 1994).

Palonen, Kari. "Max Weber's Reconceptualization of Freedom," *Political Theory* 27:4 (1999) 523–44.

Parsons, Talcott. *Sociology of Religion* (Boston: Beacon, 1963).

The Structure of Social Action (New York: Free Press, 1968).

Pettit, Philip. *Republicanism: A Theory of Freedom and Government* (Oxford: Oxford University Press, 1997).

Peukert, Detlev. *The Weimar Republic* (London: Hill & Wang, 1993).

Pippin, Robert. *Modernism as a Philosophical Problem* (Cambridge: Cambridge University Press, 1991).

Plamenatz, John. "Two Types of Nationalism," in E. Kamenka (ed.), *Nationalism: The Nature and Evolution of an Idea* (New York: St. Martin's, 1976).

Portis, Edward Bryan. "Max Weber's Theory of Personality," *Sociological Inquiry* 48 (1978) 113–20.

Max Weber and Political Commitments: Science, Politics, and Personality (Philadelphia: Temple University Press, 1986).

Praeger, Jeffrey. "Moral Integration and Political Inclusion: A Comparison of Durkheim's and Weber's Theories," *Social Forces* 59:4 (1981) 918–50.

Pufendorf, Samuel. *On the Duty of Man and Citizen* (Cambridge: Cambridge University Press, 1991).

Putnam, Robert. "Bowling Alone: America's Declining Social Capital," *Journal of Democracy* 6:1 (1995) 65–78.

Ranke, Leopold von. *The Theory and Practice of History* (Indianapolis: Bobbs-Merrill. 1973).

Rathenau, Walter. *The New Society*, trans. A. Windham (New York: Harcourt, Brace, 1921).

Renan, Ernest. "What Is a Nation?" in G. Elley and R. Suny (eds.), *Becoming National: A Reader* (Oxford: Oxford University Press, 1996).

Riedel, Manfred. "Gesellschaft, Gemeinschaft," in Brunner, Conze, and Koselleck (1972), Bd. 2.

"Bügerliche Gesellschaft," in Brunner, Conze, and Koselleck (1972), Bd. 2.

Riesebrodt, Martin. "From Patriarchalism to Capitalism: The Theoretical Context of Max Weber's Agrarian Studies (1892–3)," in K. Tribe (ed.), *Reading Weber* (London: Routledge, 1989).

Ringer, Fritz. *The Decline of the German Mandarins: The German Academic Community, 1890–1933* (Cambridge, MA: Harvard University Press, 1969).

Robertson, Hector M. *Aspects of the Rise of Economic Individualism* (Cambridge: Cambridge University Press, 1933).

Rollman, Hans. " 'Meet Me in St. Louis': Troeltsch and Weber in America," in Lehmann and Roth (1987).

Rorty, Richard. *Objectivity, Relativism and Truth : Philosophical Papers, Vol. 1* (Cambridge: Cambridge University Press, 1991).

Rosenberg, Hans. "Theologischer Rationalismus und vormärzlicher Vulgärliberalismus," *Histrischer Zeitschrift* 141 (1930) 497–541.

Rosenblum, Nancy. *Membership and Morals: The Personal Uses of Pluralism in America* (Princeton, NJ: Princeton University Press, 1998).

Roth, Guenther. Introduction to G. Roth (ed.), *Economy and Society*, by Max Weber (Berkeley: University of California Press, 1978).

"Marx and Weber on the United States – Today," in R. Antonio and R. Glassman (eds.), *A Weber–Marx Dialogue* (Lawrence: University of Kansas Press, 1985).

"Weber's Political Failure," *Telos* 78 (1989) 136–49.

Max Webers deutschen-englische Familiengeschichte 1800–1950 (Tübingen: J. C. B. Mohr/Paul Siebeck, 2001).

Rudolph, Susanne Hoeber. "From Weber to Weber (via Foucault)," *World Politics* 48:1 (1995) 21–8.

Runciman, David. *Pluralism and the Personality of the State* (Cambridge: Cambridge University Press, 1997).

Rupp, Gordon. *Culture-Protestantism: German Liberal Theology at the Turn of the Century*, American Academy of Religion: *Studies in Religion*, Vol. 15 (Missoula, MT: Scholars Press, 1977).

Ryan, Alan. "Weber and Mill on History, Freedom and Reason," in Mommsen and Ostehammel (1987).

Said, Edward. *The World, The Text and the Critic* (London: Faber, 1984).

Samuelson, Kurt. *Religion and Economic Action* (Stockholm: Svenska Bokförlaget, 1961).

Sandel, Michael. "The Procedural Republic and the Unencumbered Self," *Political Theory* 12:1 (1984) 81–96.

Democracy's Discontent: America in Search of a Public Philosophy (Cambridge, MA: Harvard University Press, 1996).

Scaff, Lawrence. "Max Weber and Robert Michels," *American Journal of Sociology* 86:6 (1981) 1269–86.

Fleeing the Iron Cage: Culture, Politics, and Modernity in the Thought of Max Weber (Berkeley: University of California Press, 1989).

"The 'Cool Objectivity of Sociation': Max Weber and Marianne Weber in America," *History of the Human Sciences* 11:2 (1998) 61–82.

Schluchter, Wolfgang. "Die Paradoxie der Rationalisierung," *Zeitschrift für Soziologie* 5:3 (1976) 256–84; trans. G. Roth as "The Paradox of Rationalization: On the Relation of Ethics and World," in Schluchter and Roth (1979).

"Value Neutrality and The Ethic of Responsibility," in Schluchter and Roth (1979).

The Rise of Western Rationalism: Max Weber's Developmental History, trans./intro. G. Roth (Berkeley: University of California Press, 1981).

Religion und Lebensführung, Bd. 2 (Frankfurt a. M.: Suhrkamp, 1988).

Rationalism, Religion, and Domination: A Weberian Perspective, trans. N. Solomon (Berkeley: University of California Press, 1989).

Paradoxes of Modernity: Culture and Conflict in the Theory of Max Weber (Stanford, CA: Stanford University Press, 1996).

Schluchter, Wolfgang and Roth, Guenther. *Max Weber's Vision of History* (Berkeley: University of California Press, 1979).

Schmidt, Gustav. *Deutscher Historismus und der Übergang zur parlamentarischen Demokratie: Untersuchungen zu den politischen Gedanken von Meinecke, Troeltsch, Max Weber* (Lübeck: Matthiesen Verlag, 1964).

Schmitt, Carl. *Verfassungslehre* (Berlin: Dunker & Humboldt, 1983).

The Crisis of Parliamentary Democracy (Cambridge, MA: MIT Press, 1988).

Political Theology (Cambridge, MA: MIT Press, 1988).

"The Age of Neutralizations and Depoliticizations," trans. M. Konzett and J. P. McCormick, *Telos* 96 (1993) 119–42.

The Concept of the Political (Chicago: University of Chicago Press, 1996).

Schorske, Carl. *Fin-de-siècle Vienna: Politics and Culture* (New York: Vintage, 1961).

Schriften des Vereins für Sozialpolitik, Bd. 116: Verhandlungen der Generalversammlung in Mannheim, 28 September 1905 (Leipzig: Dunker & Humboldt, 1906).

Schroeder, Ralph. "'Personality' and 'Inner Distance': The Conception of the Individual in Max Weber's Sociology," *History of the Human Sciences* 4:1 (1991) 61–78.

Schulin, Ernst. "Max Weber and Walter Rathenau," in Mommsen and Osterhammel (1987).

Schulz, Gerhard. *Zwischen Demokratie und Diktatur, Bd. I: Verfassungspolitik und Reichsreform in der Weimarer Republik* (Berlin: Walter de Gruyter, 1987).

Seligman, Adam. "The Representation of Society and the Privatization of Charisma," *Praxis International* 13:1 (1993) 68–84.

Sheehan, James. *German Liberalism in the Nineteenth Century* (Chicago: University of Chicago Press, 1978).

"Some Reflections on Liberalism in Comparative Perspective" in Köhler (1984).

Shils, Edward. *Center and Periphery* (Chicago: University of Chicago Press, 1975).

The Constitution of Society (Chicago: University of Chicago Press, 1982).

The Virtue of Civility: Selected Essays on Liberalism, Tradition, and Civil Society (Indianapolis: Liberty Press, 1997).

Skinner, Quentin. "Meaning and Understanding in the History of Ideas" and "Motives, Intensions, and the Interpretation of Texts," in J. Tully (ed.), *Meaning and Context: Quentin Skinner and His Critics* (Princeton, NJ: Princeton University Press, 1988).

Liberty before Liberalism (Cambridge: Cambridge University Press, 1998).

Smith, Adam. *An Inquiry into the Nature and Causes of the Wealth of Nations* (Chicago: University of Chicago Press, 1976).

Smith, Anthony. *The Ethnic Origins of Nations* (Oxford: Blackwell, 1986).

Sombart, Werner. *The Quintessence of Capitalism: A Study of the History and Psychology of the Modern Business Man*, trans. M. Epstein (New York: Howard Fertig, 1967).

Stammer, Otto (ed.). *Max Weber and Sociology Today* (Oxford: Blackwell, 1971).

Stern, Fritz. *The Politics of Cultural Despair: A Study in the Rise of the German Ideology* (Berkeley: University of California Press, 1961).

Failure of Illiberalism (New York: Knopf, 1972).

Strauss, Leo. *Natural Right and History* (Chicago: University of Chicago Press, 1950).

Strong, Tracy. "'What Have We to Do with Morals?' – Nietzsche and Weber on History and Ethics," *History of the Human Sciences* 5:3 (1992) 9–18.

Tamir, Yael. *Liberal Nationalism* (Princeton, NJ: Princeton University Press, 1993).

Tawney, Richard Henry. *Religion and the Rise of Capitalism* (New York: Harcourt Brace, 1952).

Taylor, Charles. *Hegel* (Cambridge: Cambridge University Press, 1975).

Sources of the Self: The Making of the Modern Identity (Cambridge, MA: Harvard University Press, 1989).

The Ethic of Authenticity (Cambridge, MA: Harvard University Press, 1991).

Philosophy and the Human Sciences: Philosophical Papers II (Cambridge: Cambridge University Press, 1993).

Tenbruck, Friedrich H. "The Problem of Thematic Unity in the Works of Max Weber," *British Journal of Sociology* 31:3 (1980) 316–51.

"Das Werk Max Webers: Methodologie und Sozialwissenschaften," *Kölner Zeitschrift für Soziologie und Sozialpsychologie* 38:1 (1986), 13–31.

Theiner, Peter. "Friedrich Naumann and Max Weber: Aspects of a Political Partnership," in Mommsen and Osterhammel (1987).

Thom, Martin. "Tribes within Nations: The Ancient Germans and the History of Modern France," in H. Bhabha (ed.), *Nation and Narrative* (London: Routledge, 1994).

Titunik, Regina. "Understanding the Devil: Max Weber's Political Thought" (Ph.D. dissertation, Department of Political Science, University of Chicago, 1991).

"Status, Vanity, and Equal Dignity in Max Weber's Political Thought," *Economy and Society* 24:1 (1995) 101–21.

Tocqueville, Alexis de. *Selected Letters on Politics and Society*, trans. J. Toupin and R. Boesche/ed. R. Boesche (Berkeley: University of California Press, 1985).

Democracy in America (New York: Harper & Row, 1988).

Todorov, Tzvetan. *On Human Diversity: Nationalism, Racism and Exoticism in French Thought* (Cambridge, MA: Harvard University Press, 1993).

Tolstoy, Leo. *Complete Works*, Vols. 13, 14 (New York: AMS Press, 1968).

Tönnies, Ferdinand. *Community and Society* (New Brunswick, NJ: Transaction, 1993).

Toulmin, Stephen. *Cosmopolis: The Hidden Agenda of Modernity* (Chicago: University of Chicago Press, 1990).

Treitschke, Heinrich von. *Politics*, ed. H. Kohn (New York: Harcourt, Brace & World, 1963).

Trevor-Roper, Hugh Redwaid. *Religion, Reformation and Social Change* (London: Macmillan, 1972).

Troeltsch, Ernst. *The Social Teachings of the Christian Churches*, trans. O. Wyon (London: Allen & Unwin, 1931).

   Protestantism and Progress: A Historical Study of the Relation of Protestantism to the Modern World (Boston: Beacon, 1958).

Turner, Bryan. *Max Weber: From History to Modernity* (London: Routledge, 1992).

Turner, Charles. *Modernity and Politics in the Work of Max Weber* (London: Routledge, 1992).

   "Liberalism and the Limits of Science: Weber and Blumenberg," *History of the Human Science* 6:4 (1993) 57–79.

Ulmen, Gary L. "The Sociology of the State: Carl Schmitt and Max Weber," *State, Culture and Society* 1:1 (1985) 3–57.

Vattimo, Giani. *The End of Modernity: Nihilism and Hermeneutics in Postmodern Culture*, trans. J. Snyder (Baltimore: Johns Hopkins University Press, 1988).

Verhandlungen des achten Evangelische-sozialen Kongresses (Göttingen: Vandenhoeck & Ruprecht, 1897).

Verhandlungen des ersten deutschen soziologentages (Frankfurt a.M.: Sauer & Auvermann, 1969).

Vierhaus, Rudolf. "Bildung," in Brunner, Conze, and Koselleck (1972), Bd. 1.

Villa, Dana. *Socratic Citizenship* (Princeton, NJ: Princeton University Press, 2001).

Viroli, Maurizio. *Republicanism* (New York: Hill and Wang, 2002).

Voegelin, Eric. *The New Science of Politics* (Chicago: University of Chicago Press, 1952).

Ward, William Reginald. *Theology, Sociology, and Politics: The German Protestant Social Consciousness, 1890–1933* (Berne: P. Lang, 1979).

Warren, Mark. "Max Weber's Nietzschean Conception of Power," *History of the Human Sciences* 5:3 (1992) 19–37.

Weinding, Peter J. *Health, Race and German Politics: Between National Unification and Nazis* (Cambridge: Cambridge University Press, 1989).

Whimster, Sam and Lash, Scott (eds.). *Max Weber, Rationality, and Modernity* (London: Allen & Unwin, 1987).

Williams, Bernard. "A Critique of Utilitarianism," in J. J. C. Smart and B. Williams, *Utilitarianism: For and Against* (Cambridge: Cambridge University Press, 1973).

Winckelmann, Johannes. *Die protestantische Ethik II – Max Weber: Kritiken und Antikritiken* (Gütersloh: Gütersloher Verlag, 1978).

Max Webers hintergelassenes Hauptwerk: Die Wirtschaft und gesellschaftliche Ordnungen und Mächte. Entstechung und gedanklicher Aufbau (Tübingen: J. C. B. Mohr/Paul Siebeck, 1986).

Wohl, Richard. *The Generation of 1914* (Cambridge, MA: Harvard University Press, 1979).

Wolin, Sheldon. *Politics and Vision: Continuity and Innovation in Western Political Thought* (Boston: Little, Brown, 1960).

"The Liberal/Democratic Divide: On Rawls's Political Liberalism," *Political Theory* 24:1 (1996) 97–142.

Index

Albrow, Martin, 139
Alexander, Jeffrey, 21, 62, 65
Allison, Henry, 52
Alter, Peter, 135
Arato, Andrew, 92
Arblaster, Anthony, 41
Arnold, Matthew, 57
Aron, Raymond, 11, 23, 146, 180

Bacon, Francis, 103
Baehr, Peter, 18, 29, 31, 62
Baumgarten, Eduard, 29, 60
Beetham, David, 12, 23, 139, 157
Bellamy, Richard, 16
Bendix, Reinhard, 19
Berger, Stephen, 21, 65
Berkowitz, Peter, 6, 188
Berman, Marshal, 62
Berman, Sheri, 7
Blackbourn, David, 11
Blum, Fred, 13
Blumenberg, Hans, 104
Bowen, Ralph, 161
Breiner, Peter, 12
Brentano, Lujo, 28, 32, 33,
    159
Broch, Herman, 124
Brubaker, Roger, 9, 135
Bruch, Rüdiger vom, 124

Bryant, Christopher, 3, 135
Bücher, Karl, 153
Bunyan, John, 40
Burrow, John Wyon, 141

Cahnman, Werner, 66
Calvin, John, 36, 37, 44
Carlyle, Thomas, 28
Chalcraft, David, 17
Chambers, Simone, 7
Chapman, Mark D., 59
Charnock, Stephen, 47
Cohen, Jean, 92
Comte, August, 105
Constant, Benjamin, 73, 127
Coser, Lewis, 30
Culler, Jonathan, 141

Dagger, Richard, 6
Dahlmann, Dittmar, 130
Dahrendorf, Ralph, 156
D'Alembert, Jean Le Rond, 104
Demm, Eberhard, 139
Descartes, René, 103
D'Holbach, Paul-Henri, 104
Dibble, Vernon K., 13
Diggins, John Patrick, 23, 62
Donne, John, 27
Dostoevsky, Feodor, 78, 95

Dumont, Louis, 36, 89
Durkheim, Emil, 18, 140

Eden, Robert, 53
Eisen, Arnold, 19
Eisenstadt, Shmuel, 36, 86
Eksteins, Modris, 63
Eley, Geoff, 11, 134
Elkin, Stephen, 6
Elshtain, Jean Bethke, 6
Emerson, Rupert, 167
Evans, Richard, 11

Factor, Regis, 121
Ferguson, Adam, 133
Fischer, Fritz, 10
Fischer, Karl, 18, 28
Fleischman, Eugène, 53
Forster, E. M. (Edward Morgan),
    41
Foucault, Michel, 19, 98
Franco, Paul, 181
Freud, Sigmund, 153
Freund, Julien, 23
Frommer, J., 60
Frommer, S., 60

Galileo, Galilei, 103
Galston, William, 4
Gellner, Ernest, 3, 53, 134
George, Stefan, 124
Gerth, Hans, 29
Giddens, Anthony, 19
Gierke, Otto von, 76, 77
Goethe, Johannes, 118
Goldman, Harvey, 20, 21, 28, 48,
    59, 123
Graf, Friedrich Wilhelm, 140
Gray, John, 16
Green, Bryan S. R., 17
Gross, Otto, 54
Gutman, Amy, 188

Habermas, Jürgen, 10, 24, 92,
    111, 134, 180
Hall, John A., 135

Hawthorne, Geoffrey, 105
Heckart, Beverly, 159
Hegel, Georg Wilhelm Friedrich, 3,
    91, 92, 103, 160, 182
Heidegger, Martin, 50
Helle, Horst J., 54
Helvètius, Claude, 104
Hennis, Wilhelm, 8, 20, 23, 43, 73,
    96, 151
Henrich, Dieter, 20
Herf, Jeffrey, 23, 65
Hirst, Paul, 2
Hobbes, Thomas, 51, 70
Hobsbawm, Eric, 1
Hoffmanstahl, Hugo von, 124
Holmes, Stephen, 14
Honigsheim, Paul, 62
Horowitz, Asher, 19
Hroch, Miroslav, 134
Hume, David, 104

Iggers, Georg, 141

Jameson, Frederic, 24, 97
Jaspers, Karl, 13, 20
Jellinek, Georg, 70
John, Michael, 70

Kahan, Alan, 16
Kalberg, Stephen, 9, 23, 150
Kant, Immanuel, 41, 51, 52, 53, 54,
    68, 93, 96, 97
Keane, John, 7
Kedourie, Elie, 134
Khilnani, Sunil, 3
Kierkegaard, Søren, 44
Kim, Sung Ho, 151
Köhler, Hennig, 16
Kohn, Hans, 135, 138
Kopstein, Jeffrey, 7
Kristeva, Julia, 17
Krüger, Dieter, 66, 139
Kumar, Krishan, 3

LaCapra, Dominick, 17
Landauer, Karl, 161

Landshut, Siegfried, 20
Larmore, Charles, 15, 116, 182
Lassman, Peter, 20
Levine, David, 30
Liebersohn, Harry, 21, 59, 142, 143
Lindenlaub, Dieter, 138
Locke, John, 50, 52, 68
Löwith, Karl, 14, 20, 99, 104
Lukács, Georg, 11
Luther, Martin, 33, 34, 36, 37, 45, 131, 142, 178, 185

Macedo, Stephen, 6, 81
Machiavelli, Nicolo, 40, 58, 123
MacKinnon, Malcolm H., 18
Maier, Charles, 162
Marcuse, Herbert, 11, 12, 180
Marx, Karl, 18, 68, 91
Mayer, Jacob P., 9
McCormick, John, 164
McKim, Robert, 170
McMahan, Jeff, 170
Meinecke, Friedrich, 60
Merleau-Ponty, Maurice, 50
Merquior, José Guilherme, 85
Michels, Robert, 157
Mill, John Stuart, 150, 170
Mills, C. Wright, 29
Mitzman, Arthur, 23, 24, 30, 60, 61, 78
Moellendorf, Wichard von, 161
Mommsen, Wolfgang, 7, 9, 10, 11, 12, 14, 15, 16, 17, 26, 62, 63, 64, 66, 130, 136, 139, 143, 157, 159, 162, 166, 177, 180
Mosse, George, 23, 141
Mouffe, Chantal, 187
Müller, Johannes, 160

Naumann, Friedrich, 13, 159, 162
Nehamas, Alexander, 43
Nelson, Benjamin, 21, 65
Neuenhaus, Petra, 19
Nietzsche, Friedrich, 19, 43, 53, 98, 101, 102, 106, 108, 110

Oakes, Guy, 53
Oakeshott, Michael, 133, 134, 180, 181, 182, 183, 184, 185, 186
O'Connor, Daniel, 52
Osterhammel, Jürgen, 66, 130, 139, 143, 159, 162
Owen, David, 20, 176

Palonen, Kari, 30
Parsons, Talcott, 19, 22, 29, 86
Pettit, Philip, 73
Peukert, Detlev, 63
Pippin, Robert, 104
Plamenatz, John, 135
Plato, 103, 116
Ploetz, Alfred, 142, 143
Portis, Edward Bryan, 19
Praeger, Jeffrey, 140
Preuss, Hugo, 167
Pufendorf, Samuel von, 70
Putnam, Robert, 189

Rachfall, Felix, 18, 28
Ranke, Leopold von, 138
Rathenau, Walter, 154, 161, 162
Reisebrodt, Martin, 77
Renan, Ernest, 149
Riedel, Manfred, 66
Ringer, Fritz, 23, 65, 124
Robertson, Hector M., 18
Rollman, Hans, 62
Rorty, Richard, 15
Rosenberg, Hans, 16
Rosenblum, Nancy, 5, 84
Roth, Guenther, 13, 17, 21, 59, 62, 111, 140, 171
Rousseau, Jean Jacques, 41, 52, 80
Rudolph, Susanne Hoeber, 19
Runciman, David, 76
Rupp, Gordon, 140
Ryan, Alan, 150

Said, Edward, 141
Samuelson, Kurt, 18
Sandel, Michael, 58, 73
Saussure, Ferdinand de, 141

Scaff, Lawrence, 20, 32, 78, 116, 157
Schluchter, Wolfgang, 8, 17, 19, 99,
    111, 116
Schmidt, Gustav, 121
Schmitt, Carl, 10, 163, 164, 166,
    179, 186
Schmoller, Gustav, 138
Schorske, Carl, 124
Schroeder, Ralph, 20
Schulin, Ernst, 162
Schulz, Gerhard, 167
Seligman, Adam, 93
Sheehan, James, 16
Shils, Edward, 6, 84, 85, 86
Skinner, Quentin, 17, 73
Smith, Adam, 34, 68, 80, 81
Smith, Anthony, 135
Sombart, Werner, 28, 32, 62, 143,
    154
Spencer, Herbert, 105
Stammer, Otto, 146
Stern, Fritz, 23
Strauss, Leo, 14, 15, 176, 177, 178,
    179, 180
Strong, Tracy, 53

Tacitus, 141
Tamir, Yael, 170
Tawney, Richard Henry, 18
Taylor, Charles, 21, 34, 52
Tenbruck, Friedrich H., 8
Theiner, Peter, 159
Thom, Martin, 141
Titunik, Regina, 14, 15, 147
Tocqueville, Alexis de, 3, 80, 81,
    149, 150, 170

Todorov, Tzvetan, 135, 149
Toller, Ernst, 130
Tolstoy, Leo, 78, 79, 100, 107, 108
Tönnies, Ferdinand, 62, 65, 66, 82
Toulmin, Stephen, 58
Treitschke, Heinrich von, 137
Trevor-Roper, Hugh Redwaid, 18
Troeltsch, Ernst, 21, 59, 62, 77, 79,
    80, 154
Turner, Bryan, 19
Turner, Charles, 19, 104, 186
Turner, Stephen, 121

Ulmen, Gary L., 164

Vattimo, Gianni, 98
Velody, Irving, 20
Vierhaus, Rudolf, 124
Villa, Dana, 179
Vinci, Leonardo da, 103
Vogelin, Eric, 14

Wagner, Adolf, 138
Ward, William Reginald, 159
Warren, Mark, 53
Weber, Marianne, 17, 60, 61, 118,
    124, 139
Weber, Max Senior, 60
Wehler, Hans-Ulrich, 10
Weinding, Peter J., 142
Wells, Gordon, 18, 29
Williams, Bernard, 114
Winckelmann, Johannes, 17, 18,
    28
Wohl, Richard, 63
Wolin, Sheldon, 123, 189

CPSIA information can be obtained
at www.ICGtesting.com
Printed in the USA
FSHW02n1253180718
50647FS

9 780521 036566